Maps and Meaning

Levitical Models for Contemporary Care

Nancy H. Wiener and Jo Hirschmann

D1523141

©2014

Fortress Press
Minneapolis

MAPS AND MEANING

Levitical Models for Contemporary Care

Cover design: Laurie Ingram

Cover images: Top left © Burlingham/Shutterstock; Top right © Selimaksan/iStock; Middle © Dom Augustin Calmet/Art.com; Bottom left © Squarepixel/iStock; Bottom right © Hemera/Thinkstock

Library of Congress Cataloging-in-Publication Data

Print ISBN: 978-1-4514-8294-2

eBook ISBN: 978-1-4514-8754-1

Manufactured in the U.S.A.

This book was produced using PressBooks.com, and PDF rendering was done by PrinceXML.

For Judy, Elizabeth,
Shoshana, and Dalia,
with love.

Contents

Foreword

Claudia Setzer

Professor of Religious Studies, Manhattan College

The Torah is compared to water, sustaining life, never running dry, a constant well from which to draw up new insights. We relate to the colorful narratives of Genesis and respond to the powerful liberationist themes of Exodus. The prophets call us to social justice. The language and imagery of these works have infused and sustained some of the great movements in American culture—abolitionism, first-wave feminism, and the civil rights movement.

Yet the Priestly material in Leviticus and Numbers leaves many of us still thirsty. For Jews, the material can make us self-conscious. Its seemingly bizarre and archaic rituals and practices of exclusion do not sound very spiritual. Many a *devar Torah* (mini-sermon on the weekly Torah reading) on *Tazria-Metzora* (Lev. 12:1--15:33) has begun with a rueful remark about one's bad luck in being assigned a Torah portion on skin diseases and seminal emissions. Numbers is more pliable, but most Jewish preachers shy away from its themes of war and bloodshed. A common interpreter's strategy is to take a small part of the portion and use it as a springboard to talk about other matters.

In nineteenth-century liberal religion, the "ritual and ceremonial laws" were divorced from the ethical laws, and the former were assigned to a more primitive stage of religion. Abraham Geiger (1810–1874), a founder of Reform Judaism in Germany, championed Judaism as the flagship of ethical monotheism but rejected the validity of most of the laws and promoted Judaism as a tradition evolving away from ritual and commands to more abstract principles.

Nor have Christians warmed to this material. For some, it has been useful for supersessionist interpretations, providing a bleak backdrop against which Jesus shone for his message of inclusion of social outsiders like lepers and the sick and his preaching of peace. At times the first-century Pharisees have been folded in with other sectarians and with the Priestly material to create a great anachronistic essence called "Judaism," a caricature of a legalistic religion without compassion. Jesus' teaching was then presented as its improved replacement and the religion of universalism.

Adolph von Harnack (1851–1930), a highly influential representative of liberal Protestant scholarship, was typical of this characterization of Judaism as empty, harsh, and in its death throes in the first century. Julius Wellhausen (1844–1918), the scholar most commonly associated with the Documentary Hypothesis, subscribed to the idea of progressive revelation, relegating the Old Testament and, by extension, Judaism to a more primitive stage of humanity. Although the term "late Judaism," a term for first-century Judaism that encompasses these assumptions, is no longer acceptable for New Testament scholars today, its assumptions (and occasionally the term itself) still surface.

The dichotomy of ethics and law is a false one. After all, "love your neighbor as yourself" (Lev. 19:18), the demand to give sanctuary to the runaway slave (Deut. 23:15-16), and the command to leave the edges of one's field unharvested for the poor and the foreigner (Lev. 23:22) are both laws in the Torah. Two generations of historical Jesus scholarship by Jews and Christians have reminded us that the Torah and Prophets were Jesus' Scripture, and first-century Judaism, which was really multiple groups and persuasions, was the vibrant tradition from which he drew his teaching and healing. Furthermore, rabbinic Judaism is understood now not as the forerunner of Christianity but as its sister religion. Both postbiblical Judaism and the earliest forms of Christianity are developments out of biblical Israel, or, in Alan Segal's words, all are "Rebecca's Children."

In the following pages, Rabbi Jo Hirschmann and Rabbi Nancy H. Wiener truly engage these Priestly laws, not as a superficial excuse to talk about something else but as revealing deep mythic structures that speak to humanity's needs. The writers show that the biblical categories of *kedushah* (separation, holiness), *tumah* (impurity), and *taharah* (purity) continue to function in human experience and inform the big questions around which all the world's religions coalesce. These questions include change and its inevitability, the body with its limits and possibilities for experiencing the sacred, our lives in relation to community, boundaries and boundary crossings, and the role of witness and accompaniment in suffering.

Chaplains, like the ancient priests, live in the midst of life's messiness and finitude. As individuals, they share the normal human reactions to pain, death, and illness. But this book articulates how each one is also a conduit for tradition, providing access to larger, sacred community. To be part of a tradition is to draw on its resources, to live at a nexus of past, present, and future life.

Wise and accessible, this book delightfully weaves together biblical and other scholarship with the experiences of healthcare and pastoral professionals. Classic works by Mary Douglas, Robert Alter, and

Jacob Milgrom appear alongside more recent scholarship by David Kraemer and Barbara Mann. This book will be useful not only to therapeutic professionals but also to teachers, students, and preachers. Many a sermon could be inspired and informed by this work.

As our authors dip into the waters of Torah, they reveal the hope that is at the heart of the Priestly tradition. Written from a place of exile and dislocation, this tradition uses memory as a way to maintain identity when outside a familiar time and place, and asserts that God goes with the people into exile. As they delve into the Priestly material, our authors demonstrate that the usual maps by which we orient our lives can be redrawn. They show us that *tumah* is unavoidable and essential to wholeness. Finally, they maintain that a person isolated because of illness, trauma, or military service nevertheless remains bound to community.

One need not be religious to find comfort in the humane insights of this book. The authors show that everyone has resources to draw on—ancient traditions, universal themes, and social connectedness. They show the fundamental need to be seen and known as we are, with acceptance and truth, reminding us that God is called *El Roi*, "the one who sees." Our two rabbis teach us that in brokenness, loss, or isolation, we can make meaning. Anyone journeying into "the kingdom of the sick," as Susan Sontag calls the strange territory we all visit at some point, would be privileged to have these two as their guides.

Foreword

Neil Gillman

Professor Emeritus of Jewish Philosophy, Jewish Theological Seminary

In a recent radio interview, the eminent Nobel Prize–winning neuroscientist Eric Kandel was asked to speculate about new directions for his discipline in the decades to come. This was his response: "I envision a multiplicity of fields branching out from neuroscience, fields such as neuro-aesthetics, neuro-ethics, neuro-anthropology. . . ." To which I responded, speaking to myself as I listened in my living room, "and neuro-theology."

In many ways, it was Kandel's work that prompted me to view neuroscience as the key discipline for understanding human behavior and community. The reality is that everything human beings do is affected by our minds—or, if you wish, by our brains. Therefore, there is a neuroscientific dimension to our entire life experience.

Reading Rabbis Wiener and Hirschmann's *Maps and Meaning* has expanded my perspective. In one way or another, the issues that emerge in the following pages also affect our entire life experience. These considerations can be profitably read not only by neuroscientists but also by anthropologists and sociologists, psychologists, philosophers, and, of course, by theologians. The singular accomplishment of this work is to expand the range of our understanding of what, until now, has been read as simply biblical religion or ancient Judaism. While this book devotes some space to the laws of levitical purity and to Israel's communal structure as it marched through the wilderness to the promised land, its purpose is to encompass the much broader scope of the human experience as a whole. In this way, their study opens up the conversation to include the widest possible range of humanistic studies.

It is, therefore, highly desirable that this book be read, studied, and appreciated by an audience far beyond people who seek a wider understanding of ancient Judaism. In effect, Rabbis Wiener and Hirschmann have read the Bible from a new perspective that pulls together much of contemporary scholarship on the way human beings live and make sense of their lives. This study reflects the academic work of a number of disciplines, including all of the social sciences. What the authors have succeeded in doing is nourishing their reading of biblical texts with material from all of these disciplines. More importantly, they bring biblical material and these contemporary disciplines into conversation with each other. In so doing, they have brought the Jewish study practice of *chevruta*, of studying aloud in pairs, to a new area of discourse, placing the biblical text, its accompanying commentaries, and cultural, historical, and personal associations into dialogue with one another.

As I consider how ancient Judaism structured space, time, and community, as well as the rituals used to communicate these structures to the community at large, I reflect on how this structuring of space is echoed in my life. In particular, the authors' discussion of the complex of rituals related to exiting and entering the biblical *machaneh*—literally, the "camp"—resonate with my recent experiences with illness. Being "outside the camp" as I spent time in the hospital for treatments has deepened my own understanding of what it is to be at home, or inside the camp. More than simply being in a distinctive physical space, being inside the camp means being in a situation where everything is familiar, where your comfort is guaranteed, and where it becomes possible for you to achieve whatever it is you feel you were meant to achieve.

Maps and Meaning has helped me clarify the use of ritual as a structuring device, as well as the impact this pattern has had on my own personal life experience. A small but meaningful example: when in the hospital, I regularly resist the demand that I put on a gown. Wearing a gown not only ritually marks that I am in unfamiliar territory, but its symbolic resonance also transports me spiritually to the striped pajamas of the concentration camp. Conversely, putting on my own clothes now has meaning far beyond wearing something familiar and comfortable; it is the first step in the longed-for process of reentering the familiar territory I call home.

Rabbis Wiener and Hirschmann's unique accomplishment, then, has been not only to illuminate biblical Judaism but also to probe deeply into the ways in which doctrines and rituals affect the everyday life of the wider community. In the broadest sense, this book is about how doctrines and rituals have a transformative effect on the state of mind of the members of that community. In addition to this, *Maps and Meaning* takes us beyond a new understanding of a purely social-science appreciation of biblical religion. It also explicitly addresses professional caregivers, for whom it will serve as a mind-broadening experience and a source of more profound appreciation of their lives' work. Whether in our personal or professional lives, we have all experienced shifts in our states of being or our spheres of function. This book gives all of us a deeper understanding of the many ways we negotiate life's transitions, and of how our choices about honoring these transitions affect our understandings of our selves, the world, and the transcendent.

Introduction

To study in *chevruta*, with a partner, is a mainstay of Jewish life. Over the years, both of us have enjoyed the fruits of *chevruta* study, but never with the intensity and creativity that led to this book. Five years ago, our mutual curiosity about Jewish teachings that might inform contemporary pastoral caregiving led us to embark on an exploration of biblical texts about sickness and healing. Each study session gave rise to an ever-expanding number of questions and associations, triggering extended forays into fields with which we were already familiar, and new arenas altogether.

We began by looking at the *metzora*, often translated as "leper," the biblical figure with a skin condition who spent time *michutz lamachaneh*, meaning outside the camp. Intrigued by Leviticus's description of a place set aside for the management of an illness, we entered into a world far more expansive than we had first imagined. The *metzora* raised questions for us that dovetailed with contemporary discussions in fields ranging from anthropology to neuroscience to literary and ritual theory. It soon became clear to us that we and other professional caregivers would benefit greatly from a deeper understanding of these questions and issues.

We dove into a rich hermeneutical process in which we placed diverse voices in dialogue with each other. These voices included biblical and rabbinic stories, contemporary scholarly material from a range of disciplines, clinical material from our own work as rabbis and chaplains, and our own experiences of being both patients and family members. Later in the process, we interviewed a number of colleagues who work as military chaplains, bringing their voices into our conversation too. Woven into all of this was God's presence, a reassuring reminder that text study is an ancient and reliable means of connecting with holiness and divinity.

Ultimately, this book is about how human beings maintain our sense of rootedness to, and interconnectedness with, all of life. Our shared love of learning was the crucible that kept the two of us connected to these very things. This book is a product of the synergy and synthesis to which the Jewish community's cherished practice of *chevruta* study gives rise.

In this book, we begin by exploring how humans maintain their sense of orientation during times of both stability and transition. In the opening chapter, we use the medical terminology of "alert and oriented" to present a model of orientation and attunement. We also summarize how contemporary neuroscientists understand the brain's propensity to "map" the world around us, and we describe studies that show what happens to the brain when it is "de-centered" through participation in meditation or ritual. We suggest that the experience of losing our usual axes of orientation might, paradoxically, allow for growth and change. In chapter 2, we present Leviticus's "maps," describing the levitical geographical and spiritual terrain. We pay particular attention to the place known as *michutz lamachaneh* and to the categories of people who spent time there. We propose that hospitals, nursing homes, and military bases are just a few of the contemporary corollaries of the Bible's *michutz lamachaneh*.

In chapter 3, we turn our attention to the *metzora*, exploring the biblical and contemporary significance of his skin condition and describing his journey to *michutz lamachaneh*, his sojourn there, and his return home again. We also describe the priest's relationship with the *metzora*, proposing that he served as "priest, prophet, and pastor," a widely used framework for understanding modern-day clergy's work. These three roles combined to make the priest the *metzora*'s *Moreh Derekh*, or Guide for the Way. Chapter 4 continues this focus on the priest with an exploration of how ancient and contemporary caregivers were and are affected by our journeys between the camp and *michutz lamachaneh*. Drawing on a ritual of return described in the Torah for the priest who had come into contact with the powerful substance used to disperse death's pollution, we propose that all professional caregivers, not only clergy, have much to learn from how the Bible approached these kinds of transitions.

Chapter 5 compares the experiences of today's patients to the *metzora*. Drawing on biblical descriptions of a Tent of Meeting that lay outside the boundaries of the camp, we describe the creation of sacred space in institutional settings such as hospitals and nursing homes, and we look at various rituals marking the numerous transitions through time and space that today's care-receivers offer. In chapter 6, we turn our attention to the Bible's war camp that was *michutz lamachaneh*, drawing parallels to the experiences of contemporary military personnel. We explore war's effects on soldiers and on those who stay behind in the camp, and we examine ancient and contemporary means of leaving for war and returning home again. Finally, in chapter 7, we discuss the social marginalization that often accompanies physical marginalization. Looking at the priest and those of the *metzora* through a fresh set of biblical stories, we propose that the margins and the center are inextricably interconnected and, when allowed to interact fully and freely, offer new avenues that lead to *shalom* (peace) and *shleimut* (wholeness).

As we worked on this book, many people provided assistance along the way. While the two of us are responsible for any errors or shortcomings, we are grateful for the role that each of these people played in imbuing the finished product with a sense of completion that we call *shleimut*.

Heather Borshof, Bob Feinberg, Bonnie Koppell, Harold Robinson, and Emily Rosenzweig, all of whom serve as both rabbis and military chaplains, graciously allowed us to interview them. They vastly expanded our understanding of this critical arena for pastoral caregiving, and their experiences, insights, and torah fill chapter 6. Additionally, Ron Lemmert added a great deal to our understanding of prison as a *michutz lamachaneh* setting, and Shlomo Fox deepened our understanding of pastoral accompaniment. Daniel Coleman, Curtis Hart, David Kraemer, Adriane Leveen, Judy Roth, Claudia Setzer, S. David Sperling, and Robert Tabak all read draft chapters along the way and offered invaluable feedback. Margaret Groarke connected us to Claudia Setzer, facilitating a rich and fruitful partnership, and Dianne Hess helped us create the index for this book. We also thank Benjamin Wiener for providing us with a copy of an Israeli Supreme Court decision.

We frequently turned to Alyssa Gray, Adriane Leveen, and S. David Sperling with questions about biblical and rabbinic passages. Their expertise contributed significantly to our understanding of key issues, and David Sperling generously spent a whole day with us, joining us in our immersion in the *metzora*'s story. The staff of the Hebrew Union College–Jewish Institute of Religion library in New York City assisted us with our many queries. We are grateful to Yoram Biton and, especially, to Tina Weiss, who conducted numerous literature searches for us and tracked down obscure sources, all with great patience. We also acknowledge and thank our patients, congregants, and students. At the bedside, in the synagogue, in the classroom, and in numerous community settings, they have been our teachers, allowing us to grow and evolve as rabbis, chaplains, and human beings.

We are immensely grateful to the team of editors and production staff at Fortress, who turned our computer-typed pages into a coherent book. Thank you to Kevin Brown, Lisa Gruenisen, Carolyn Halvorson, Maurya Horgan, Laurie Ingram, Amy Sleper, and Marissa Wold. We extend particularly heartfelt thanks to Neil Elliot, who graciously believed that our years of *chevruta* study could become the book you now hold in your hands.

Finally, we extend our deepest love and gratitude to the people with whom we most intimately share our lives. For five years, Judy Tax, Elizabeth Wilson, and Shoshana and Dalia Hirschmann generously permitted the process that led to the creation of this book to disrupt their lives, all the while offering their steadfast love and support. We thank the five of you for making it possible for us to bring this project to fruition and, with great love, dedicate it to you.

1

"Alert and Oriented" in the Hebrew Bible and Contemporary Life

In emergency rooms, at hospital bedsides, at nurses' stations, at accident scenes, and in theaters of war, medical staff use a common language to describe patients' mental status. The shorthand "A&O" indicates that someone is alert and oriented, and medical teams refine this information by describing the number of axes of orientation a patient displays. Oriented times three (which is abbreviated as "O times 3" or "O × 3") means the patient is oriented to person, place, and time. She can identify who she is, where she is, and what time it is (most often day, month, and year, or sometimes the more exact time of day). In an emergency or traumatic situation, oriented times four (abbreviated as "O × 4") indicates the patient's ability to identify the event that precipitated the need for care. These assessments provide essential medical information and they also acknowledge how frightening and life-threatening situations have the potential to knock us off our moorings.

This medical jargon gives expression to a basic truth about human existence: we operate best as individuals and as members of communities when we perceive and understand ourselves in relation to self, place, and time. Our ability to connect the current situation to the past—both the distant past and the recent past—increases our sense of well-being, centeredness, and balance. It contributes to our sense of wholeness and integrity. Things may be unfamiliar but we still know who we are, where we are, and what our relationships are to the world around us. Should any one of these axes of orientation fail to function correctly, we lose our ability to navigate in our personal, communal, physical, temporal, and geographic spheres. We find ourselves working with a malfunctioning compass, a map that is not drafted to scale, a cloud-filled sky that obscures the North Star.

This truth about orientation is juxtaposed with another significant reality, that to exist is to be in flux. We are constantly changing in large and measurable ways, as well as in tiny and often imperceptible ones. In emergency settings, medical personnel may ask a patient her name, meaning how she is identified on her driver's license and other official documents. Who we actually are, however, is far more complex; we each function with composite identities that encompass far more than our names, our current location, and the present moment. Many factors, including space, time, and circumstance, determine which of the multiple facets of our identities is of primary importance at any given moment. Most often, a person's identity as a father, for example, is not immediately relevant in a business meeting, but it is essential when he interacts with his daughter. A building or a geographic location is unremarkable until we connect it with a particular memory. One hour might seem like the next, days might blur together, unless we choose to name and mark them. Finding ourselves in a room surrounded by friends can be a wonderful experience; knowing how and why we are there heightens our sense of awe.

For millennia, religious and philosophical systems have explored two seemingly opposing truths. On the one hand, we have a deep need to anchor ourselves. On the other hand, we live in a constant state of change. While in a medical setting, the "A" of the "A&O" assessment refers to the identifiable state of being awake and conscious, we believe that faith traditions have long operated with their own corollary. We suggest that, from a religious or spiritual perspective, "A" describes the awareness that life consists of an additional dimension, one that transcends the self and the human. Much like the addition of a "z" axis in geometry produces the perception of depth through which a two-dimensional representation becomes three dimensional, this awareness deepens and enriches human experience. It is through this axis of awareness that all of creation's seemingly disparate elements appear connected. In deistic faiths, this awareness is at the heart of a belief in God; many other people operate with this awareness without relating it to a deity. For spiritual and pastoral caregivers, an individual's awareness and attunement become the focus of the "A" of any assessment of the people in our care. In this book, we will refer to this added dimension as spiritual awareness or attunement.

We all have the capacity to attune ourselves to what lies beyond the self. As pastoral educators Barbara Breitman, Mychal B. Springer, and Nancy H. Wiener explain, "In Hebrew, the word for musical 'attunement,' tuning one's voice or instrument to vibrate with everyone else's, uses the same root as *kavanah* (intention). In pastoral care, as in music and prayer, intentionality directs the heart and enhances sacred connectivity."[1]

Clergy and other pastoral caregivers serve a unique function. We draw people's attention to that additional dimension of awareness

1. Barbara E. Breitman, Mychal B. Springer and Nancy H. Wiener, "*P'tach Libi B'Toratecha* [Open My Heart to Your Torah]," *CCAR Journal: The Reform Jewish Quarterly* (Summer 2012): 135.

that transcends the present yet also allows us to locate ourselves in the current moment and find attunement to it. By making space for this consciousness, we seek to support individuals and communities as they find purpose and make meaning. We encourage them to imagine different or new times, places, or states of being and to translate these imaginings into reality. By fostering interpersonal relationships and by facilitating rites and rituals, we identify the holy and affirm the existence of this spiritual dimension for individuals and communities. Offering presence and accompaniment, we walk with individuals and communities as they negotiate transitions in a constantly shifting world. We do this regardless of which of a person's many selves is in the foreground, and no matter the time or the place.

Through our work as pastoral caregivers, the two of us know that individuals and groups seek out and are most receptive to our support, care, and counsel when their axes of orientation have loosened or failed to serve them. This can happen because of trauma, an unexpected life transition, or even an anticipated change. As pastoral theologian Carrie Doehring expresses it, "People become most aware of their values when they reach turning points in their lives and must make choices or when they are thrust into decision making because of a crisis. . . . [T]heology is a way to talk about people's deepest values."[2] In this way, pastoral caregivers help people to articulate these beliefs, explore how the flow of life's events and changes might challenge these beliefs, and, if necessary, forge new belief systems.

In our exploration of the theologies that underpin pastoral caregiving, we began to study the biblical *metzora*, commonly translated as "leper."[3] Of the many categories of people represented

---

2. Carrie Doehring, *The Practice of Pastoral Care: A Postmodern Approach* (Louisville: Westminster John Knox, 2006), 111.

in the Bible, the *metzora* provides an example of an individual who suffered from a physical condition that required him to spend a period of time outside the community's encampment in the place known as *michutz lamachaneh* (literally, outside the camp). In its narration of the *metzora*'s story, the Bible recounts how the *metzora* (the care-receiver), the priest (the caregiver), and the broader community were all affected by the *metzora*'s diagnosis and subsequent movements in and out of the camp. The *metzora*'s separation from the community was replete with repercussions for him and it also had ripple effects on innumerable others.[4]

The more broadly we read, the more profoundly we appreciated two intertwined aspects of our lives as social beings: first, our ability to remain oriented is dependent on the ways we process information arriving from different sources; and, second, our lives are inextricably interconnected, meaning that we do not and cannot understand ourselves or thrive in isolation. The Talmudic maxim, *o chevruta o metuta*, either companionship or death,[5] as well as the words of Virginia Woolf, "To be myself, I need the illumination of other people's eyes,"[6] took on new meaning and resonance for us. Guided by these insights, we came to realize that they found expression in virtually every field we encountered. As our initial narrow scope broadened, we explored diverse fields including biblical studies, anthropology, sociology, theology, ritual studies, neuroscience, and psychology. By placing these disciplines in conversation with each other, we constructed an integrated understanding of the efforts

---

3. In chapter 3, we will explore the range of possible translations of the word *tzara'at*, the skin disease with which the *metzora* was afflicted.

4. Throughout this book, we use male pronouns to refer to the *metzora*, as Leviticus does.

5. Mishnah *Ta'anit* 3:23; Babylonian Talmud *Ta'anit* 16b.

6. Virginia Woolf, *The Virginia Woolf Reader*, preface and notes by Mitchell A. Leaska (New York: Harcourt Brace, 1984), 103.

human beings make to maintain and regain their senses of orientation during times of transition.

An ever-expanding body of questions captured our imaginations and helped us conceive of broader and more varied implications for pastoral care. Finding answers to our new questions became the heart of our work. We sought to understand: What can we learn from the Bible about our human propensity to orient ourselves to geography, time, and self, and to remain aware of the transcendent? How can our experiences of the *metzora* and other biblical figures who spent time separated from the community at large help us understand the impact of losing one or more of the axes of orientation? How does a person transition from one state of being, or one understanding of self, to another? During these transitions, what are the roles and functions of other people, communal norms, and rituals? What impact does the loosening of one person's axes of orientation have for her family, friends, and community? And, after a period of disconnection or disorientation, how does everyone who was affected regroup and reengage with daily life, the community, and the transcendent? In the following pages, we present the framework we used to explore these questions.

Mental Maps

While our ancestors who collected and transmitted the Torah's teachings did not have access to the teachings of modern science about the brain and its workings, they did understand the human need and ability to create mental maps of ourselves and our environs. Through stories, human beings helped each other "map out" the terrain of their inner and outer worlds. In antiquity and now, our mental maps allow us to situate ourselves, others, and objects in time, to orient ourselves in space, and to locate people in the landscape of our relationships. While we might still intuit that our minds hold "maps" of our lives and our world, the findings of modern neuroscience explain how this happens.

As psychiatrist Daniel Siegel explains, different parts of the brain transmit information to the frontal lobe, causing it to fire "neurons in patterns that enable us to form neural representations—'maps' of various aspects of our world."[7] In order for us to be oriented along all of the axes that healthcare workers routinely use in their "A&O" assessments, the brain's distinct parts need to communicate with each other. The interconnectedness of our existence with everything else in the universe is mirrored in the ways that all the different areas of the brain work together. Understanding more about the brain's functioning sheds light on how we perceive and operate in the world. Moreover, it helps us find the insights and healing powers embedded in the ancient stories we will be exploring in this book. To better understand this, we present here a simplified account of how our brains and minds function.[8]

The brain's two hemispheres serve discrete functions. The right brain lives only in the present, responding to sensations and relating them to a reality that is not bound by time or space. It registers similarities that exist between current input and previous experiences but it does not interpret them. For example, the right hemisphere has known cold before and recognizes the sensation of goose-bumps on the skin. However, the exact circumstances of those prior experiences are not important to the right brain, nor are the meaning or consequences of the goose-bumps. In contrast, the left brain's primary function is to "make sense" of all of this sensory input by analyzing it and considering it in relation to prior experiences. Being

7. Daniel J. Siegel, *Mindsight: The New Science of Personal Transformation* (New York: Bantam, 2011), 7.

8. For further details about the different areas of the brain and their functions, we recommend the sources cited in the following notes.

cold and having goose-bumps cause the left brain to consider how *this* cold and *these* goose-bumps compare to other times the body has experienced them. The left brain also considers whether goose-bumps could indicate something other than that the body is cold, since other stimuli, such as the "chilling" experience of watching a horror movie, have caused goose-bumps in the past. In this way, the left brain creates a narrative, a story line that draws together life's otherwise disparate experiences.

The hippocampus connects these two hemispheres, running between them so the sensory "now" of the right brain can communicate with the analytical left brain. Sitting at the front of the brain, the prefrontal cortex interacts with every other part of the brain, and it maintains an internal monologue with itself as well.[9] Ultimately, the prefrontal cortex makes executive decisions about how to respond to sensory input and to the disparate responses coming from the brain's different regions. In order to have a sense of self in time and space and to derive meaning from our experiences, we utilize our ability to create and maintain mental maps. These maps depend upon information crossing from one hemisphere of the brain to the other, which transforms sensory input and data collection into something meaningful and useful. All this means that the presence of functional neural pathways within and among the two hemispheres is the key to our remaining oriented along all four axes.

The numerous parts of our brain function best when they are highly interdependent and can communicate effectively with one another. The neural firings that constitute communication between different parts of our brains lay down networks that can be thought of as the grids for our mental maps. Our mental maps, which chart

---

9. Mark B. Moss, "Understanding the Frontal Lobes: Emotional Regulation, Social Intelligence and Motivation" (course offered by the Institute for Brain Potential, May 8, 2013, New York, NY).

time, space, and relationships, contain all of our experiences and reactions. Because of this, each person's mental map is uniquely hers. At the same time, our mental maps are markedly similar to those of others in our families and communities; mental maps do not stand in isolation, and they are not objective representations. Neural pathways are activated by personal experiences, but these experiences overlap with relational and communal experiences, including the stories we tell ourselves, the stories we hear, the activities and rituals in which we participate, and the things we observe others doing.

Mirror neurons are the parts of our brains that "figure out" what another person intends to do. They also prepare observers' brains and bodies to engage in the same activity they are watching.[10] In studies in which one person performs an action and a second person observes it, images on an fMRI (functional magnetic resonance imaging) machine show that the same parts of each person's brain light up.[11] Whether we play a game of tennis ourselves or watch someone else play, the same areas of the brain and the same neural pathways are engaged. This means that the brains of both the viewer and the player record and store the images and the muscular reactions. (This is why watching a skilled player play can be an essential part of training.) Similarly, an infant observing and mirroring an adult's reactions to oncoming traffic or a loud noise learns about responses to danger, timing, and myriad other factors that will inform her daily existence.

This ability to relate to another's inner life has implications beyond imitation. Mirror neurons seem to provide us with the capacity for understanding the minds of other people. In Marco Iacoboni's words, "The properties of these cells seem to solve—or better, dis-solve—what is called the 'problem of other minds': if one has access

10. Siegel, *Mindsight,* 60.
11. Marco Iacoboni, "Imitation, Empathy, and Mirror Neurons," *Annual Review of Psychology* (2009): 60, 664–66. Online publication date: September 15, 2008. http://www.nmr.mgh.harvard.edu/~bradd/library/iacoboni_annurevpsychol_2009.pdf

only to one's own mind, how can one possibly understand the minds of other people? How can one possibly share one's own mental states with others?"[12] On an individual level, our mirror neurons connect us to the people around us, allowing us to imitate their actions, to create relationship maps, and to imagine what is going on inside their minds.

On a communal level, mirror neurons create what Siegel calls "we-maps," which "enable us to look beyond our immediate and individually focused survival needs, and even beyond the present version of our relationship maps, to a vision of a larger and interconnected whole."[13] Much as a person using a map relies on a key to explain its symbols, our ability to quickly use our mental maps depends on the meanings we come to ascribe to the happenings of the world. We learn these meanings from our families, from our society, and from our own idiosyncratic experiences. In addition to creating resonance with others' activities, Siegel explains, "At the most complex level, mirror neurons help us understand the nature of culture and how our shared behaviors bind us together, mind to mind."[14] Ultimately, these "we-maps" are the key to our sense of connection to people and groups beyond our isolated selves.

As Matthew D. Lieberman explains in his book *Social: Why Our Brains Are Wired to Connect*, the human brain's "default network supports social cognition—making sense of other people and our selves."[15] We seem to be hardwired to connect with other people and to understand ourselves in the world through our relationships. In our human communities, we survive and thrive when we acknowledge and act upon our interdependence with each other and with the

---

12. Iacoboni, "Imitation, Empathy, and Mirror Neurons," 666.
13. Siegel, *Mindsight*, 29.
14. Siegel, *Mindsight*, 60.
15. Matthew D. Lieberman, *Social: Why Our Brains Are Wired to Connect* (New York: Crown, 2013), 19.

entire universe. In fact, as Lieberman explains, "our brains are built to practice thinking about the social world and our place in it."[16] Just as the brain's neural firings lay down networks and create mental maps, so too do the stories we tell ourselves about society and our place in it lay down grids. Helpfully, these grids allow us to process huge amounts of data very quickly; less helpfully, they ignore potentially important data when the information does not appear relevant to the majority of information that is being processed or to the problem at hand. However, the brain's inherent neuroplasticity means it possesses infinite potential to grow and develop by laying down new neural pathways throughout the course of our lives. When something novel occurs, or when we make a concerted effort to break the typical patterns of our neural pathways, we might find that we see, hear, perceive, feel, connect, or think in hitherto unknown ways.[17]

Narrative

In his description of the human capacity to construct narrative, Siegel explains, "We make sense of our lives by creating stories that weave our left hemisphere's narrator function with the autobiographical memory storage of our right hemisphere."[18] While we experience the world as disparate, distinct sensations, each experienced in the here and now, we do not remember or understand them as such. In the moment of the actual experience, our right brain registers it. As neuroscientist Jill Bolte Taylor explains, to the right mind "the moment of *now* is timeless and abundant."[19] In contrast, the left brain takes these moments and "strings them together in timely succession."[20] What we make of the discrete moments, interactions,

16. Lieberman, *Social*, 22.
17. Siegel, *Mindsight*, 38–44.
18. Siegel, *Mindsight*, 73–74.
19. Jill Bolte Taylor, *My Stroke of Insight: A Brain Scientist's Personal Journey* (London: Viking, 2006), 30 (italics in original).

and experiences of our lives depends on the stories we tell ourselves. Those stories, in turn, are determined by how the left brain processes all the sensory information the right brain receives.[21]

Neuroscience, anthropology, sociology, linguistics, and countless other fields all conclude that the stories we tell ourselves are linked to the larger meta-narratives of our families and our cultures. Citing Sallie McFague, pastoral counselor Andrew Lester puts it this way, "We learn who we are through the stories we embrace as our own—the story of my life is structured by the larger stories (social, political, mythic) in which I understand my personal story to take place."[22] Given this, our stories are not unique products of our own lives and brains. As Lester explains, they are "communal products" that are not possessed by any one individual but arise, rather, from shared social interactions.[23]

Sometimes these stories remain useful over a lifetime; at other times their efficacy diminishes and they become a source of pain or paralysis. Indeed, both the substance of our narratives and our sense of self are fluid, responding to our ever-evolving and ever-changing web of relationships.[24] Each moment contains the potential to foster within us new ways of thinking and being in the world. Just as our neuroplastic brains have the capacity to continually change and grow, so do our perceptions and behaviors. Our stories hold this potential too.[25]

20. Taylor, My Stroke of Insight, 31.
21. Moss, "Understanding the Frontal Lobes."
22. Andrew D. Lester, Hope in Pastoral Care and Counseling (Louisville: Westminster John Knox, 1995), 38, citing Sallie TeSelle McFague, "Experience of Coming to Belief," Theology Today 32, no. 2 (July 1975): 160.
23. Lester, Hope in Pastoral Care and Counseling, 38, citing Gergen and Gergen, "Social Construction of Narrative Accounts," in Historical Social Psychology, ed. Kenneth J. Gergen and Mary M. Gergen (Hillsdale, NJ: Lawrence Erlbaum Associates, 1984), 173.
24. Bonnie J. Miller-McLemore, "The Living Human Web," in Images of Pastoral Care: Classic Readings, ed. Robert C. Dykstra (St. Louis: Chalice, 2005), 40–46.
25. Siegel, Mindsight, 84.

Whether we are the storyteller or the story listener, narrative has the capacity to change us on emotional, spiritual, and neurological levels. Sociologist Arthur Frank has written extensively about the human need to narrate experience. In his book *The Wounded Storyteller: Body, Illness, and Ethics*, he reflects on the transformative impact of stories on both tellers and listeners. Frank employs a map metaphor to convey the power of stories, describing them as "a way of redrawing maps and finding new destinations."[26] This insight is invaluable to pastoral caregivers because we offer care to others during transitional moments *as their stories are evolving*.

All caregivers who depend on narrative create a resonance with the people in our care. We do this by listening empathically to the stories of people who might be feeling disoriented, dislocated, or isolated. Barbara Breitman describes this as "feeling felt." She explains,

> By linking affective, visual/imagistic, sensorimotor and somatic parts of the brain, the mirror neuron system enables us to attune to another and to achieve a form of bodymind synchrony with them. When we bring ourselves into relationship with our whole being, we are actually harnessing the neural circuitry that enables two beings to "feel felt" by each other.[27]

This experience of "feeling felt" affords people a greater sense of who they are, where they are, and even of meaning and purpose. It also puts them at their ease as they tell their evolving stories.

When people find themselves in changed or changing circumstances, they might discover that their current story—and, thus, their current meaning structure—is severely challenged or even

---

26. Arthur W. Frank, *The Wounded Storyteller: Body, Illness, and Ethics* (Chicago: University of Chicago Press, 1995), 53.
27. Barbara Breitman, "Wired for Connection: Contemporary Neuroscience, the Mystery of Presence and Contemplative Jewish Spiritual Practice," in *Seeking and Soaring: Jewish Approaches to Spiritual Direction*, ed. Rabbi Goldie Milgram (New Rochelle, NY: Reclaiming Judaism Press, 2009), 380.

ruptured. While some therapeutic models focus on the development of new personal narratives, the pastoral model is distinctive. It helps an individual move from what Carrie Doehring calls embedded theology, a long-held default set of beliefs that we invoke at critical moments, to deliberative theology. These new belief systems are "deliberately thought out"; they require that we evaluate old beliefs, hopes, and values and, if necessary, formulate new ones.[28] As new theologies and belief systems are created in tandem with new narratives, new neural pathways also form. Uniquely, pastoral caregivers utilize collective religious myths, stories, and liturgies as sources of strength, hope, and connection. For people seeking to modify an old story or create a new one, these resources provide a broader narrative in which to place an individual story. At the same time, pastoral caregivers offer guidance and support to those seeking a new, deliberative theology that gives meaning and focus to their new understanding of self.

Meditation and Ritual: Their Role in Loosening and Forming Moorings

Illness, accident, injury, and war all have the potential to loosen or rupture our moorings. Difficult as the precipitating events might be, being unmoored is not inherently undesirable or problematic. In fact, such experiences can lead to growth and change. Although it might at first sound counterintuitive, certain spiritual and religious activities also give rise to the feeling of being unmoored. Andrew Newberg and Mark Waldman, who have explored the intersection of neuroscience and religion, demonstrated that the parts of the brain that help individuals remain oriented to person, place, and time are temporarily deactivated during meditative states or moments

28. Doehring, *Practice of Pastoral Care*, 112.

that people subjectively describe as "religious" or "spiritual." In these "hyperquiescent" states, the brain's impaired or deactivated area is on the left side.[29] As a result, the left hemisphere cannot weave the narratives we use to keep ourselves oriented to person, place, and time. All of this leaves us with the sense of being unmoored.

When sensory inputs to the left brain are blocked, as they are during a period of meditation, the brain no longer makes the distinction between self and not-self.[30] In this meditative state, the bounded self with which most of us navigate through the world is no longer a functional reality. With no information arriving from the senses, the left orientation area cannot find any boundary between the self and the world. As a result, the brain seems to have no choice but "to perceive the self as endless and intimately interwoven with everyone and everything."[31] In this state, people experience a sense of timelessness and placelessness. In religious and spiritual traditions, this sense of expansiveness, along with the awareness that there is no discernible or meaningful distinction between inner and outer worlds, are the hallmarks of a transcendent experience.

Neuroscientist Jill Bolte Taylor suffered a stroke at the age of thirty-seven. Her memoir, *My Stroke of Insight*, tells the story of this experience. She provides a clear and poignant account of her loss of a functioning left brain. Following her recovery, she put into words her experience of being unmoored yet still connected to the universe in ways she had not previously known. She writes:

> Feeling detached from normal reality, I seemed to be witnessing my activity as opposed to feeling like the active participant performing the

29. Andrew Newberg and Mark Robert Waldman, *Why We Believe What We Believe: Uncovering Our Biological Need for Meaning, Spirituality, and Truth* (New York: Free Press, 2006), 173–80.
30. Eugene G. d'Aquili and Andrew B. Newberg, *The Mystical Mind: Probing the Biology of Religious Experience* (Minneapolis: Fortress Press, 1999), 116.
31. Sharon Begley, "Religion And The Brain," *Newsweek*, May 6, 2001, online http://www.newsweek.com/religion-and-brain-152895.

action. I felt as though I was observing myself in motion, as in the playback of a memory. . . . [M]y verbal thoughts were now inconsistent, fragmented, and interrupted by an intermittent silence. . . . As the language centers in my left hemisphere grew increasingly silent and I became detached from the memories of my life, I was comforted by an expanding sense of grace. In this void of higher cognition and details pertaining to my normal life, my consciousness soared into an all-knowingness, a "being at *one*" with the universe. . . . I was aware that I could no longer clearly discern the physical boundaries of where I began and where I ended. I sensed the composition of my being as that of a fluid rather than that of a solid.[32]

Taylor's first-person narrative illustrates that, paradoxically, this experience of being unmoored from what usually keeps us connected to person, place, and time also has the potential to foster an altered sense of connection. It might also allow for the development of new stories—particularly ones that unite personal experience with larger religious, spiritual, or mythic narratives. Curiously, a similar effect can be achieved through what is called simultaneous hyperactivation of different parts of the brain. This refers to communal experiences, such as participation in a drumming circle, in which multiple senses are stimulated, causing different parts of the brain to communicate with each other. As d'Aquili and Newberg explain, this can also be experienced and explained within a religious or spiritual framework.

If the arousal and quiescent systems are activated during ritual, then [participants in the ritual] may experience a brief breakdown of the self-other dichotomy. This breakdown will be interpreted within the theology and stories of the religion, and this powerful experience will give the participants a sense of unity with each other because they are all taking part in the same ritual. Furthermore, the participants may have a sense of being more intensely united to God or to whatever the religious object or prayer or sacrifice may be. This liturgical sense of unity can allow everyone (not just monks or mystics) a chance . . . to experience

32. Taylor, *My Stroke of Insight*, 37–42 (italics in original).

the mystical—a sense of unity with God, with the universe, or with whatever is "ultimate."[33]

Through studies such as these, neuroscientists have corroborated what educational theorists, ritual scholars, and scholars in other disciplines have noted: that ritual and repetition are central mechanisms for teaching a social group's newest members its value system and behavioral and social norms. Religious rituals the world over provide multisensory experiences that engage mind and body, punctuated with times of quiet and introspection. Because they simultaneously engage many different regions of our brains, such religious activities can have the same impact as meditation but on a collective rather than an individual scale. Patrick McNamara uses the term "de-centering" to describe this sense of being unbounded and of transcending the limits of ordinary experience. In scientific terms, he describes de-centering as "a temporary decoupling of the Self from its control over executive cognitive functions." Another way to describe this is to say that the individual has entered a "liminal state,"[34] which is perhaps similar to what happened to the *metzora* as he traveled from the camp to *michutz lamachaneh*.

Our Stories, Our Selves

Since time immemorial, individuals and communities have transmitted stories in which people find themselves in uncharted territory—geographically, intellectually, psychologically, and spiritually. These stories describe such a rupture in the world as it has been known and experienced. They relate precipitating events, the journey from the familiar to the less known or the unknown, and a sense of radical dislocation with all of its attendant fears and trauma.

33. d'Aquili and Newberg, *Mystical Mind*, 106.
34. Patrick McNamara, *The Neuroscience of Religious Experience* (New York: Cambridge University Press, 2009), 5.

In a description of the ways that rupture manifests neurologically, Siegel writes, "Grappling with loss, struggling with disconnection and despair, fills us with a sense of anguish and actual pain. Indeed, the parts of our brain that process physical pain overlap with the neural centers that record social ruptures and rejection. Loss rips us apart."[35]

Whether losses are physical, emotional, or existential, they are painful and undermine our sense of personal integrity. To cope with and make sense of these experiences, personal and communal stories offer models that benefit both those directly affected and the community at large. As upsetting as the details of these stories can be, many of them underscore how encounters with what lies beyond established boundaries offer the potential for transformation. These stories provide hope by projecting a vision beyond the present moment into a future in which individuals and communities can survive and thrive. They are what Lester calls "future stories." In his words:

> Projecting ourselves into the future and creating stories about the "not yet" is a central process of any person's ongoing identity, the self in process. The content of these future stories is both a contributor to and an expression of a person's hoping process. Future stories, of course, can also be a source of despair.[36]

At best, our future stories provide us with images with which to envision ourselves and others overcoming obstacles and growing and changing in positive ways. When they do, they create a future into which we want to live. Alternatively, as Lester says, they can be a source of despair, presenting us with images that are so frightening and overwhelming we cannot find the motivation to move toward them.[37]

35. Siegel, *Mindsight*, 6.
36. Lester, *Hope in Pastoral Care and Counseling*, 6.

The entire book of Leviticus is itself a future story intended to encourage a demoralized people to live into it. Although it was written for Israelites living in exile in the wake of the destruction of the First Temple in 587 B.C.E., it was a story of the past that functioned as a future story. With no access to their homeland and with no shrine to house their deity, the exiled Israelites could have told stories focused solely on loss and despair. Instead, Leviticus emphasized priestly duties and the ways in which God's presence could be felt even during a period of uncertainty, fear, and wandering. Like their ancestors, whose time in Egypt ended with a new generation entering the land of the patriarchs, these exiled Israelites heard this retrojected story of wandering and projected themselves into a future of restored wholeness and communion with God. Leviticus assured the Israelites that God accompanied them during their own journey of exile and promised that, once they returned home, they would reconstruct God's dwelling place.[38]

This frame, which regards stories as lifelines of hope in the face of loss and adversity, helps us understand the Hebrew Bible's stories about three types of individuals, all of whom found themselves in a state of radical dislocation. These three types were the *metzora,* the priest who came into contact with the substance used to disperse the impurity of death, and the warrior who had shed blood. Each of them spent time away from the community and away from the familiar. Their stories are our stories, offering lessons that enrich and add meaning to our lives. The three sets of stories teach us that not all of the sojourns that unmoor us and lead us far from our comfort zones result in permanent distance and dislocation. In many cases, we can eventually experience return and restoration. We can repair the

37. Lester, *Hope in Pastoral Care and Counseling,* 72–74.
38. Baruch A. Levine, *Leviticus, Va-yikra: The Traditional Hebrew Text with the New JPS Translation,* JPS Torah Commentary (Philadelphia: Jewish Publication Society, 1989), xxxvi.

sense of being torn apart. We can reconnect to ourselves, others, and God. We can tell new stories that incorporate our new insights and perspectives.

To fully grasp how these biblical stories convey this message, we must first consider the geographic and spiritual mental maps contained in the levitical writings. These were the maps that helped the *metzora*, the priest who came into contact with death's dispersant, and the warrior to retain a degree of orientation along the four different axes. These were the maps that enabled them to find meaning in different contexts, which was at the heart of their ability to create usable future stories. It is to these maps that we turn our attention in the next chapter.

2

Mapping Human Communities

A Layering of Maps

Years ago, some atlases took the form of books filled with multilayered, translucent maps. The base map provided the earliest known contours of the country. Subsequent superimposed layers showed how the contours changed over time and indicated topographical features, natural resources, precipitation rates, and the like. This multilayered presentation enhanced the reader's understanding of the country's interrelated, yet distinct, aspects. In the following pages, we offer a similar layering of mental maps to present the Priestly imagination, contextualize the specific biblical stories we will explore, and explicate some of the more obscure details contained in them.

In the Priestly imagination,[1] two overlapping mental maps—one geographic and the other spiritual[2]—provided ancient Israelites with tools to orient themselves whether they were in familiar or unfamiliar territory. These "we-maps" served a dual purpose: to maintain community cohesion and to facilitate individual transitions. They explicated the roles and functions of each individual, family, and tribe, and they enabled each one of these entities to understand itself as a component of the larger whole. These maps were accompanied by a set of narratives that prescribed behavior during times of predictable and unpredictable change.

To grasp the experience of the *metzora* and others destined to spend time outside the camp, we must keep in mind three interrelated yet distinct features of the levitical writers' worldview. First, everything in the world was defined by its relationship to *kedushah*, usually translated as "holiness," and *taharah*, usually translated as "purity." Second, everything in the world had an essential nature. And, third, the geographic world contained two main regions: the *machaneh* (camp) and *michutz lamachaneh* (outside the camp).

---

1. In *The Divine Symphony: The Bible's Many Voices* (Philadelphia: Jewish Publication Society, 2003), Israel Knohl explains the distinctive features of the two strata of writings that relate to the priesthood and the sacrificial system. The earlier strand, known as P for Priestly, focused on the unique functions of the priesthood, identified the sacrificial system as the means to draw near to God and holiness, and articulated strict purity laws. The later strand, associated with the Second Temple period, recognized the unique functions of the priesthood but also had a democratizing tendency that allowed the populace, regardless of purity, to participate in and have access to the cult. This strand also stressed ethical behavior as a means to draw near to God. For this reason, it is known as the Holiness writings, which scholars abbreviate as H. (While Knohl's entire book explicates these distinctions, see particularly pp. 63–69.) In the schema presented in this chapter and in this book as a whole, we utilize the Priestly writings. Throughout this book, we use the words "priestly" and "levitical" interchangeably. They are not intended to describe a historical reality but, rather, the biblical world as portrayed by the Priestly authors.
2. While the word "cultic" might be a more apt adjective, we choose to use "spiritual" because of its greater relevance to our own time and context.

Kedushah, Taharah, and *Tumah*

In the Priestly rendering of the Israelites' world, only God could designate a person, people, place, object, day, or season as *kadosh*, meaning holy. That which was holy deserved special honor and treatment, and it was set apart from the ordinary for the purpose of serving God. In Hebrew, the words "consecrate" and "holy" have the same root —*kuf-dalet-shin*—because consecration is the act of setting something aside for holy purposes. God's designation of the Sabbath as a day set apart from the rest of the week for the purpose of serving and honoring God is probably the clearest and best-known example of this phenomenon.[3] God also designated the priests as a holy class set aside for the service of God and the cult.[4] Interestingly, a separate biblical strand identified the entire people as a "nation of priests" and holy to God.[5]

Regardless of whether or not they were *kadosh*, people, objects, and covered places had an additional characteristic: they were either *tamei*, usually translated as "impure," or *tahor*, usually translated as "pure." Everything in the world, whether holy or profane, could experience the transient states of *tamei* and *tahor*. Specific activities and circumstances rendered people, places, and things *tamei*; prescribed procedures and rituals enabled a person, place, or thing to reclaim its state as *tahor*. For example, the skin condition *tzara'at* rendered a person *tamei*. Once a person had recovered from his *tzara'at*, he participated in a series of rituals that restored him to a state of *taharah* (purity). Best imagined as an invisible, miasmic substance, *tumah* (impurity) was communicable to other Israelites and to objects.

---

3. Genesis 2:1–4.
4. Exodus 28:36; 29:1, 44; Numbers 8:14–16.
5. Exodus 19:6. This strand is associated with the Holiness writings; see n. 1 above. We return to this notion of a "nation of priests" in chapter 7.

For this reason, the *metzora* had to reside *michutz lamachaneh* for the duration of his illness.

Essential Nature

The Priestly imagination spoke of a world in which everything, including God, had an essential nature. Nothing in the created world could simultaneously be X *and* the opposite of X. However, something could be X and temporarily not behave as X, seemingly running counter to its essential nature. In this construct, when X's essential nature (its X-ness) was ambiguous, its own well-being and the well-being of the community were at risk. Without its essential X-ness, neither X nor those who interacted with X knew which boundaries and rules should guide their actions and interactions. Both X and those who interacted with X might inadvertently act in inappropriate ways, trespassing the boundaries of their shared mental maps and potentially destabilizing group identity and cohesion.

We offer some examples to clarify this aspect of the Priestly worldview. In the world of the ancient Israelites, all creatures were either male or female, and gender-bound rules and expectations helped each individual remain oriented to self. However, if someone had ambiguous genitalia, neither that individual nor the community could know which of the rules and boundaries relating to gender should be followed. Centuries later, the rabbis of the Talmud attempted to honor the diversity of the human forms they encountered by providing detailed descriptions of multiple gender categories, not only the two mentioned in the Hebrew Bible.[6]

Similarly, time was divided into two major categories: holy and appointed time, called *moed*, and normal time, called *chol*. All holy

---

6. See Margaret Moers Wenig, "Male and Female, God Created Them? The Intersex, Transgender and Transsexual in Jewish Tradition and in Our Lives," *CCAR Journal: The Reform Jewish Quarterly* (Fall 2012): 130–42.

days, the Sabbath included, fell into one category; workdays fell into another. It was easy to distinguish between the two when a festival was one or two days long. However, the Bible instructs that pilgrimage festivals were a week long, with work prohibited on the first and last days. Did this mean that the interim days were not holy days? Later generations of rabbis devised a way of describing this interim period as *chol hamoed*. By fusing the words for ordinary and appointed time they allowed for a period that had some features of both the sacred *and* the profane.

These examples highlight the difficulties that exceptions pose in a binary system. The Priestly system worked with two interrelated binary systems: holy/profane and pure/impure. Lawrence Hoffman, summarizing the pioneering work of anthropologist Mary Douglas, suggests another way of understanding purity and impurity:

> [R]ules about impurity . . . are actually rules about categorization of experience, or, to be more exact, rules about dealing with those things which do not fall easily into the categories. They are rules about anomalies and ambiguities, things that, in the first instance, do not fall neatly into place but are caught betwixt and between, or that, in the second instance, are susceptible to two alternative interpretations as to their essential nature.[7]

In her landmark work *Purity and Danger*, Douglas writes that "dirt" is "matter out of place." By "dirt," Douglas means substances that pollute or are taboo. She includes in this designation various categories described in Leviticus: unclean animals, bodily discharges, improper sexual relationships, and *tzara'at*. For Douglas, dirt contravenes social order. Societies categorize matter into polluting and nonpolluting substances and, by doing so, they differentiate between what can be present in social spaces and what must be

---

7. Lawrence A. Hoffman, *Beyond the Text: A Holistic Approach to Liturgy, Jewish Literature and Culture* (Bloomington: Indiana University Press, 1987), 38.

excluded.[8] In Douglas's words, a society's efforts to control "dirt" constitute "an attempt to relate form to function, to make unity out of experience."[9] A culture's efforts to name that which pollutes and to control its entry into social spaces are imbued with symbolic meaning. Within this conceptual framework, a body—whether human or animal—is "a model which can stand for any bounded system." The body's borders, then, "can represent any boundaries which are threatened or precarious."[10]

We take this to mean, first, that the body can be mapped and, second, that the body itself is a "map" that stands in for society at large. This helps us understand Leviticus's interest in the *metzora*, a person whose boundary—that is, skin—between himself and the world had been compromised.[11] What was supposed to remain contained within the human body had emerged to mingle with the world beyond it. As the solid and bounded became fluid and mottled, the *metzora*'s skin eruptions called into question the essential nature of the human form and rendered him *tamei*. These eruptions also threatened the well-being of the "body" of the community as a whole.

Geographic and Spiritual Planes

The bulk of the Torah's narrative follows the Israelites' journey through the desert as they made their way from slavery to the promised land. After redeeming the people from Egyptian bondage, God accompanied them on their journey as they moved through the

8. Mary Douglas, *Purity and Danger: An Analysis of Concepts of Pollution and Taboo* (London: Routledge, 1966), 36.

9. Douglas, *Purity and Danger*, 2.

10. Douglas, *Purity and Danger*, 116.

11. Rachel Adler, "Those Who Turn Away Their Faces: *Tzaraat* and Stigma," in *Healing and the Jewish Imagination: Spiritual and Practical Perspectives on Judaism and Health*, ed. William Cutter (Woodstock, Vt.: Jewish Lights, 2007), 145.

desert as a single body. During this journey, they stopped to set up camp at locations along the way, with the edges of the encampment serving as a boundary between the community and any number of dangers. However, the Torah records specific times when particular Israelites were required to go outside the boundaries of the camp. To appreciate the significance of these times, we describe the Israelites' geographic mental map and its relation to *kedushah*, *tumah*, and *taharah*.

Within the Camp

The portable Tabernacle stood at the heart of the encampment and at the geographic and spiritual center of the ancient Israelites' world. This structure was known by two names: *Ohel Moed* and *Mishkan HaEdut*.[12] Throughout this book we will refer to it as the *Ohel Moed*. According to the Priestly writings, the *Ohel Moed* was the only holy precinct in which God's presence could dwell.[13] God's presence in the *Ohel Moed* was dependent on four conditions: first, the cleanliness and purity of the *Ohel Moed* and the objects within it; second, the ritual purity of the priests who entered it; third, the ritual purity of the Israelites who approached it to make their offerings; and, fourth, the purity and integrity of the sacrificial animals. Any person who entered, or any object that was brought into, the *Ohel Moed* had to be physically clean, ritually purified, and consecrated to God. Anyone or anything directly involved in the rituals of the *Ohel Moed* had to be consecrated, which is to say, set apart for holy service. For example, the priests went through a ceremony of ordination that consecrated them to God.[14] Similarly, before bringing crops or animals to the

12. Richard Elliott Friedman, "Tabernacle," in *The Anchor Bible Dictionary*, ed. David Noel Freedman, 6 vols. (New York: Doubleday, 1992), 6:292.
13. Baruch A. Levine, "Mythic and Ritual Projection of Sacred Space," *Journal of Jewish Thought and Philosophy* 6 (1997): 59–70, here 65.

Ohel Moed as an offering to God, Israelites consecrated them by restricting their uses to holy purposes.[15]

The *Ohel Moed* was always *kadosh* and the priests were responsible for ensuring that it retained its status as *tahor*. In order to do this, all *tamei* people and things were kept at the greatest possible distance from it. The *Ohel Moed* stood at the center of the camp but was cordoned off from the community by hanging material.[16] Any Israelite—that is, someone who did not belong to the priestly class—who wished to enter the outer court of the *Ohel Moed* had to pass through a gate.[17] Even then, an Israelite could only enter the outer precinct.[18] From this courtyard, the Israelites could see the doorway, the *petach*, to the inner precincts of the *Ohel Moed*. According to Leviticus, sacrifices had to be made at this *petach*. This was a liminal space that represented the beginning of the holy precinct; it could be seen, but not traversed, by those who brought their sacrifices. Standing at a distance, ordinary Israelites served as witnesses to the priestly activities, which brought everyone, either directly or vicariously, into God's presence.

The inner precinct, accessible only to priests, had two interior sections: an outer chamber known as the Holy Place, and an inner chamber known as the Holy of Holies.[19] The Holy of Holies, which contained the Ark of the Covenant, was the actual site of God's dwelling[20] and was entered only once a year and then only by the

14. Exodus 28–29, Leviticus 8–9.
15. Deuteronomy 15:19.
16. Exodus 40:21-22, 28.
17. Exodus 27:16.
18. The outer precinct consisted of a large courtyard, an altar for burnt offerings, and a basin for washing. See Exodus 40:22-27.
19. Exodus 26:31-35. The Holy Place contained an altar for incense, a candelabrum, Aaron's "flowering" staff, and a table for showbread.
20. David P. Wright, "Holiness in Leviticus and Beyond," *Interpretation* 53 (1999): 356.

High Priest. No one else witnessed, or even knew, what transpired in the Holy of Holies.

Each Israelite tribe (with the exception of the Levites) had a designated dwelling area on a specific part of the periphery of the *Ohel Moed*, thus completely encircling it.[21] These areas were not *kadosh* and could therefore contain some impurity. Each family unit within a tribe had a dwelling place, an *ohel*, generally translated as "tent." Like God's *Ohel*, an individual family's *ohel* was subject to *tumah* and could be declared unfit for habitation if priests determined it could not be properly cleansed and restored to a state of *taharah*.[22] The entire camp was the locus of the community's ritual, social, commercial, and communal life.[23] It was home to the community declared by God to be "chosen among all the people," a "nation of priests," and a "holy people." Through sacrifices to God, the priests were responsible for conveying the sentiments—such as gratitude and guilt—of individuals and the community as a whole. In this way, the priests ensured God's continued presence among the people.[24] These understandings of individual and collective holiness were central to the stories the ancient Israelites told themselves, stories that we have inherited from them.

Beyond the Camp

For the ancient Israelites, the areas that constituted the *machaneh* and *michutz lamachaneh* were fluid and constantly changing. Because this was a community in transit, the camp frequently moved. The Hebrew root of the word *machaneh* is *chet-vav-nun*, meaning "to park" or "to rest," which underscores the camp's transient nature. As the

---

21. See Numbers 2. We return in chapter 7 to the topic of where the Levites lived.
22. Wright, "Holiness in Leviticus and Beyond," 356. See also Leviticus 14:33-53.
23. Exodus 19:5-6. We will explore the idea of a "nation of priests" in chapter 7.
24. Knohl, *Divine Symphony*, 76.

Israelites moved and rested, today's *machaneh* became tomorrow's *michutz lamachaneh*. The very territory that was "in" became "out," and vice versa. For these wanderers, territory and boundaries were not fixed; protection, safety, and a sense of boundedness had to be repeatedly recreated and reasserted.

Key stories about the Israelites' understanding of themselves were tied to the world that lay *michutz lamachaneh*. During their travels, the Israelites had regular contact with the people who inhabited some of these lands.[25] In addition, the Israelites' collective mental map included information about other *michutz lamachaneh* territories that had specific names like *midbar* (literally, "desert" or "wilderness") and *p'nei hasadeh* (literally, "the face of the field"). Each of these areas presented its own perils and possibilities.

As they journeyed from Egypt to the promised land, the Israelites were in a place known generically as the *midbar*. In addition, the Torah's narrative identifies more specific *midbar* locations that surrounded the camp as it moved. The terrain of the *midbar* was varied.[26] Some *midbar* areas had names (for example, *Midbar Tzin, Midbar Yehudah,* and *Midbar Maon*); others did not. Many different peoples inhabited specific parts of the *midbar*. Some lived in transient camps; others lived in fixed cities or towns. As the Israelites traveled through the *midbar*, their safety depended on their relationship with the local inhabitants, as well as on God's protection.

The *midbar* was a place for journeys, both geographic and spiritual. For individual Israelites and for the group as a whole, significant

25. The book of Numbers, in particular, describes many such encounters. See especially chapters 21–35.
26. Some *midbar* areas abutted the Sea of Reeds (Exodus 13:18; 15:22; Numbers 33:11; Deuteronomy 1:40), and others abutted towns with roads or open fields or encampments (Judges 20:42, 45; 1 Samuel 13:18). Some were near oases (Exodus 16:1), and some contained heights (Numbers 27:12; Judges 1:16). Some offered excellent places to hide from a pursuer (1 Samuel 23:25; 26:3).

identity and status transformations occurred in the *midbar*. Moses encountered God at a burning bush in the *midbar*.[27] Later, the people encountered God at mountains in the *midbar* known variously as *Har HaElohim*[28] and *Har Sinai* or *Har Chorev*.[29] Ultimately, the *midbar* was the place where the generation of Israelite slaves gave way to a new generation of freeborn Israelites who could enter and conquer the promised land.

The Bible describes two rituals in which animals were sent away to the *midbar* or to *p'nei hasadeh*. On Yom Kippur, Aaron placed his hands on a goat's head, confessed the community's sins over it, and then sent the goat off into the *midbar* with the Israelites' *tumah*-bearing transgressions. To ensure that the goat traveled sufficiently far from the camp, a designated man accompanied the animal to an *eretz gezerah*, literally, a "cut-off place," and left it there.[30] Similarly, priests sent birds to *p'nei hasadeh* as part of purification rituals for the *metzora* and a house with *tzara'at*.[31] As with the Yom Kippur scapegoat, the birds carried the *tumah* of *tzara'at* away from the camp. Elsewhere in the Bible, *p'nei hasadeh* was the area in which things that bore *tumah* were placed: refuse from the camp and from the sacrifices—particularly dung and carcasses—and human bodies denied proper burial.[32]

The accounts of the Yom Kippur scapegoat and the birds used in the *tzara'at* purification rituals suggest that the *midbar* and *p'nei hasadeh* were capable of containing or bearing *tumah* that the camp could not. Building on David Kraemer's work, we propose that the

27. Exodus 3.
28. Exodus 3:1 and 4:27.
29. Deuteronomy 4:10, 15.
30. Leviticus 16:20-22.
31. Leviticus 14:7, 53. According to Leviticus 13 and 14, outbreaks of *tzara'at* appeared on human skin, in houses, and in fabric. In this book, we are concerned only with *tzara'at* on human skin.
32. 2 Kings 9:37; Jeremiah 9:21.

scapegoat and scape-bird were sent from the human realm to "the realm of God." Writing about the similarities among various forms of "impurity," Kraemer proposes that everything *tamei* belongs in the realm of God. He writes, "God claims the territory of pregnancy and birth. . . . God even claims the pig and lobster—just two among thousands of God's creatures that God retains a full claim on and which we, therefore, may not consume."[33] Extrapolating from Kraemer's approach, we understand the *midbar* and *p'nei hasadeh* as places that had the capacity to hold things that were part of God's realm. Given this, we assume that holiness was accessible in these regions, and we proceed from the understanding that *kedushah* could be accessed by moving far into the *Ohel Moed*'s center *and* by moving far out beyond the borders of the camp.

On the Immediate Borders of the Camp: *Michutz Lamachaneh*

The area that the Priestly authors call *michutz lamachaneh* was on the immediate borders of the camp and played a significant role in the life of the Israelites. To retain the purity of the holy precincts of the *Ohel Moed* and the community at large, some individuals were required to spend time there. The priests traveled to this zone to carry out specific tasks; other individuals were sent *michutz lamachaneh* for bodily reasons. This category included those who had had contact with a corpse, those with genital discharges,[34] and those with *tzara'at*.[35] Those sent out for these reasons did not leave of their own volition but on the basis of the divine laws that governed the community. Individuals who had come into contact with a corpse and those with bodily emissions spent a specified length of time

33. David Kraemer, "The Logic of Impurity," *The Forward*, July 8, 2005, online, http://forward.com/articles/3783/the-logic-of-impurity/.

34. Numbers 5:1–4.

35. Leviticus 13:45–46; Numbers 5:4.

michutz lamachaneh, at the end of which they participated in prescribed rituals and reentered the camp. In contrast, the person with *tzara'at* was sent from the camp for an indefinite period of time.

The Torah tells two stories about another category of people who were sent *michutz lamachaneh*: those who did not honor God in word or deed and consequently faced the death penalty. One of these stories concerns a blasphemer with a non–Israelite parent;[36] the second is about a person found chopping wood on the Sabbath.[37] In both stories, the fates of the accuser and the transgressor were bound together, with the former taking responsibility for carrying out the punishment of the latter. The entire community accompanied both types of transgressor as they left the camp, and community members were then responsible for stoning the transgressor. In the story about the blasphemer, all those within earshot of the blasphemy were also expected to lay their hands upon the transgressor's head. Again, we adopt Kraemer's interpretation and propose that the community accompanied these transgressors to "God's realm," where they would die.

Michutz lamachaneh included one other place where God's presence could be sought: the second *Ohel Moed*, which Moses first erected outside the camp in the wake of the golden calf debacle. In this *Ohel Moed*, no sacrifices were needed as a prerequisite for communicating with God. There, Moses sought God directly without the mediation of a priest.[38] In this book, we choose to highlight this variant tradition, found in a number of Priestly passages,[39] because it opens up important possibilities for those *michutz lamachaneh* to connect to and maintain a relationship with God. According to this variant

---

36. Leviticus 24:10-23.
37. Numbers 15:32-36. We will return to these two stories in chapter 7.
38. Exodus 33:7-11.
39. Exodus 33 and Numbers 11-12.

tradition, this was the *Ohel* to which any community member, not only Moses, could go when she sought God or wished to present a question to God.[40]

In our reading, this *Ohel Moed* became the "Tent of Special Appointments."[41] Here, Moses met Aaron and Miriam to hear their grievances against him.[42] This was also the gathering place for those Israelites upon whom God had bestowed the spirit of prophecy.[43] Moses' activities at this *Ohel* had significance for the entire Israelite camp. When Moses went to this tent, all of the people would rise and stand within their own doorways in the camp and gaze toward Moses as he entered the Tent of Special Appointments.[44] Even though this *Ohel* was not part of the community's cultic practice, each person within the camp was intimately tied to it through his connection to Moses' communion there with God. These intriguing passages suggest that *michutz lamachaneh* was the location for yet another out-of-the-ordinary event: it was potentially the locus of each individual's private relationship with God.[45]

One last *michutz lamachaneh* place needs to be mentioned: the locations reserved for the storage of *kadosh* things and the disposal of *tamei* things. Just as holy things had their proper place within the camp, so too they had their proper place *michutz lamachaneh*.

---

40. Exodus 33:7-11. Verse 7b reads: *ve'hayah kol-me'vakesh Adonai*, "all those who sought God used to . . ." or "all those who had a question for God used to. . . ." According to *The Brown-Driver-Briggs Hebrew and English Lexicon* (Peabody, Mass.: Hendrickson, 2001), the semantic range of the root *bet-kuf-shin* includes seek, desire, demand, ask, and request (pp. 134–35).

41. According to the *Brown-Driver-Briggs Hebrew and English Lexicon*, *moed* can mean "appointed time, place, meeting" (p. 417).

42. Numbers 12.

43. Numbers 11:16-17, 24-28. Two helpful articles by Benjamin Sommer explore redactional traditions related to the outer Tent. See Benjamin Sommer, "Reflecting on Moses: The Redaction of Numbers 11," *Journal of Biblical Literature* 118 (1999): 601–24; and Benjamin Sommer, "Conflicting Constructions of Divine Presence in the Priestly Tabernacle," *Biblical Interpretation: A Journal of Contemporary Approaches* 9 (2001): 41–63.

44. Exodus 33:7-9.

45. See chapter 5 for a fuller exploration of this dynamic.

The red heifer was a holy animal, the ashes of which were the essential ingredient in the mixture used to disperse death's pollution from a person who had had contact with a corpse. The animal's body was burned and its ashes were then stored *michutz lamachaneh* in a *makom tahor*, literally, "a pure place." Just as only the priests, who were consecrated people, could be in contact with consecrated objects within the camp, a pure person, referred to in the Bible as an *ish tahor*, was responsible for carrying these ashes to the *makom tahor* that lay beyond the camp's boundary.[46] In a similar fashion, the remains from the priests' *chatat*, which we translate as "purification offerings,"[47] were also placed *michutz lamachaneh* in a *makom tahor*. Most offerings stayed in the *Ohel Moed* to be consumed by the priests. However, since the priest could not "eat his own sin," a place for proper disposal was required.[48] Finally, *michutz lamachaneh* was also used for the disposal of *tamei* materials, including the remains of a house rendered uninhabitable by an outbreak of *tzara'at*, which had to be taken to a *makom tamei* (literally, "an impure place") that was *michutz la'ir* (literally, "outside the city").[49]

The Military Camp: A Camp beyond the Camp

During times of war, God sent warriors *michutz lamachaneh*.[50] Unique among all those who made temporary homes *michutz lamachaneh*, the warriors established a separate, external camp for themselves. There, God walked through the war camp, moving intimately among the

---

46. David P. Wright, *The Disposal of Impurity: Elimination Rites in the Bible and in Hittite and Mesopotamian Literature*, Society of Biblical Literature Dissertation Series 101 (Atlanta: Scholars Press, 1987), 134.
47. In chapter 4, we explain this choice of translation, which we borrow from Jacob Milgrom.
48. See N. H. Snaith, "The Sin-offering and the Guilt-offering," *Vetus Testamentum* 15 (1965): 75. We return to this topic in chapter 4.
49. Leviticus 14:45.
50. Deuteronomy 23:10–15.

warriors.[51] While separated from the Israelites' main camp and its *Ohel Moed*, the military camp shared a distinct characteristic with the *Ohel Moed*'s altar: in both places life and death were mixed in God's presence. Warriors who had killed in battle had to remain in this external military camp to clean and purify themselves, their kit, and their weapons and wait a prescribed amount of time before reentering the camp.[52] This carefully choreographed transition was essential for those making the journey from a place that mixed life and death to a place—the community's *machaneh*—that was unequivocally the land of the living. Additionally, upon the conclusion of a war, the community's leaders—specifically, Moses, Eleazar the priest, and the chieftains—went *michutz lamachaneh* to greet the warriors.[53] We propose that, unlike the average Israelite, these divinely-recognized leaders had a special status that allowed them to travel with ease between the camp and *michutz lamachaneh*.

Contemporary Corollaries

We have provided such a detailed description of the ancient Israelites' mental maps because we believe these stories have something to teach contemporary readers about navigating transitions and finding holiness in the midst of adversity. These maps recognized the need for spatial, ritual, spiritual, and temporal containers to accommodate people whose lives were in a state of flux. Illness, the breakdown of the body, death, the breach of social norms, and going to war are all inevitable parts of life. Leviticus's mental maps offer a model for how we might navigate transitions between the known and the unknown, integrate new experiences, and create a livable future for ourselves. The world of the ancient Israelites, and the maps and

51. Deuteronomy 23:15
52. Numbers 31:12-13
53. Numbers 31:13.

stories that helped them navigate it, may seem far removed, even inscrutable, to us. The concentric regions that indicated distance from the central shrine and primary area of residence may be hard to imagine. However, our modern lives are filled with parallels to Leviticus's *michutz lamachaneh* that can breathe new life into our contemporary understandings.

With regard to Leviticus's need to contain death, we see a parallel to cemeteries and burial grounds. At least in the period since the beginning of the nineteenth century, cemeteries have been intentionally placed beyond residential zones, in part because of the fear that death carried a polluting "miasma," which offers an intriguing parallel to the levitical notion of *tumah*.[54] Although the expansion of urban and suburban areas means that cemeteries may now abut residential areas, they are still strictly set-aside places used only for burying corpses and naming and remembering the deceased. Garbage dumps, meanwhile, are an example of a contemporary physical parallel to the way that specific areas *michutz lamachaneh* were used to dispose of items that were too powerful or too dangerous to store within the camp.[55] This is especially true of toxic

54. In the colonial period, graveyards were built within the confines of settlements, sometimes in areas adjacent to churches. But, as Marilyn Yalom explains in her history, *The American Resting Place*, by the turn of the nineteenth century "many people began to believe in the miasma theory" in which "city burial grounds were [regarded as] contaminating agents that emitted noxious vapors." This erroneous belief that decomposing bodies posed a danger to public health resulted in cemeteries' "exodus from urban to rural locales." In sharp contrast to earlier generations, "[A] religious congregation would sell a valuable piece of central-city real estate, disinter hundreds of bodies, and then re-inter them in less expensive acreage outside the city limits. . . . Increasingly, all across the nation, city limits were extended and cemeteries relocated farther and farther away from the city center." See Marilyn Yalom, *The American Resting Place: Four Hundred Years of History through our Cemeteries and Burial Grounds* (Boston: Houghton Mifflin, 2008), 42–45.

55. In their exploration of the archaeology of garbage, William Rathje and Cullen Murphy track the development of modern trash disposal methods (*Rubbish! The Archeology of Garbage: What Our Garbage Tells Us about Ourselves* [New York: HarperCollins, 1992], 41–42, 84–86, 90–91). They report that New York City was the first municipality to develop a system for the collection and removal of garbage. This replaced the earlier practice of throwing garbage out of doors or windows, or burying it in a pit dug on one's own property. From 1895, public

waste dumps. Compost heaps, in contrast, are set up near residences and contain noncontaminating, reusable refuse.

For the purposes of this book, we are most interested in contemporary corollaries that hold up a mirror to biblical stories about the *metzora* and the warrior. Hospitals, nursing homes, and other healthcare settings offer an intriguing parallel to the *michutz lamachaneh* known to the *metzora*. Although we do not directly address the experience of prisoners, correctional facilities are also arguably *michutz lamachaneh* places. With regard to the war camp, there are obvious parallels to military bases.

We will consider parallels to the levitical priests and the *ish tahor* who were involved in the management of *kedushah* and *tumah*. These include people who work in healthcare settings, group homes, long-term care facilities, and correctional facilities. Arguably, it can also include people who work in funeral homes and cemeteries. Clergy constitute an interesting category of people who, like the priests of old, work deep inside the formal centers of holiness (that is, places of worship) *and* are frequently asked to journey to the margins to visit people who are removed from the ordinary settings of daily life.

employees "cleared the streets of rubbish and offal and carted off their cullings to dumps, incinerators . . . and . . . the Atlantic Ocean" (until the owners of shorefront properties complained). These early municipal solutions created the "twin problem of garbage incinerators that befouled the air and the malodorous open dumps that ringed American cities like vile garlands." Interestingly, the reformers who called for sanitary landfills feared that open dumps emitted a contagious miasma that could cause illness—much like contemporaneous anxieties about cemeteries' polluting miasma. By the beginning of the twentieth century, cities began to replace these open dumps and polluting incinerators with "sanitary landfills," in which each day's new garbage deposit is "covered with six inches or so of some material that is relatively inert and won't decompose." Landfills caught on slowly: in 1945 only about a hundred cities had sanitary landfills; by 1960, there were fourteen hundred. Unlike their open-dump predecessors, landfills are not necessarily located on the edges of population centers—and, in some cases, might be literally right underneath them. In coastal cities, landfill has been used to build solid land out of former wetlands. In most cases, landfills "are landscaped and developed, and embark on second careers as golf courses, parks, or industrial estates." They are, however, hermetically sealed to demarcate a clear boundary between the parts of the land on which we live, work, and travel, and the parts of the land where we store municipal waste. In this way, we suggest that they can be considered *michutz lamachaneh*.

Finally, we regard chapels in hospitals and other institutional settings as corollaries of the Tent of Special Appointments and believe that they hold meaning for contemporary caregivers and care-receivers.

Radical Dislocation

Becoming a patient, a nursing home resident, or a soldier presents dramatic changes in role and identity, in geographic location, and in the passage and measurement of time. Upon first arriving in these settings, people frequently realize how thoroughly disconnected they are from the daily and communal rhythms that usually orient them to time, and from the communal landmarks that orient them to place. In this book, we explore how people's relationships to themselves and their surroundings change when they are *michutz lamachaneh*. Before looking in depth at biblical and contemporary stories about being in such places, we offer some approaches to space and time that will undergird these discussions.

Human geographer Yi-Fu Tuan explains that "space" turns into "place" when it becomes, in some way, familiar or known.[56] When we are dis-"placed," we lose our orientation markers. However, we might come to regard losing an attachment to a specific place as an opportunity. In her book on Jewish conceptions of space and place, Barbara Mann explores literary representations of the "wandering Jew," a figure who epitomizes rootlessness and "placelessness." Mann turns this negative stereotype on its head by suggesting that, with their "productive attachment to multiple locations and their sensitivity to both mobility and the relations between ostensibly disparate places," these Jews are "place-makers par excellence."[57]

56. Cited in Barbara E. Mann, *Space and Place in Jewish Studies*, Key Words in Jewish Studies 2 (New Brunswick, N.J.: Rutgers University Press, 2012), 17. Tuan writes, "The ideas 'space' and 'place' require each other for definition. From the security and stability of place we are aware of the openness, freedom, and threat of space, and vice versa." Yi-Fu Tuan, *Space and Place: The Perspective of Experience* (Minneapolis: University of Minnesota Press, 2001), 6.

Following Mann's lead, we will explore how displacement from familiar zones might allow for place-making that changes both people and spaces, fostering the formation of new identities and insights.

Similarly, over the course of our lives, we measure time in many different ways. Anthropologist of religion Mircea Eliade offers an understanding of time that helps to explain the coexistence of two temporal realities. We live our lives following what Eliade calls "profane" time, the passage of one day to the next.[58] As one day turns into another, our lives follow their private trajectories. We might understand this as the daily minutiae of our lives—our disappointments and our victories—and the arrival and passing of significant life transitions. These might include births and deaths, coming-of-age rituals and weddings, as well as events associated with illness, such as the first onset of symptoms, diagnosis, surgery, admission to and discharge from various facilities, and receiving

---

57. Mann, *Space and Place in Jewish Studies*, 100.

58. For a full discussion of Eliade's understanding of time, see Mircea Eliade, *Patterns in Comparative Religion*, trans. Rosemary Sheed (New York: Meridian, 1958), 388–408. We recognize that Eliade's standing as a scholar has been compromised by revelations of his active involvement in the Romanian fascist movement, which he concealed when teaching at the University of Chicago after World War II. Adriana Berger explores the connections between Eliade's political involvements and his academic writing, arguing that the former influenced the latter. She concludes, "Eliade's case raises the never-boring question: What is the relation (if any) between the artist's moral integrity as reflected in his writings and the message of his work? In the end, Eliade's statements and actions . . . will forever compromise his scholarly prestige, leaving a disturbing mark on his integrity. . . . And, finally, what are we to do with Eliade's 'tainted greatness'? How are we to reconcile his case? It is not possible—it would not even be wise—to dismiss his achievements out of hand. But it is necessary to consider their source and analyze what in his works is still of value" ("Mircea Eliade: Romanian Fascism and the History of Religions in the United States," in *Tainted Greatness: Antisemitism and Cultural Heroes*, ed. Nancy A. Harrowitz, Themes in the History of Philosophy [Philadelphia: Temple University Press, 1994], 51–74). For another view, see Robert S. Ellwood, *The Politics of Myth: A Study of C. G. Jung, Mircea Eliade, and Joseph Campbell*, Issues in the Study of Religion (Albany: State University of New York Press, 1999). Ellwood also documents Eliade's fascist affiliations but sees less overlap between the political and scholarly realms of his life. The present authors are not qualified to assess the relationship between Eliade's politics and scholarship, though we recognize the controversy that surrounds his work. We have chosen to include here Eliade's understanding of time because it sheds helpful light on the present discussion.

difficult news. At the same time, we live in "mythical time," which connects us to the grand narratives of our communities. In Eliade's words, these are the "rhythms of the cosmos" that reveal a "fundamental sacred power" in the natural world.[59]

Our experience of the profane time of which Eliade writes is highly subjective. It can be measured by the face of a clock, by the activities in which we engage, or through comparisons to how others have spent the same span of time. William Kaufman builds on the work of philosopher Henri Bergson to present an understanding of time that explains how we experience time differently in different contexts. While the neat divisions of time on a clock face suggest that each moment is homogeneous, "experience reveals that moments of time are not alike; each moment has its own distinctive qualitative tone."[60] The passage and measurement of time are contextual, and so are the ways in which we orient ourselves to them. This means that, as we spend time in and between settings where time feels different, we must constantly renegotiate our orientation to it.

Sacha Stern also explores our subjective experiences of time. Writing about early rabbinic approaches to time, Stern proposes that this model eschewed a scale that divides time into regular units. Contrasting early Judaism's world-view with the Greek concept of *chronos*, in which time was understood as a continuum and "an independent entity," Stern explains that early Judaism is grounded in a "process-related world-view." By this he means that

[R]eality can be described in terms of an infinity of concrete, individual processes . . . [T]he key concept is . . . not time but *process*. By 'process' I simply mean a structured or meaningful sequence of events. [61]

59. See Eliade, *Patterns in Comparative Religion*, 388.

60. William E. Kaufman, "Time," in *Contemporary Jewish Religious Thought: Original Essays on Critical Concepts, Movements, and Beliefs*, ed. Arthur A. Cohen and Paul Mendes-Flohr (New York: Free Press, 1987), 983.

By way of example, Stern describes rabbinic discussions about the ordering of halakhically-prescribed activities, such as the recitation of certain pieces of liturgy. In that model, time was measured according to events such as sunrise or nightfall. To maintain an orderly relationship to time, the Rabbis established relationships (such as precedence or simultaneity) between two events. One such example is the relationship between the rising of the sun and the timing of morning prayers.[62]

For the purposes of our discussion, the questions become: When illness, war, or imprisonment interrupt the expected order of events, how do we respond? When society does not provide a prescribed string of activities with which to mark transitions, what do we create to fill this void? When the past, present, and future of our lives do not follow the story we had expected, how do we create new, livable stories? When we do not know how long we must wait, how does this change our perception of the passage of time?[63]

Our social brains and our interdependence with other human beings help us know ourselves in the world. The absence of familiar faces, narratives, and routines often leaves us feeling deracinated—or, as McNamara puts it, "de-centered." In the case of the *metzora* or the warrior, ancient Israelite society may indeed have created conditions that promoted this type of de-centering. Traumatic as it was, the experience of being temporarily "off-line" held possibilities for transformation and reintegration. Isolated in times and places lacking the markers that would typically trigger their left hemispheres' analytic functions, the *metzora* and the warrior might have found

61. Sacha Stern, *Time and Process in Ancient Judaism* (Oxford, UK; Portland, OR: Littman Library of Jewish Civilization, 2003), 2, 8, 98.
62. Stern, 47.
63. For a valuable perspective on this last question, see Maria Konnikova, "You're So Self-Controlling," *New York Times*, November 16, 2013. In this article, Konnikova explores how psychologists and neuroscientists understand perceptions of time, waiting, and reward.

themselves altered by their experiences. They might have discovered new answers to familiar questions related to identity, such as: Who am I in relation to my body, my family, my community, and the transcendent? How do I experience time and relate to other people? What are the daily rhythms that currently shape my life?

Like the *metzora* and the warrior, when we travel from one "camp" or sphere of life to another, we make visceral and concrete journeys through geographic space. Simultaneously, we might also travel along temporal, emotional, neurological, and spiritual planes. These journeys are replete with opportunities for change and growth. This loosening or absence of the axes of orientation might increase our sense of expansiveness and heighten our sense of having a religious or spiritual experience. Reflecting on different types of existence, Irvin Yalom writes,

> In the everyday mode we are consumed with and distracted by material surroundings—we are filled with wonderment about *how things are* in the world. In the ontological mode we are focused on being *per se*—that is, we are filled with wonderment *that things are* in the world. When we exist in the ontological mode—the realm beyond everyday concerns—we are in a state of particular readiness for personal change.[64]

The *metzora* and warrior's experiences of radical dislocation might have placed them in an ontological mode, just as our contemporary experiences of dislocation might also. Perhaps this is why the Priestly geographic and spiritual maps show God walking among the soldiers, or ready to be sought at the Tent of Special Appointments. The Priestly mental maps underscore the many-layered impact that one person's radical dislocation had on the individual himself and on a host of other people. With these mental maps as our backdrop, we will explore the experiences of the *metzora* and the warrior as they

---

64. Irvin D. Yalom, *The Gift of Therapy: An Open Letter to a New Generation of Therapists and Their Patients* (New York: Harper Collins, 2002), 127 (italics in original).

are depicted in the biblical text, but first we turn our attention to the priest.

3

The Levitical Priest as a Guide for the Way

In this chapter, we take as our starting point the modern view of clergy as professionals who straddle three roles: priest, prophet, and pastor. Through these three roles, clergy help people connect to themselves, communities, and God. Although the origins of this model are unclear, it is widely invoked by contemporary clergy. Across denominational and religious spectra, seminaries train would-be clergy to fulfill all three of these roles and congregants generally expect their clergy to be competent in all three areas.[1] While this model is obviously of most relevance to members of the clergy, we present it here because it offers a means of unpacking the role of the levitical priest, and because we think all professional caregivers will find resonance with some elements of it.

In the tripartite division of priest, prophet, and pastor, the "priest" role encompasses officiation at religious services and life-cycle events. The "priest" has a command of the breadth of her tradition, which includes literature, liturgy, customs, teachings, and values, and uses it

---

1. See, for example, Lawrence A. Hoffman, "Rabbinic Spiritual Leadership," *CCAR Journal: A Reform Jewish Quarterly* (Summer 2006): 36–66, especially 64–65.

to facilitate meaningful connections for her congregants. In this way, the "priest" helps people maintain their orientation to holy times, places, and rituals. The "prophet," meanwhile, speaks articulately and passionately about his era's most pressing social justice concerns, reminding people of their obligation to respond to these conditions, in part because doing so affirms their ongoing relationship with God. The "prophet" helps people locate themselves within a larger social map that is defined by relationships and responsibilities. He also leads communities as they imagine and map new, more just social relationships that will improve life for all people.

Finally, the "pastor" works with individuals and families in intimate settings—at a sick person's bedside or in a premarital counseling session, for example—to offer support and accompaniment through life's transitions. The "pastor" walks with individuals as they map their inner worlds, their relationships with others, and their transcendent experiences. Like the shepherd of a flock of sheep, she guides and accompanies the collective and the individuals who constitute it. Writing about the task of training seminary students, Nancy H. Wiener, Julie Schwartz, and Michele F. Prince describe shepherds' daily activities and relate them to the work of pastoral caregivers.

> To be a biblical pastor, one had to: treat each sheep differently, providing each the space or distance it needs from him/her and the others in the flock to be comfortable; lead all members of the flock to where they can find nourishment; bring the group together when danger is at hand; keep each individual member of the flock in sight, taking note of changes in behavior and environment; offer extra protection to the young or weak, until they are able to appropriately care for themselves. Like the pastor with a flock, a skilled clergy person moves people toward the holiness they are pursuing, comforts and guides, encourages, strengthens the weak, refreshes, restores and protects. A well-trained pastoral caregiver offers all of these skills and sensitivities to individuals, families and communities.[2]

Pastoral counselor James Dittes offers various iterations of the typology of pastor, prophet, and priest. He notes that the three roles are sometimes characterized, respectively, as "turned inward, outward, and upward," or as fostering "self-centeredness, other-centeredness, and God-centeredness," or as conveying "grace, responsibility, and holiness." However, he cautions that "these tidy distinctions are too casual, too peripheral, and too polemical" because such tightly drawn differences mask the inevitable and necessary overlap among the roles.[3] As we explored Leviticus, we were surprised to observe that this is true also for the levitical priest. Although the "priest" role is the most fully developed, there are also aspects of the levitical priests' interactions with the *metzora* that encompass the roles of "prophet" and "pastor."

In their "priest" capacity, the levitical priests offered sacrifices and performed other rituals, such as the release of the scapegoat on Yom Kippur, the mixing of the concoction of water and ashes used to disperse the pollution of death, and the elaborate purification process for the healed *metzora*. The overarching purpose of these rituals was to maintain the people's proper relationship with God. The bulk of the biblical material devoted to the priests comprises prescriptions and descriptions related to this "priestly" function. However, to make the case that the roles of "priest" and "pastor" are somewhat blurred, Dittes describes how the priestly function is informed by pastoral imperatives. In this construction, the priest's ultimate function is to change individuals' consciousness and self-consciousness. Writing about contemporary aspects of the priest role, Dittes explains,

---

2. Nancy H. Wiener, Julie Schwartz, and Michele F. Prince, "Seminary-Based Jewish Pastoral Education," in *Judaism and Health: A Handbook of Practical, Professional, and Scholarly Resources*, ed. Jeff Levin and Michele F. Prince (Woodstock, Vt.: Jewish Lights, 2013), 111.

3. James E. Dittes, *Pastoral Counseling: The Basics* (Lousiville: Westminster John Knox, 1999), 153.

People do not necessarily *behave* differently as a result of the priest's mediation; rather, they *see* themselves differently, for having been brought into relationship with the Other. . . . Pastoral counseling aspires to just such awareness and self-consciousness as a result of communication with, and befriending of, powers that loom out of reach, out of ken, clouded with mystery and awakening dread.[4]

In this way, both priestly rituals and pastoral counseling present opportunities for the exploration and mapping of mysterious and perhaps untraversed territory, whether this is our relationship with the transcendent or the inner workings of our own minds and hearts. Through ritual and liturgy, priests help those whom they serve and pastor to enter into the realm of the numinous and the ineffable, accompanying them through journeys into the self and far beyond the self. While rituals serve a great many purposes, one of them is of particular relevance to the present study. Jonathan Z. Smith defines ritual as a means of integrating loss. He explains that ritual "provides an occasion for reflection on and rationalization of the fact that what ought to have been done was not, what ought to have taken place did not."[5] In other words, in a controlled and choreographed manner, we acknowledge that things did not turn out as we expected, and we express our desire to move on.

In his role as "pastor," meanwhile, the levitical priest entered into an intimate relationship with the *metzora* centered on accompaniment, witnessing, and boundary crossing. This role is captured with the word "presence," which Barbara Breitman defines as the simple act of "being with another person," adding that "[o]ne of the greatest mysteries of pastoral caregiving is the healing power of presence." She goes on to explain, "Presence creates the bridge

4. Dittes, *Pastoral Counseling,* 154–55 (italics in original).
5. Jonathan Z. Smith, *To Take Place: Toward Theory in Ritual* (Chicago: University of Chicago Press, 1987), 109. Smith is writing about communal losses, including the destruction of the Temple, but his approach has relevance for our study of individual losses.

across which people can walk when they endeavor to communicate with one another."[6] A key aspect of presence is the ability to look and to notice. As we will discuss in this chapter, the repeated uses of the verb "to see" (the Hebrew verb root *resh-aleph-heh*) in Leviticus 13 offer a means of understanding the sight, which includes insight, hindsight, and foresight, inherent in the work of both the "pastor" and the "prophet."

Interestingly, the words for shepherd and he-who-sees are both pronounced (and transliterated) *ro'eh*, even though they are spelled differently in Hebrew. This inadvertent wordplay invites us to draw out the intimate connection between shepherding and seeing. To properly pastor a flock, we must look carefully so we can attend to those sheep that stumble or wander, or appear lost or confused. It is this insightful watching that allows us to be present with the entire flock, with those in the center and those at its margins. We look back at our prior experiences, personal and collective, and this informs how we view our flocks and their behavior. We also bring to bear our foresight, anticipating patterns and developments that might emerge. By looking carefully, we discern the different types of presence—a gentle hand, a directive word, a guiding nudge—that meet the needs of each member of the flock. (In a further interesting parallel, the Torah offers the example of Jethro, the father-in-law of Moses, who served the Midianites as both a shepherd and a priest.[7])

The prophet also sees. He sees the bigger picture and understands how one individual's situation relates to society's overall structure and functioning, and vice versa. Elsewhere in the Torah, we learn that the priests had an oracular function, which involved the Urim and Thummim, two stones placed inside Aaron's breastplate.[8] In Levitcus,

6. Barbara Eve Breitman, "Foundations of Jewish Pastoral Care: Skills and Techniques," in *Jewish Pastoral Care: A Practical Handbook from Traditional and Contemporary Sources*, ed. Dayle A. Friedman (Woodstock, Vt.: Jewish Lights, 2001), 96, 98.
7. Exodus 3:1.

the priest was responsible for observing and managing the ways in which *kedushah*, *tumah*, and *taharah* ebbed and flowed through people's bodies and homes, as well as through the camp and the community. As they enacted this aspect of their responsibilities, the priests were similar to prophets or seers—hence our use of this frame for this aspect of the priests' work.

We acknowledge that, in this typology, the levitical priests took on only a piece of what might be described as the prophet's role. Unlike the fiery and tempestuous prophets of the Hebrew Bible, the priests who spent time with people sickened by *tzara'at* were not generally concerned with society's ethical and moral lapses. However, in his groundbreaking work on these prophets, Abraham Joshua Heschel focuses on an aspect of prophecy that will undergird our discussions of the levitical priest in his role as "prophet." Heschel writes, "The prophet's ear...is attuned to a cry imperceptible to others." He goes on to say that the prophet "perceives the silent sigh."[9] This description captures our understanding of a prophetic dimension to the levitical priest's intimate attunement to the *metzora*.

In a similar spirit, we follow Dittes's proposition that there is important overlap between the roles of "pastor" and "prophet." In his words, "The prophet is not out primarily to change people's behavior, but instead wants to change people's awareness and self-perception in a way that will change their approach to *any* issue they may face."[10] In other words, the prophet helps people to map for themselves new realities that are more whole, fulfilling, and oriented toward justice, which captures another aspect of our perception of the levitical priest's prophetic role.

8. Exodus 28:30.
9. Abraham J. Heschel, *The Prophets* (1936; Peabody, Mass.: Prince, 1962), 7, 9.
10. Dittes, *Pastoral Counseling*, 158 (italics in original).

We recognize that the priestly office, as presented in the Hebrew Bible, is hierarchical, hereditary, and exclusively male. In the final chapter of this book, we reimagine the priestly role in terms that have implications for all professional caregivers—and for all community members in general. For now, we take as our starting point Leviticus's detailed description of the interactions between the priest and the *metzora*. Chapters 13 and 14 of Leviticus present an intriguing set of instructions involving the person with an actual or suspected outbreak of *tzara'at* on his skin. We use this material, along with verses culled from other parts of the Hebrew Bible, as a means of exploring the priests' tripartite role. We propose that the three roles add up to make the priest a *Moreh Derekh*, a Guide for the Way—meaning, the way to establish, maintain, or return to balance. The levitical priests attended to disrupted relationships among the individual, the community, and God, and guided people through the necessary steps to repair these relationships in order to restore balance to the world.[11] In the levitical construct, when the borders of the human body broke down, it was as if the borders of society as a whole were breaking down. When this happened, the community needed a map to lead them through uncertain and sometimes frightening new terrain. Every map needs its reader and guide, and the priests were the guides to Leviticus's maps. They were expert map readers who were intimately familiar with the smallest details and with the big picture, with the human body and with invisible miasmic substances.

---

11. The expression *moreh derekh* appears in rabbinic literature in *Exodus Rabbah* 12:1, as well as in *Pesikta Zutra* and *Sechel Tov* on Exodus 9:19, where it is applied to Moses and used to describe his ability to lead Pharaoh to repentance. In Isaiah 2:3 and Proverbs 4:11 the two Hebrew roots that form the phrase *moreh derekh* appear together, but not in this specific form. We are grateful to S. David Sperling who drew our attention to these verses.

Tzara'at in Leviticus

Although the priests dealt with illness, they were not healers; they did not bring either medical or miraculous cures to those afflicted with *tzara'at* or any other illness. In contrast to other ancient Near Eastern cultures, the Hebrew Bible presents only God and God's prophets as healers.[12] Indeed, the Bible reports accounts of prophets bringing miraculous healing to the sick, but these types of stories are notably absent from Leviticus. One such story involves Naaman, a *metzora* and commander in the Aramean army, who sought and received healing from Elisha, an Israelite prophet. Elisha also had the power to inflict *tzara'at* as a punishment. When Elisha's servant, Gehazi, tried to exact payment from Naaman in exchange for the miraculous healing, Elisha punished him, declaring that Naaman's *tzara'at* would cling to Gehazi and his descendants for all time.[13] In these stories, those who benefitted or suffered because of Elisha's miracles recognized that his words and deeds were manifestations of the will of the God of Israel. In contrast to prophets like Elisha, the levitical priests did not enjoy this type of connection with God. They were God's servants rather than God's spokespeople, God's functionaries rather than God's miracle workers. Their role was to understand and enforce rules and, through these rules' accompanying rituals, ensure the well-being of both God and the people.

12. See Hector Avalos, *Illness and Health Care in the Ancient Near East: The Role of the Temple in Greece, Mesopotamia, and Israel*, Harvard Semitic Monographs 54 (Atlanta: Scholars Press, 1995), especially 260–74, 289. See also God's declaration in Exodus 15:26, "For I, the Eternal, am your healer."

13. 2 Kings 5. See also Ephraim Shoham-Steiner, "Al Tzara'at Naaman ve'Repuyah," in *Rishonim v'Achronim*, eds., Joseph Hacker, B. Z. Kedar and Joseph Kaplan (Jerusalem: Zalman Shazar Center for History, 2009), 213–36, especially 214, where Shoham-Steiner explains that the priests diagnosed rather than cured *tzara'at*. In the Hebrew Bible, Naaman, whose story appears in 2 Kings 5, is the only non-Israelite who becomes ill with *tzara'at*. In this story, the word *ripui* (healing) does not appear; rather, Naaman's Israelite serving girl uses the phrase *ye'esof oto mi'tzra'to* ("he would cure him of his *tzara'at*") to express her hope that her master would be cured.

Leviticus 13 and 14 are unique in that nowhere else does the Bible present a detailed account of an illness or condition and its management. According to Leviticus, *tzara'at* refers to both a skin condition and a fungal growth in houses and fabric. In this book, we are concerned only with the *tzara'at* that appears on the skin of the human body. Leviticus 13 describes numerous permutations of skin conditions that had to be inspected by priests and delineates those that were *tzara'at*, those that were not *tzara'at*, and those that were ambiguous and, thus, had to be inspected again after a seven-day quarantine period. Leviticus 14 prescribes the ritual for purifying a person who had recovered from *tzara'at*.

Although it is often translated as "leprosy,"[14] the *tzara'at* described in the Bible is not the same as the illness we know today as Hansen's disease—or, indeed, any other medical condition known to modern doctors. Robert Alter sums up the current scholarly consensus:

> [M]odern scholars are virtually unanimous in rejecting th[e] identification [of leprosy with *tzara'at*]. The symptoms do not correspond, and there is scant evidence that leprosy was present in the Near East before the Hellenistic period. No positive identification with a disease known to modern medicine has been made.[15]

Alter chooses to translate *tzara'at* as "skin blanch" on the grounds that it "is associated with a ghastly white loss of pigmentation."[16] Jacob Milgrom, who laid the groundwork for much subsequent biblical scholarship on Leviticus, adopts a similar approach by translating *tzara'at* as "scale disease."[17] Since *tzara'at* cannot be equated with a single medical condition, Milgrom and Alter both focus on how the

---

14. See, for example, the JPS Bible. A note explains, "[T]he traditional translation "leprosy" has been retained without regard to modern medical terminology" (*JPS Hebrew-English Tanakh* [Philadelphia: Jewish Publication Society, 2000], 232).
15. Robert Alter, *The Five Books of Moses: A Translation with Commentary* (New York: W. W. Norton, 2004), 592, note on *skin blanch*.
16. Alter, *Five Books of Moses*, 592.

symptoms appear on the body. For Milgrom, *tzara'at*'s significance lies in the ritual, not the pathological, realm. Citing the story of Naaman, he notes that *tzara'at* is evidently not infectious since, in his role as army commander, Naaman was allowed to interact freely with others. Had Naaman been an Israelite, he would have been separated from the broader community; but, as Milgrom points out, this would have been for ritual reasons, not because of a fear of contagion.[18]

In his *Five Books of Moses*, Everett Fox uses the straightforward transliteration of the Hebrew, *tzara'at*,[19] which is the approach we also adopt. Although Fox does not offer an explanatory note, his word choice appears to be an acknowledgment that the Hebrew defies both medical classification and easy translation. Given that scholars cannot draw any contemporary medical parallels to the condition known in the Bible as *tzara'at*, the questions then become: What did *tzara'at* mean in its levitical context, and what lessons might Leviticus teach us about our own relationship to the rupture and disorientation associated with illness?

In Milgrom's schema of the ancient world, *tzara'at* is "an aspect of death."[20] Milgrom notes that, in the Bible, there are two key similarities between *tzara'at* and death. First, both *tzara'at* and corpses contaminate "by overhang"—that is, by being under the same roof. Second, there are striking similarities in the purification rituals for *tzara'at* and for corpse contamination. In Milgrom's words, "both

17. Jacob Milgrom, *Leviticus 1–16: A New Translation with Introduction and Commentary*, Anchor Bible 3 (New York: Doubleday, 1991), 775.
18. Milgrom, *Leviticus 1–16*, 818. In a similar vein, in their entry in the *Anchor Bible Dictionary*, David P. Wright and Richard N. Jones suggest that Leviticus "extrapolat[es] other symptoms which are consistent with its system of purity and impurity but which do not reflect medical reality" ("Leprosy," *The Anchor Bible Dictionary*, ed. David Noel Freedman, 6 vols. [New York: Doubleday, 1992], 4:279).
19. Everett Fox, *The Five Books of Moses: Genesis, Exodus, Leviticus, Numbers, and Deuteronomy. A New Translation with Introductions, Commentary, and Notes* (New York: Schocken Books, 1995).
20. Milgrom, *Leviticus 1–16*, 819.

require aspersion with animal blood that has made contact with cedar, hyssop, and scarlet thread and has been diluted in fresh water."[21] *Tzara'at*, it seems, contains within it a warning or an echo of death; it connotes decay. For this reason, of all the forms of bodily *tumah*, it is the closest in Leviticus's schema to death, both in its modes of transmission and in its rituals for purification.

For anthropologist Mary Douglas, all of the aberrant bodily conditions described in Leviticus deal with "a breach of the body's limits."[22] A healthy body contains and releases its fluids appropriately; the skin of a healthy body maintains its integrity. In Leviticus's worldview, unexplained genital discharges, the blood of the parturient, and eruptions of the skin all indicated that something was wrong. They were signs that the body, as a container, had been breached. These atypical discharges were *tamei*; they threatened everyone's well-being and undermined God's ability to dwell in the camp. Douglas stresses that all of these discharges were involuntary, plainly stating that, "Nowhere does Leviticus say that the disease can be attributed to sin of the victim."[23] Although *tzara'at* is associated with sin and stigma elsewhere in the Hebrew Bible,[24] this is

21. Milgrom, *Leviticus 1–16*, 819. See also Rashi's note to Numbers 12:12. Commenting on Numbers' account of Miriam's *tzara'at* and Aaron's urgent plea to Moses that Miriam "please not be like the dead," Rashi explains: "Because the *metzora* is considered to be like a corpse; just as a corpse causes ritual impurity upon entering [a room], so too does a *metzora* cause ritual impurity upon entering [a room]." We will discuss the purification ritual following contact with a corpse in more depth in chapter 4.
22. Mary Douglas, *Leviticus as Literature* (Oxford: Oxford University Press, 1999), 185.
23. Douglas, *Leviticus as Literature*, 185.
24. Elsewhere in the Bible, *tzara'at* is explicitly a punishment for wrongdoing, and rabbinic literature amplifies this idea. According to Yair Zakovitch, in all such biblical stories, the *metzora*'s transgression is the "failure to submit to the proper authority" (Yair Zakovitch, *Every High Official* [Tel Aviv: Am Oved, 1986], 142–45, cited in Shalom David Sperling, "Miriam, Aaron and Moses: Sibling Rivalry," *Hebrew Union College Annual* 70–71 [1999–2000]: 39–55, especially 48). For example, in 2 Chronicles, King Uzziah is afflicted with *tzara'at* on his forehead, apparently as a divine punishment for offering incense in the Temple without proper authority (2 Chronicles 26:16-21). A version of this story also appears in 2 Kings 15:1-5. In Numbers 12, Miriam and Aaron speak against Moses, casting aspersions on his unique claim to prophecy and muttering against his Cushite wife. Speaking through a pillar of cloud, God

emphatically not the case in Leviticus. In the levitical context, *tzara'at* was a manifestation of *tumah*, which did not necessarily bear any relation to sin or to stigma. Because both the wider community and God's earthly precinct could become *tamei*, the suspected *metzora* had to be isolated from the community to prevent transmission of *tumah* that threatened the overall integrity of the community. Again, it is worth repeating that it was not the *tzara'at* itself that was contagious but the *tumah* that emanated from it.

The Priest and the *Metzora*: A Case Study

Leviticus 13 proceeds from the understanding that illness disrupts life's usual maps, that it sends people to spatially and existentially unfamiliar places, and that it requires new maps as well as guides who can read them. Much of Leviticus 13 is presented as a flow chart in which the priest examined people with ever multiplying permutations of symptoms and determined the appropriate course of action: declare the person *tahor*, isolate the person for one week and then reexamine him, or declare the person *tamei* and, therefore,

rebukes the pair. As the cloud withdraws from the Tent of Meeting, Miriam's skin is covered with *tzara'at* "like snow," a metaphorical image generally assumed to allude to dry, white, flaking skin (Numbers 12:11). For the Rabbis who added layers of commentary to the biblical text, the connection between *tzara'at* and improper speech was of particular interest. *Vayikra Rabbah* includes a string of four *midrashim* on Leviticus 14:1 (which read, "This will be the teaching for a *metzora* . . ."). Each *midrash* describes an incident involving *lashon ha'ra* (speaking badly about another person). All four *midrashim* conclude with the formula: "As it is written, This will be the teaching for a *metzora*, [which is the same as] the teaching of *motzi shem ra*." Best translated as "bringing forth bad speech," *motzi shem ra* is a play on the similar-sounding *metzora*. The point is clear: *tzara'at* is a punishment for careless speech (*Leviticus Rabbah* 16:1–4). Tractate *Arachin* of the Babylonian Talmud expounds on this same idea. Embedded within a longer discussion about *lashon ha'ra*, we find a number of references to *tzara'at*. This includes the assertion that, unlike other people with bodily manifestations of *tumah*, the *metzora* dwells outside the camp as a punishment for driving rifts between others with his slanderous speech (Babylonian Talmud *Arachin* 16b). *Leviticus Rabbah* also posits that women who disregard the laws of *niddah* (proper sexual relations between husbands and wives) and have sexual intercourse while menstruating will give birth to babies with *tzara'at* (see, for example, *Leviticus Rabbah* 15:5).

a *metzora*. The priest had to look for afflictions that were white, reddening white, and those that lay deeper than the skin. He had to assess whether the surrounding hair had turned white, and whether the affliction itself had white, yellow, or black hair growing from it. He had to follow the course of wounds from burns to see whether they healed properly or whether they turned into *tzara'at*. He had to examine afflictions on every part of the body, in the hair and beard, and in bald patches on the head.

In a case where the priest initially determined that the lesion was something other than *tzara'at*, the person was nevertheless isolated for seven days so that the priest could reexamine him a week later. Leviticus does not tell us where the person was isolated, but it is probable that it was *michutz lamachaneh*, which is the conclusion the Rabbis reach. According to a discussion in Tractate *Megillah* of the Babylonian Talmud, the only difference between someone with suspected and confirmed *tzara'at* is that a person with a confirmed case was obliged to rend his clothes and make his hair unruly. Given this, confinement *michutz lamachaneh* was a common factor in both situations.[25] (These three actions—rending the clothes, making the hair unruly, and residing outside the camp—were prescribed for the confirmed *metzora* and are discussed in detail below.)

After seven days, the priest once again examined the person's skin. Depending on the nature of the symptoms, at this point the priest might reaffirm the person's status as *tahor* or isolate him for another seven days. If at the end of this additional seven-day period the skin remained unchanged, the priest declared the person *tahor*. Regardless of how much time had elapsed since the original discovery of a suspicious skin condition, the newly *tahor* person laundered his

---

25. Babylonian Talmud *Megillah* 8b. The Talmudic discussion does not address whether the suspected *metzora* should cover his upper lip and publicly declare himself *tamei*.

clothes and returned to ordinary life. Significantly, the person with a suspected case of *tzara'at* was not automatically declared *tamei*. Suspicion of a *tzara'at* outbreak did not change his status before God or in the community. However, he had to move *michutz lamachaneh* and he was temporarily excluded from ordinary social interactions with other people and from the sacrificial rites that allowed the people to draw near to God.

Leviticus only provides examples for these specific cycles of examination and quarantine. Extrapolating from the available information, we assume that in any case in which a person's *tzara'at* persisted, or a case in which *tzara'at* could not be definitively ruled out, the priest returned to the *metzora* every seven days to conduct another examination. Although the major rituals took place at the onset and conclusion of the skin disease, we proceed from the assumption that the priest continued to visit the isolated person weekly.

In a case in which the priest determined that a person had *tzara'at*, the priest pronounced him *tamei*. Upon receiving this diagnosis, the *metzora* rent his clothes, made his hair unruly, covered his upper lip, and called out "*Tamei! Tamei!*" The *metzora* dwelled outside the camp, away from the *Ohel Moed* and the rest of the community, until he was healed from his disease. When this happened, the priest ordered that two live birds be brought outside the camp, along with cedar wood, crimson material, and hyssop. One of the birds was slaughtered over an earthenware vessel that held *mayyim chayyim*, fresh water. The other bird was held in a bundle with the cedar wood, crimson stuff, and hyssop and dipped into the vessel. The priest sprinkled the bloody water onto the *metzora* and set the live bird free over *p'nei hasadeh*, literally "the face of the field" but best translated as "the open field."[26] The *metzora* then bathed his body, shaved all his hair, and laundered his clothes. At this point he could return to the camp but had to sit outside his tent for seven days. On the eighth day he again bathed, shaved, and laundered his clothes. He then brought oil, flour, and animals or birds to make a series of sacrifices.[27]

At this point in the proceedings, the priest slaughtered the animal brought for one of these offerings[28] and then daubed some of the blood on the person's extremities—the ridge of his right ear, the thumb of his right hand, and the big toe of his right foot. The priest then poured oil into the palm of his hand, daubed it over the blood, and poured the remaining oil over the *metzora*'s head. This ritual bears remarkable similarities to the ordination rite for priests.[29] Upon conclusion of these rituals, the person could return to the fullness of the life he knew before he contracted *tzara'at*, which included approaching the *Ohel Moed* to participate in sacrificial rites. The rituals that allowed a person to make the journey from being *tamei* to being *tahor* are rich with interpretive possibilities connected to the contemporary experience of being a patient. We will turn our attention to this in chapter 5; for now, the priests are our focus.

Moreh Derekh: Priest

In his most public role, the levitical priest was responsible for all cultic activities. It is this work that constitutes the priests' "priestly" role. The overriding purpose of the sacrificial system was to manage the spread of *tumah*, one form of which was *tzara'at*. To ensure the well-being of both God and the people, the priests were in possession of specialized knowledge that allowed them to assess the

---

26. Leviticus 13:45-46. As described in chapter 2, *p'nei hasadeh* is a space uninhabited by humans that is distinguished from both the camp and *michutz lamachaneh*.
27. Leviticus 14:1-20.
28. This was the reparation offering.
29. See Exodus 28–29 and Leviticus 8–9. This parallel will be discussed in greater detail in Chap. 7.

presence of *tumah* and prescribe and oversee rituals that marked a person's transition from a *tahor* to a *tamei* state and back again. There was nothing rarefied about the priests' work. They oversaw rituals intended to manage life's messiness—but these rituals were steeped in precisely that same messiness. The priests were in intimate contact with human and animal bodies; they conducted their work amid the blood and guts of sacrificial animals and the suppurating sores of undiagnosed skin conditions. The levitical system instituted measures to restore balance to human and divine relationships that had been thrown off-kilter by the presence of *tumah*. In the case of the *metzora*, the rituals were multilayered and involved both animal bodies and human bodies. In these rituals, two elements are particularly salient: the importance of kinesthetic symbolism, and the intermingling of life-related symbolism and death-related symbolism.

Kinesthesia

The first set of animal-related rituals involved the two birds, one of which was slaughtered and one of which became a "scape-bird," similar to the scapegoat that was set free as part of the Yom Kippur ritual. First, and on the most obvious level, the flight of the bird represented a kinesthetic removal of the *tumah*. In the Yom Kippur ritual described in Leviticus 16, Aaron placed his hands on the head of the scapegoat, kinesthetically transferring the community's transgressions to the goat.[30] Then, through the second kinesthetic mechanism of its journey into the wilderness, the goat carried away these *tumah*-bearing sins.

In the ritual for the *metzora*, a similar kinesthetic and visceral transfer happened. Before setting the bird free over *p'nei hasadeh*, the priest sprinkled some of the bloody water from the bird onto the

---

30. Leviticus 16:21.

metzora. With its ability to fly far away, the bird represented freedom. The sprinkling action transferred this freedom to the *metzora*, who was now at liberty to return to his home and community. Interestingly, the bird and the *metzora* moved in opposite directions—one away from the habitation of the camp and one toward it. Nevertheless, both the bird and the *metzora* moved toward holiness, which could be accessed by moving as far out as possible and as far in as possible. As described in chapter 2, holiness could be accessed by moving inward toward the *Ohel Moed* and its altar, and by moving outward toward *p'nei hasadeh* or the *midbar.* God was found in the intimacy of the *Ohel Moed's* curtained recesses, and God was also found in the wide-open expanse of the uninhabited environs beyond the boundaries of the camp.

Life and Death

On a symbolic level, the *metzora*'s ritual operated at the place where life and death meet. The first bird was slaughtered over a vessel of water so that its blood would mix with the water. Its blood—the substance that was once its life force—was mixed with *mayyim chayyim,* literally "living water," but best translated as "fresh water."[31] Before it was released, the live bird was dipped into the bloody water as the priest held it in a bundle with cedar wood, hyssop, and crimson material. These three materials were also involved in the creation of the *mei niddah,* the watery mixture made from the ashes of the red heifer used to purify a person who had come into contact with a corpse.[32] Rachel Adler notes that both of these mixtures combine life and death; because of this she calls them "nexus fluids."[33] In a similar vein, Jill Hammer writes that the three materials represent "life-

31. We will return to the topic of *mayyim chayyim* in chapter 5.
32. See Numbers 19.

consciousness" because they are connected to the physical structure or accoutrements of the *Ohel Moed*. She explains, "All of these things are elements of the sanctuary: hyssop used by priests for sprinkling, cedar for the wooden poles, scarlet thread for the curtains."[34]

The priests oversaw a ritual that was rich in both life and death symbolism because their task was to manage the frequent and inevitable breaches in the line between life and death. As they did this, they worked with all the materials and symbols available to them. This included, most viscerally, the bodies of two birds. One bird was slaughtered and dead. The body of the other bird dripped with bloody water as it was ensconced in powerful symbols of life and was then set free to fly away from the healed body of the former *metzora*. To perform these rituals correctly, the priests interacted with people's bodies and beings in distinctly non-normative ways. They had to look; they had to prescribe when and how to bathe, shave, and launder clothes; and they had to touch, daub, and sprinkle others' bodies with liquid substances. In the parlance of contemporary pastoral care, we might say that they became witnesses of *tumah* and its effects on people's lives.

Moreh Derekh: Pastor

As we have already noted, *ro'eh* means both "shepherd" and "he-who-sees," which underscores the connection between pastoring and seeing. In Leviticus 13, the root *resh-aleph-heh*, meaning "to see," appears in a variety of forms more than thirty times.[35] Leviticus could

33. Rachel Adler, "Those Who Turn Away Their Faces: *Tzaraat* and Stigma," in *Healing and the Jewish Imagination: Spiritual and Practical Perspectives on Judaism and Health*, ed. William Cutter (Woodstock, Vt.: Jewish Lights, 2007), 151.
34. Jill Hammer, "Parashat Hukkat," online at http://ajrsem.org/2010/06/chukat577/.
35. The verb is used twenty-one times in its active form, in which the priest is the subject of the verb and the *metzora* is the object. It also appears twelve times in the *hifil* and *nifal* forms. In both of these forms, it is best translated as "to appear." In these usages, the verb describes how the skin appeared to the priest as he conducted his investigation.

not more explicitly state that the priest looked closely at the *metzora's* body in order to make an accurate assessment and diagnosis. As he looked, the priest took in aberrant skin conditions that Leviticus describes using words that often fell outside the bounds of ordinary life and language.[36] In this way, the priest traversed the boundaries of ordinary social interactions. The priest also crossed spatial boundaries. While much of his work took place in the highly ordered environment of the *Ohel Moed*, he was also expected to travel and work *michutz lamachaneh*.

In Leviticus 13 and 14, as well as in the Hebrew Bible as a whole, the "priest" aspects of the levitical priests' work are the most fully developed. To describe the "pastor" and "prophet" roles, we must extrapolate and imagine because we lack detailed information and the text leaves many questions unanswered. Chief among these questions is this one: What happened in the case of a long and chronic illness or condition when a person was confined *michutz lamachaneh* for weeks, months, or years without getting better? Leviticus includes no information about this eventuality.[37] However, it is our contention that the priest was likely involved in the ongoing assessment of chronic illnesses, which encompassed the possible outcome of the *metzora's* death. In such a tightly managed system that required meticulous examination of multiple different skin conditions, we can only imagine that the priest—who was the only approved arbiter of these diagnoses—was involved in assessing whether a person's ongoing confinement *michutz lamachaneh* was warranted. This means

---

36. For example, Leviticus employs the words *se'eit, baheret, sapachat,* and *mispachat* (see, for example, Leviticus 13:2, 6) to describe aberrant skin conditions. These words do not appear anywhere else in the Hebrew Bible.

37. We speculate that it was unnecessary for Leviticus to explore this possibility because, in a series of chapters devoted to defining and managing boundaries, this *metzora's* status was no longer in question. He was now a corpse (in rabbinic Hebrew, a *met*) that could transfer *tumah* to the living and that carried with it clearly defined rules regarding contact and purification.

that the priest's involvement in intimate witnessing and accompaniment might spread over months or years with the same person. The *metzora* was separated from the community and might have been experiencing steady loss of health and eventual death. Only the priest accompanied him on this journey.[38]

In a similar vein, we might imagine that the priest was the only figure present with the *metzora* at the time of his initial diagnosis of *tzara'at*. Upon receiving his diagnosis, the *metzora* rent his clothes, made his hair unruly, covered his upper lip, and called out, "*Tamei! Tamei!*" We do not know if the priest stayed while this happened, but it seems likely, if only so that someone could confirm that the *metzora* had followed the prescribed steps. In addition to ensuring that the *metzora* behaved in an appropriate manner, which was part of the "priest" role, there was also a "presence" element at play here. As Adler notes, the *metzora's* actions mimicked those of a mourner expressing ritualized grief. She describes the *metzora's* actions as a "charade of death."[39] Just as a mourner is surrounded by comforters who offer their presence as witnesses, perhaps the priest offered his comfort, presence, and witness to the one absorbing the news that he was *tamei*, isolated, and restricted from participation in ordinary activities.

The name Levi, which is one of the terms used to refer to the priests, is drawn from the root *lamed-vav-yud*, meaning "to accompany." According to one *midrash*, Abraham, who is the Hebrew Bible's paragon of hospitality, was in the habit of offering travelers food, drink, and accompaniment as they moved from one

38. In Leviticus 13 and 14, there is no mention of any other person who traveled outside the camp to be with the *metzora*. However, in the overall biblical schema, priests were not the only people who could go outside the camp. Numbers19:9, for example, mentions an *ish tahor* who was involved in transporting and storing the ashes used in the *mei niddah*. See chapter 2 for a fuller description of this person.
39. Adler, "Those Who Turn Away Their Faces," 153.

place to another. The rabbis neatly bundled his threefold demonstration of compassion and companionship into an acronym that explains why Abraham planted an *eshel* (tamarisk) tree in one of the places he called home.[40] Spelled *aleph, shin, lamed,* each letter of the tree's name represents an element of Abraham's hospitality: *achilah* (food), *sh'tiyah* (drink), and *levayah* (accompaniment). In the 1990s, Dayle Friedman coined the term *livui ruchani,* meaning spiritual accompaniment, to describe the work done by spiritual caregivers. She suggests that these practitioners might be called *milaveh ruchani* (for a male) or *milavah ruchani* (for a female), which literally means "spiritual accompanier."[41] In contemporary Israel, this is one of the primary terms that has emerged to describe the work of spiritual caregivers.[42]

While the priests did not extend the typical hallmarks of hospitality to community members, they did offer sustained, steady, and reliable accompaniment. The priest was present with the sick person from the initial inspection of a condition that might pose a threat to the broader community, beginning with weekly examinations of the lesions and continuing until the *metzora*'s death *michutz lamachaneh* or his full reintegration into the community. Through this steady presence, the priest offered to the *metzora* the possibility that he might find new anchors and a new sense of orientation as he adjusted to his new reality. Cut off from his family, from the community, and from formal ritual access to God, the *metzora* was nevertheless in regular contact with the priest. Despite his *tamei* status, the *metzora* was granted ongoing interactions with a person who embodied and

40. Genesis 21:33.

41. Dayle Friedman, "Livui Ruchani: Spiritual Accompaniment," in Friedman, *Jewish Pastoral Care,* xvii.

42. See http://www.livui-ruhani.org/en/, the website of the Israel Spiritual Care Network of Organizations.

represented *kedushah*. This is a powerful example of what accompaniment means—in the biblical context and for our own time too.

Moreh Derekh: Prophet

As already noted, Leviticus 13 is organized around multiple uses of the verb "to see," reminding us that the priests were expected to examine skin lesions in all of their minute aspects. In their capacity as "prophets," the priests engaged in a different type of seeing. As seers (literally, those who see), the priests saw and interpreted the bigger picture of the relationship between one individual's body and the overall state of the community's relationship with God. One person's sickness or condition, or a death in one family, had implications for the rest of the household, for the community at large, and for God. In this schema, individuals, the community, and God existed as inextricably bound entities in which the well-being of the whole depended on the integrity of its constituent parts. The priests understood how this landscape was mapped and they knew how to guide community members along its paths.

Within this framework, the priests were responsible for seeing, interpreting, understanding, and managing the flow of *tumah* from one person's body to other parts of the communal entity. As they did this work, it was essential that the priests concern themselves with justice and honesty. In the Bible's worldview, containing *tumah* was a serious matter. An inaccurate diagnosis—whether because of an innocent mistake or malicious attack—could result in an individual's unwarranted exclusion from the community. Building on Douglas's work, Adler writes,

> It is significant that *tzaraat* can be diagnosed only by a priest. As Mary Douglas points out, this means that accusers with a grudge or panicked

mobs, who in other societies are the usual source of witchcraft accusations, cannot make a determination of *tzaraat*. The priest guarantees a ritual version of due process, and it is careful and lengthy.[43]

As Adler points out, the priests offered protection to individuals within the community. They were entrusted with the role of diagnostician, and they were also the arbiters of what was just and right. A mere religious functionary could not perform this work; rather, it had to be done by someone with a larger view of right and wrong. Implicit in Leviticus 13 and 14 is the idea that the priests dealt with weighty matters of *tumah* and *taharah*, order and disorder, life and death. Two passages in Deuteronomy draw out these themes more explicitly.

In each of these passages, the priests mediated difficult cases of civil and criminal law that raised questions about how to determine the line between life and death. The priests negotiated the dangerous spaces that opened up when one person committed an act of violence or caused another human's death. By deciding matters involving these types of disruption to the social order, which included the flow of *tumah* from a person's body, the priests maintained life and death in their proper relationship to each other. To do this, the priests needed specialized knowledge, a broad vision, and a commitment to taking care of society's deepest needs—needs that were at once visceral and transcendent. This required insight, foresight, and hindsight, and a commitment to everyone's well-being. In ritual, medical, civil, and criminal matters, the priests were seers who saw and adjudicated. They turned vision into action to protect individuals, the community, and God. To do this, they had to understand a complex

---

43. Adler, "Those Who Turn Away Their Faces," 150. S. David Sperling points out to us (personal communication) that Douglas's contrast is imprecise because in Hammurabi's laws witchcraft accusations were subject to judicial procedure. This point, and the relationship between witchcraft and illness, both factors that posed threats to God and to community, are worthy of further exploration. However, this is beyond the scope of the present study.

and multilayered map, and they had to honor the diverse elements that each layer contributed to the broader picture.

We selected the following two passages from Deuteronomy because they use the word *nega* (or its plural form *nega'im*), a term that also appears in Leviticus 13's descriptions of *tzara'at*. There, the word appears as both *nega hanetek*[44] or *nega hatzara'at*[45] and is best understood as "affliction," as in "an affliction of *tzara'at*." Elsewhere in the Tanakh, a *nega* can be inflicted by God as a punishment. Generally translated as "plague" in these contexts, the word *nega* appears in a warning of the impending death of Egypt's firstborn sons; in the description of God's punishment of another Pharaoh's household; in the description of the *nega* Isaiah suffers because of the people's sins; and in the psalmist's plea to God to take away God's affliction.[46] These types of *nega'im* are unequivocally in God's realm; they are God's punishment for transgression. Because the ebb and flow of *tumah* in a person's body is beyond the individual's control, a *nega hatzara'at* is best understood as something that is also in God's realm. The *nega* that one person inflicts on another, meanwhile, is in the human realm. Best translated as "strike" or "blow," it is to these *nega'im* that we now turn our attention.

An Example of *Nega'im* in a Criminal Matter

We will look first at an example of priestly involvement in a criminal matter. Chapter 21 of Deuteronomy provides instructions for handling a murder case in which the body was found lying in an open space and the identity of the slayer was unknown. In such a case, the elders and judges would measure the distance between the

44. See Leviticus 13:31.
45. See, for example, Leviticus 13:2.
46. Exodus 11:1; Genesis 12:17; Isaiah 53:8; Psalm 39:11.

body and the surrounding towns. The elders of the town closest to the corpse would find a heifer that had never pulled a yoke and take it to a wadi, where they would break its neck. At this point in the proceedings, the Torah instructs:

> The priests, the sons of Levi, shall approach because the Eternal your God has chosen them to serve [God] and to make blessings in [God's] name, and according to their rulings shall every quarrel and case of assault (*kol naga*[47]) [be settled].[48]

The elders of the community washed their hands over the body of the heifer and recited a formula stating that they did not shed the blood of the murdered person or witness the act, and they asked God to absolve (*le'kaper*) the Israelites of responsibility for this murder. This loss of human life, like any other death, upset the balance between life and death and (implicitly, since these terms are not used here) between *tumah* and *taharah*. With this cleansing ritual, the elders, judges, and priests brought about *kapparah*.[49] Often translated as "atonement," *kapparah* was a means of restoring balance to the world. Although Deuteronomy does not give us precise details about the priests' role in this ritual, we do learn that their presence was required. We also learn that ritual and civil matters were somewhat indivisible; the same people who served God in the *Ohel Moed* and offered blessings in God's name were also the ones who adjudicated civil disagreements, physical assaults, and murder cases.

---

47. Literally, "every strike of blow." The word *nega* appears here as *naga* because it is in the pausal form.
48. Author's translation.
49. We will explore *kapparah* in greater detail in chapter 5.

An Example of *Nega'im* in a Civil Matter

This same line of connection appears in our second passage from Deuteronomy. In the midst of miscellaneous instructions about life in the promised land, Deuteronomy states:

> When a matter is too extraordinary for you to judge, whether [a matter of] blood and blood, or law and law, or blow and blow (*nega la'nega*), [or a matter of] quarreling within your gates, you shall rise and go up to the place that the Eternal your God will choose. You shall come to the levitical priests and to the judge that will be in those days, and you will inquire and they will tell you the matter of the law.[50]

Here, God instructs the people that if they are unable to determine the just resolution of a homicide, a civil dispute, or an assault case, a judge or priest must adjudicate the matter. Again, the word *nega* appears, reminding us that disparate types of *nega'im* required the priests' close and careful inspection. Underscoring the seriousness of the topic, the passage continues with the warning that the penalty for disregarding a ruling handed down by the judges or priests would be death.[51]

In the first of these two examples, the *nega* involved death. In the second example, the *nega* involved physical violence. Like *tzara'at*, murder upset the balance of the community's life because it involved the release of *tumah*. Physical assaults did not necessarily involve *tumah*, but they upset the balance of life in more straightforward ways by bringing conflict into communal life. In all of these cases, the priests were called in to conduct an examination, draw conclusions, and manage the well-being of all of society's constituent elements—individuals and their households, the community, and God. In addition, they helped individuals and community to see more

50. Deuteronomy 17:8-9. This translation draws on Fox, *Five Books of Moses*, 929.
51. Deuteronomy 17:11.

broadly—by demonstrating that the well-being of the individual had wide implications for the entire community, for its different precincts, and for God.

The priests were responsible for naming, defining, and prescribing in matters related to illness. Like contemporary caregivers, they engaged deeply and attentively. For the priests, this revolved around looking; for contemporary professional caregivers who interact primarily through talking, the engagement is primarily about listening. However, since so much communication is nonverbal, today's caregivers also rely heavily on sight and on close visual attending. They also rely on their willingness and ability to become closely attuned to another human being, and on their curiosity about how they and others attune themselves to that which is beyond us. Both the priests of biblical antiquity and contemporary caregivers name, mirror, and reflect back what they see and hear. This includes acknowledging everything that cannot be named or known or truly understood; it requires that we leave room for bafflement and mystery.

Other professional caregivers might also see reflections of themselves in the levitical priest. For example, doctors and nurses attend to patients by looking closely and intimately at people's bodies. They do this with their attention also attuned to the bigger picture. As they assess, diagnose, and prescribe, they make use of their understandings about wider patterns of wellness and illness. They also attend to the implications of one person's illness for those around them. In some cases, they consider how a person's interactions with other parts of society (for example, a school, a workplace, or a place of worship) might contribute to, or detract from, the patient's overall well-being and support. In this way, they depend heavily upon a knowledge of society's multilayered maps, helping the patient to place herself within these maps and, if necessary, describe her changed relationships to person, place, and time.

In a world that was (and is) constantly in flux, the priests understood the larger map and the ways in which each translucent layer related to the others. They understood how individuals traversed the pages of the maps, transitioning from the camp to *michutz lamachaneh*, from *tahor* to *tamei*, and back again. In a world fraught with dangers to individuals, the community, and God, the priests were expected to make the journey as safe as possible for everyone—including themselves. As the next chapter describes, the priests were not immune to the hazards of the journey, and the levitical system had built-in mechanisms through which they could negotiate their own passage along the trail of life.

4

Empathy, Overload, and the Ash Heap: The Unmoored Caregiver

With his threefold role, the levitical priest was a *Moreh Derekh* who accompanied community members along their physical, emotional, and spiritual journeys. In the last chapter, we explored some of the parallels between the levitical priest and contemporary clergy. In this chapter, we expand our lens to include all trained, professional caregivers. Clergy represent but one type of professional caregiver, all of whom encounter profound and enduring similarities in their journeys from the camp to *michutz lamachaneh* and back again. Drawing on a single, terse biblical verse that describes the priest's movement from *michutz lamachaneh* to the camp, we invite others in helping professions to read themselves into the life of the levitical priest and to consider what he teaches all of us about our own transitions.

Being *michutz lamachaneh* has a profound effect on caregivers because of the depth of our empathic attunement to the people in our care. Pastoral educator Barbara Breitman cites the work of psychologists to explain the steps involved in the experience of empathy. First, we perceive the other person's verbal and nonverbal affective cues; then we surrender to affective arousal ourselves, as if the other person's affective cues were actually our own; finally, we have a period of resolution in which we regain a separate sense of self. In Breitman's words, "[E]mpathy requires both a capacity to identify with others and a capacity to differentiate oneself from others. It also requires a capacity to move in and out of these psychological states with fluidity."[1] This ability to identify and differentiate, and to do it with comfort and ease, is the ideal. However, we are all familiar with the reality that sometimes we struggle to separate ourselves after an encounter that profoundly touches us.

Truly seeing another's pain has the potential to cause us pain. With our mirror neurons activated, the neural loops that trigger our physical and emotional responses can be identical to those experienced by the people to whom we are offering care. This can lead us to feel genuine pain as we become aware that someone with whom we have developed a caring bond is suffering. The circumstances that are causing that person to suffer, or the depth to which we identify with the person, have the potential to knock us off our moorings and shake everything we have come to believe. In the words of Ann and Barry Ulanov, "The work of ministry requires one to put oneself in such places where one's entire safety is in jeopardy."[2] These words are a prescient description of the profound risks all caregivers take as they enter relationships of meaning.

We find a rich parallel in the experience of the levitical priest to this notion of danger. Paradoxically, preparing a substance that would help someone else regain *taharah* left the priest in a state of *tumah*. As he prepared the *mei niddah*—the watery substance by

---

1. Barbara Eve Breitman, "Foundations of Jewish Pastoral Care: Skills and Techniques," in *Jewish Pastoral Care: A Practical Handbook from Traditional and Contemporary Sources*, ed. Dayle Friedman (Woodstock, Vt.: Jewish Lights, 2001), 99.
2. Ann and Barry Ulanov, *The Healing Imagination: The Meeting of Psyche and Soul* (New York: Paulist Press, 1991), 102.

which others regained their *tahor* status after coming into contact with a corpse—the priest was rendered *tamei*. Numbers 19 describes how Eleazar (one of the priests) took an unblemished red heifer *michutz lamachaneh* to be slaughtered and burned. Its ashes were then stored in a special place, known as a *makom tahor* (literally, "a pure place"), also outside the camp, to be saved until they were needed.[3] Addressing the paradox of the priest's resulting state of *tumah*, David Kraemer explains that "the impurity of death 'leaks,' and when you are involved in 'cleaning up' this impurity, it is inevitable that you will be stained in the process. There is no protective garb that could be powerful enough to avoid the consequences."[4]

To return to the camp and reenter the holy precincts, Eleazar had to go through a purification process, which is described as follows:

And the priest laundered his clothes

and washed his body in water.

After that he entered the camp,

but the priest was *tamei* until evening.[5]

Before he could resume his cultic tasks, the priest needed to participate in this cleansing ritual and to allow for the passage of time. At first glance, the process appears to involve four discrete steps. Upon closer inspection, it becomes clear that it is more complex, necessitating many additional steps. Before laundering his clothes, the priest had to disrobe. After bathing, he had to dry off. His newly washed clothes needed time to dry before they could be worn again. Then, and only then, could the priest get dressed and walk back into

3. Numbers 19:1-10.
4. David Kraemer, "The Logic of Impurity," *The Forward*, July 8, 2005, online, http://forward.com/articles/3783/the-logic-of-impurity/.
5. Numbers 19:7.

the camp. Once inside the camp, he entered into another period of waiting before regaining his *tahor* status and being fit for service in the *Ohel Moed*.

In the Hebrew Bible, the priest was not the only individual who worked in *michutz lamachaneh* settings. An *ish tahor* was also involved in the preparation of the *mei niddah*.[6] After completing his task, he had to bathe and wait until nightfall before returning to the camp. Leviticus prescribes similar cleansing rituals in the wake of the Yom Kippur scapegoat ritual. Both Aaron, who placed his hands on the scapegoat's head, and the individual who accompanied the goat into the wilderness, had to cleanse themselves before they could reenter the camp.[7] The levitical priest and other cultic functionaries faced the shared difficulty of transitioning back to life in the camp after spending time *michutz lamachaneh,* where they had been in contact with *tumah*—whether this was the *tumah* of the *mei niddah* or the *tumah* of the Israelites' sins that were transferred to the goat's head.

These snippets of biblical material suggest that the priest functioned as part of what we might today understand as a team dedicated to caring for others in the community. In healthcare settings, numerous people interact with patients, from doctors and nurses, to chaplains and social workers, to X-ray technicians and hospitality staff. All of these people are changed in small and large ways by their daily interactions with patients and family members. In congregations, clergy are part of teams comprised of professional and lay leaders who may not themselves travel *michutz lamachaneh* but are nevertheless touched by clergy people's journeys there. This might include the administrator who receives a distressed congregant's call, the volunteer who orders a meal to be delivered to a mourning

6. Numbers 19:9-10. See chapter 2 for a description of this *ish tahor*.
7. Leviticus 16:23-26.

family's home, and the cleaning person who encounters recently bereaved and tearful congregants entering the rabbi's study. The levitical priest's multistage transition back into the camp invites all contemporary caregivers to explore our own spatial, physical, spiritual, temporal, and emotional journeys as we travel between the settings where we work and the other spheres of our lives.

A New Take on *Ivrim*: The Caregiver as Boundary Crosser

In biblical narratives, those who were *michutz lamachaneh* were, by definition, out of their element. As Rachel Adler astutely notes, this truth applied both to the one whose state of *tumah* placed him or her *michutz lamachaneh* and to the priest who traveled there to check on the *metzora*. She writes, "The priest [had to] go out to the very antithesis of his home territory, from the shrine of the ever living God to . . . outside the camp to perform the [purification] ritual."[8] As professional caregivers, we regularly traverse the border that separates a modern-day *michutz lamachaneh* setting from the rest of the community. However, as we focus on the individuals and communities in our care, we are prone to forget how removed *michutz lamachaneh* is from the places we live, shop, exercise, visit friends, and conduct most of the other activities of our daily lives. While we become far more familiar with, and accustomed to, spending time *michutz lamachaneh* than many other people, we must still pay attention to how we navigate these journeys, both as we move away from normative daily life *and* as we return to it again.

As we move from the camp to *michutz lamachaneh* and back again, we are boundary crossers. The Hebrew root *ayin-bet-resh* appears in

---

8. Rachel Adler, "Those Who Turn Away Their Faces: *Tzaraat* and Stigma," in *Healing and the Jewish Imagination: Spiritual and Practical Perspectives on Judaism and Health*, ed. William Cutter (Woodstock, Vt.: Jewish Lights, 2007), 155.

the verb "to cross" or "to trespass." The noun refers to "a region beyond or a distant side."[9] Professional caregivers constantly cross boundaries. Indeed, since family members and the general public are denied free access to emergency sites, morgues, hospitals, prisons, and military bases, most people who enter the spaces we do would be deemed trespassers. We regularly find ourselves in a region beyond what is familiar to many, invited to the far side of people's physical, emotional, and spiritual worlds.

In the biblical worldview, being a boundary crosser is an integral part of Hebrew/Israelite identity. The adjectival form of the root *avar*—*Ivri* in the singular, and *Ivrim* in the plural—means Hebrew. In the early biblical narratives, individuals and groups were identified as *Ivrim* when they went outside their home territory. In Genesis, Abram was identified as an *Ivri* when he dwelled among "a foreign people."[10] To the local people, the *Ivri* was a foreign sojourner who had crossed a boundary to enter their land. If the *Ivri* ever returned home, he would have to cross this boundary again.

Our exploration of the word *Ivrim* adds another dimension to an arena already rich in contemporary interpretations.[11] By embracing boundary crossing as an essential element of our professional identity, we enrich our understanding of our needs as caregivers. Just as we must wait in line to show a passport when we enter another country, we must similarly show identification before entering a prison, military base, healthcare facility, or accident scene. Often, we must repeat this procedure when we leave. The time it takes to wait in line, show our identification, and receive a visitor's pass presents

9. F. Brown, S. Driver, and C. Briggs, *The Brown-Driver-Briggs Hebrew and English Lexicon* (Peabody, Mass.: Hendrickson, 2001), 716–18.
10. Genesis 14:13.
11. In recent years, a growing number of Jewish writers have applied this notion of boundary crossing to contemporary transitions. For example, in his blessing for those transitioning genders, Rabbi Elliot Kukla invokes the image of a boundary crosser (www.transtorah.org).

an opportunity to recognize the significance of the movement from one distinct territory to another, each of which has its own norms, culture, and expectations. This waiting period invites us to engage deeply with the significance of such transitions and to reflect on the differences between the place we are leaving and the place we are entering. In particular, it is an invitation to consider how *tumah* and *kedushah* flow through each type of precinct.

Journeying into the Heart of *Tumah* and *Kedushah*

The levitical priests held an inherited office that was affirmed through an elaborate ordination ritual.[12] While contemporary caregivers do not necessarily enter into the roles held by their parents, they go through a period of study, hands-on training, and examinations, followed by specific rituals that confirm an ability to commence work as a caregiver. In coursework and fieldwork, contemporary students go through some process of initiation. These tend to involve interactions between experienced practitioners and the initiate and they rarely take place in the public sphere. Following a prescribed period of preparation, and frequently much soul-searching to discern that her path is the right one, the caregiver participates in a public ritual. At religious ordination ceremonies, or at graduations where new doctors receive a stethoscope, among other examples, the training institution and the assembled public affirm the new caregiver's change in status. From this time forward, the caregiver is expected to assume the mantle of responsibilities associated with her new status. When exercising these responsibilities, she now has license—in many cases both literally and metaphorically—to breach social norms. This might include crossing into spatial, spiritual, or emotional territories that are generally considered off-limits, such

---

12. Exodus 28–29; Leviticus 8–9.

as prisons, or people's private homes, or their inner spiritual and emotional lives.

Professional caregivers often describe how they are both drawn to and repulsed by the same things as other people—death, disease, trauma, and primal emotional expressions, to name but a few. While most people can choose whether to approach or retreat in such situations, many contemporary caregivers are first responders who do not generally have this option. For example, like fire and medical first responders who provide immediate and essential physical care in an emergency, contemporary clergy are expected to enter these highly charged situations and provide spiritual care there. Accident or disaster sites and intensive or critical care units constitute a unique category of human space. Family members are given only restricted access that proscribes visitation, but first responders and other professional caregivers have unrestricted access and are expected to use it. In these spaces, we and those whom we accompany have a sense of sharing time-out-of-time and space-out-of-space; a sense of unboundedness reigns. These moments that defy description are times when *yirah va'fachad*, often translated as "fear and awe," converge.[13]

Typically, most people seek the holy in their places of worship, at sites of natural beauty, or as they eat around a table with their loved ones. Curiously, places that at first sight seem the most removed from such settings sometimes evoke a similar sense of the holy. In the levitical construct, these are places where the *tumah* of illness and/ or death is strongly present. These locations foster a heightened state

13. Both *yirah* and *pachad* can be translated as fear. *Yirah* has the double meaning of both fear and reverence; it captures the experience of being overwhelmed by an experience and feeling awe and fear simultaneously. *Pachad* is a more visceral experience of fear, that is sometimes translated as dread. Together, they are used to describe the sensation of being in the presence of the holy. For an example of a liturgical usage, see the *Magein Avot* prayer, which is part of the Shabbat evening *Amidah*.

of consciousness, focus, and attunement; they are situations in which we often feel open to something beyond ourselves, to being in the presence of something apart and transformative. In the language of the Bible, the places of greatest *tumah* actually have a lot in common with those places designated as having the greatest *kedushah*. Perhaps it is caregivers' desires for these heightened, unbounded experiences that explains why we are drawn to situations that include undeniably frightening and repelling elements.

At disaster sites or by the deathbed, we and those with whom we are in contact often have an awareness of transcendence. Like the levitical priests who interacted with the *metzora*, we do this outside the communal spaces designated for communing with God, and often outside normative areas for social and communal interaction. Like the priests, we meet people on the margins and accompany them during their sojourn there. This reality puts us into regular contact with the messiness of life, reminding us that our bodies, our minds, our emotions, and the circumstances of our lives are more often than not out of our control. It is precisely when individuals cannot contain the world around them or their responses to it that professional caregivers are with them. At these times, we receive people in all their rawness and vulnerability. When familiar boundaries are breached, axes of orientation loosened, and the left brain's meaning-making functions least able to function, we help people open to the expansive possibilities available to them in their altered states.

Tzara'at, which constitutes a breach of the body's boundaries, is a physical expression of our vulnerability and a medical metaphor for life's unpredictability. Leviticus's discussions of *tzara'at* acknowledge and address these realities, providing us with ancient parallels for what we today call professional caregiving. By taking a close look at the interactions between the *metzora* and the priest, we find a window through which to view our own work. Each encounter we have—in houses of worship, agencies, healthcare facilities, offices, or neighborhoods—parallels that of the ancient priests. In these settings, we examine and assess the state of the individuals before us, interacting with them in ways that defy normal social intercourse. People expose parts of themselves to us that they would never expose to others, inviting us to see their most delicate, painful, and even shameful spots.

The teens who tell us they've been cutting and show us their scars, those who reveal their sexual infidelities or their civil or criminal offenses, those who speak of the chasm between their self-images and how they are acting toward those they love—they all come to us with their open wounds seeking assessment and guidance about how to reorient themselves. They fear the worst, that they may never regain a sense of wholeness, never find their wounds healed. Yet, at the same time, by seeking us out, they reveal their enduring hope that these transformations are possible. They trust our knowledge, expertise, and sensitivity, whether or not we feel we have earned it or deserve it.

Avot hatumah: Caregivers and the Chain of Transmission

Professional caregivers frequently describe how much meaning we find in our work with people who are suffering. We recognize the sanctity of the work we choose to do and would not willingly give it up. However, after we experience one of these transcendent moments, we often find ourselves distracted, short-tempered, or distant from the people we encounter in the hours or days that follow. We return from *michutz lamachaneh* bearing the rawness and messiness that dominates the realities of life there. When we immediately throw ourselves back into everyday tasks, we transmit the disturbing effects of these experiences to the people with whom we are next in contact. In the midst of this, it is sometimes difficult for us and for those around us to understand what is happening. The rabbinic category of *av hatumah* sheds light on these troubling spirals of unintended consequences.

In the levitical system, *tumah* could be passed from one individual to other individuals and to certain objects. For this reason, the *metzora* had to reside *michutz lamachaneh*, the priests had to make a dispersant for death's pollution, and warriors who had shed blood had to cleanse themselves and their weapons and wait a prescribed period of time before returning to the camp. The rabbis of the Mishnah and Tosefta[14] elaborated on the Hebrew Bible's concerns about the unintended transmission of *tumah*, calling the source of the contamination *av hatumah*—literally, "the father of the *tumah*." Their use of familial language conveys the ineluctable reality that traits can be unwittingly passed from one "generation" to the next. In the case of *tumah*, the *av* transmitted it to both people and to things; the object or person who contracted the *tumah* could only transmit it to food and drink, not to people or vessels.[15]

This schema offers an astonishingly apt corollary for the present discussion about self-care. Being *michutz lamachaneh* affects not only us but also the people with whom we are in direct contact and then, frequently, the people with whom they have contact. The effects of our work lives radiate outward, creating secondary and tertiary effects, as this vignette illustrates.

> After her weekly visit with Fred, a terminally ill congregant, Rabbi Sarah Katz got in her car and drove to the synagogue to meet with the nursery school students. She couldn't get the image of the younger,

---

14. The Mishnah and Tosefta are the earliest layer of rabbinic commentary.
15. Mishnah *Makhshirin* 4:8; Tosefta *Keilim* 4:18. For a concise explanation about the transmission of *tumah* in the Talmud, see Adin Steinsaltz, *The Talmud, The Steinsaltz Edition: A Reference Guide* (Jerusalem: Israel Institute for Talmudic Publications, 1988; English translation New York: Random House, 1989), 157 (4) and 186 (1).

more vital Fred of just a few years ago out of her head, an image that stood in stark contrast to the man whom she had just seen. As Sarah walked into the nursery school, the shouts of the children were a welcome, but only temporary, distraction. Their high energy presented such a contrast to her own mood that she found her thoughts wandering. Miriam, the children's teacher, noticed the distant look on Sarah's face and attempted to get her attention. When she had to call to her several times, Miriam got frustrated. When Sarah only half-heartedly engaged with the children, Miriam's irritation grew. When Sarah left the room, Miriam's frustration spilled over to the children. Their silly comments and jokes didn't bring a smile to her face; instead, she felt overwhelmed by their playful and rambunctious behavior and tried to cut it off. A few of the children were caught off guard by her response and began to cry. Miriam was so upset she just wanted to join them, but knew she couldn't. When she got home, she was feeling so miserable about the way the day had gone, she had no energy for her own family.[16]

In contemporary parlance, when we return from *michutz lamachaneh* we are not fit for human contact, and this unfitness ripples out to those with whom we interact. Regardless, we and others collude in the charade that we can immediately and successfully gather ourselves and have meaningful interactions. Our coworkers, friends, and families feel in subtle and not so subtle ways the impact of the traumas only we have actually witnessed. Our dis-ease becomes theirs. How different Miriam's expectations would have been if Sarah had sent an e-mail or text letting her know that she would be coming to the class after a particularly upsetting *bikkur cholim* visit.[17] Miriam could have then adjusted her classroom plan to reflect her previous experiences with Sarah after she returned from visits that stretched her emotional and spiritual resources. Without this type of communication, both Sarah and Miriam were trying to function normally in abnormal circumstances. What is true for Sarah and

16. In this vignette and all others in this book, identifying characteristics have been changed.
17. This is the rabbinic term for visiting the sick.

Miriam is often also true for caregivers' families and friends. If we don't acknowledge when our inner resources are drained, we make it nearly impossible for others to support us, and we leave them with little option but to shoulder the burden of our *tumah* along with us.

Levitical Priests and Contemporary Professional Caregivers

As we seek healthy ways of naming and letting go of these burdens, the priest's relationship with the *metzora* provides a model for multiple different elements of our professional lives. Like the levitical priest, we need to understand that we accompany others on journeys similar to that of the *metzora*. The pacing of the priest's assessment reminds us not to jump to conclusions and to give ourselves time to absorb a great deal of information. In her work as a hospice chaplain, Jo met Edith, a woman in her seventies with metastatic lung cancer. A long-time churchgoer with a deeply religious sensibility, Edith told Jo she was ready to die. In her words, Edith reported that she wanted "to enter the light and meet God." For some weeks, Jo's conversations with Edith stayed here, focused on Edith's relationship with God and on her professed readiness for her own death. Over time, however, Edith mentioned that she had had a twin sister who died in an accident when they were both seven. Curious, Jo asked Edith more about this sister. Slowly, Edith unraveled the story of this twin's death and, most devastatingly, of an incident that took place some months later in which Edith shoplifted a small amount of candy. When Edith's mother learned of this petty crime, she lashed out at Edith with grief-stricken rage, stating that the "good twin" had died and the "bad twin" had lived.

In the months before Edith died, she and Jo explored these events through the lens of Edith's own approaching death. While Edith continued to be buoyed by her relationship with God, she was also able to express the grief, anger, pain, and confusion that had haunted her for six decades. In the waning weeks of her life, Edith found some freedom from the moniker of the "bad twin" that had gripped her so tightly for so much of her life. Ultimately, she approached her death with a greater sense of ease and calm. Through all of these conversations, Jo moved slowly, collecting what she needed to assemble a three-dimensional picture of the woman before her in order to affirm Edith's complexity, wholeness, and humanity.

In rare situations, we are in the ancient priest's position of making a decision about the next step. Just as the levitical priest had to inform the *metzora* of his *tamei* status and instruct him to rend his clothes, cover his lip, and announce his status to the community, there are times when we must also name what we see and inform others that immediate action must be taken for their own safety and for the safety of others. With threatened suicides or homicides, or with situations involving abuse or self-harm, our assessments might lead us to initiate immediate, emergency interventions. In other situations, it is incumbent upon us, as it was upon the levitical priests, to share our assessment. If our professional roles allow us to work with someone over an extended period of time, we can offer the assurance that we will be there, checking in regularly.

When Nancy received the call from Ann, she could immediately tell something was wrong. Ann's voice cracked and her breathing was labored as she narrated the terror she felt when she learned that her mother had been rushed to the hospital because she had wandered out of her apartment and into traffic. Nancy had spoken frequently with Ann about her mother's dementia. In these conversations, Ann had always assured Nancy that the situation was under control and that she and her mother were "fine." When Nancy arrived at the hospital, Ann reported that her mother had had a particularly bad day and that she, Ann, should have kept a closer eye on her.

Over the course of the conversation, Nancy gently reminded Ann of the things that had occurred over the past six months, each on a day that Ann had labeled as "particularly bad." Nancy noted that these incidents had become more frequent and that Ann's mother's cognitive losses were making her a danger to herself and others. As Ann came to the realization that she was going to have to place her mother in a facility that could offer twenty-four-hour care, Nancy assured Ann that she would not be going through these painful changes alone. She, along with the rest of the congregation, would be there to assist and accompany both of them, checking in on them and visiting. In this way, Nancy and the congregation pledged to mirror the steady, steadfast presence of the levitical priest.

We can also care for ourselves by monitoring how frequently we go *michutz lamachaneh* and how much time we spend there. The priest was not expected to be in daily contact with the *metzora*. Instead, he had regular and predictable visits—in this case, on a weekly basis. We can adopt this model by pacing our visits and caring for others without allowing their needs to dominate our lives. In some communities, clergy from the same faith community create a rotation for routine visits to healthcare facilities. Congregants and noncongregants alike know there will always be a clergy person visiting, and each clergy person knows that his congregants will have a daily visit. This model also assures clergy that, in the absence of an emergency, they have predictable days when they don't need to visit the facility. In some large congregations with multiple clergy, calls about deaths are sent to the clergy in a particular order so that no clergy member will be inundated with funerals at which to officiate in a given week. These clergy examples mirror the model in other professions where colleagues share a rotating on-call schedule.

During each trip *michutz lamachaneh,* the priest had intimate interactions with the *metzora* and was privy, literally and figuratively, to the most tender spots of his being. As the priest monitored whether the condition had spread, the *metzora* exposed more of his body to him. We speculate, however, that neither the priest nor the *metzora* expected reciprocal intimacy. This type of uni-directional exposure established boundaries that helped both parties stay focused on the matter at hand. The interaction was bounded by a clear contract and goals. Today, we recognize the importance of establishing clear goals, contracts, and boundaries as we offer care, and we hope the benefits of doing so are clear to our patients, clients, and congregants as well. For many years, articulating a clear care plan was not part of spiritual care. Now, seminary students, pastoral care students, and clergy follow the examples of caregivers in other disciplines by learning how to prepare such plans. Setting realistic goals improves the care we offer and expands our capacity to work sustainably over the long term.

Just as we are dependable and resolute with those who are in our care, we can train this type of attention on ourselves, noticing what unsettles or rattles us. In particular, we can pay attention to the changes we notice in ourselves as we function as *Ivrim*, crossing boundaries between the camp and *michutz lamachaneh* and back again. At these times, we might develop a practice of regulating our breathing, taking a moment to center ourselves, or saying a brief prayer. This need not delay our work; rather, these acts can become part of our routine as we are *en route*. In the face of the disorientation that *michutz lamachaneh* engenders, actions such as these help us remain attuned to ourselves and perhaps also to the transcendent. When Nancy walked with a group of rabbis toward one of New York City's hospitals on the morning of September 11, 2001, they moved up the ash-covered streets in silence. Before they entered the building, Nancy encouraged everyone present to take a few deep breaths and then she chanted from Psalm 23, "Yea, though I walk through the valley of the shadow of death, I will fear no evil, for You are with me." She did this as much for herself as for the group, knowing that no one among them had any idea of what they would encounter on the other side of the hospital's main entrance.

At Calvary Hospital, a painted line at the threshold of each patient's room serves as a visual and visceral reminder to patients, family, and staff that the hospital room is holy ground that should be considered as separate from the rest of the facility.[18] Meanwhile, when Jo leaves a patient's room or home, she takes the time spent washing her hands as a moment for quiet transition. Required for the purpose of infection control, Jo adds a second meaning to handwashing, using it to acknowledge that this particular visit is over and that she is crossing into the next part of her day.

When we are *michutz lamachaneh* and feel we are beyond our physical, emotional, or spiritual comfort zones, we might find renewed strength by visiting the *Ohel Moed* that is there. Hospital chapels, gardens, and off-duty rooms are some of our contemporary corollaries to the Tent of Special Appointments. As with the ancient Israelites, this is an invitation for us to trust that an *Ohel Moed* accompanies us on all of our journeys and that, wherever it is, God may "come down."[19] The extraordinary placement of this Tent of Special Appointments outside the camp serves as a reminder that God will meet us for whatever unscheduled appointments we need. When the levitical priests entered the *Ohel Moed* that was inside the camp, they were required to wear their priestly vestments.[20] Extrapolating from this, we imagine that they wore this clothing *only* while working in this *Ohel Moed*. If and when individual priests

---

18. Calvary Hospital is a palliative care hospital in New York City for people with advanced cancer and other terminal illnesses. For more information, see www.calvaryhospital.org.
19. Exodus 33:9; Numbers 11:17, 12:5.
20. Exodus 28:42-43.

sought out God at the Tent of Special Appointments, we assume they appeared without their cultic finery. Similarly, when we break from our professional tasks to seek out the transcendent, we are invited to shed our outward, protective layers, presenting our raw vulnerability instead.

Finally, we can care for ourselves by paying attention to the social boundaries between ourselves and the people whom we serve. Caregivers often complain that we don't get proper care but, upon reflection, admit that we erect boundaries that lead others to believe we have transcended the need for care. In reality, no matter how often our professional lives bring us *michutz lamachaneh* to accompany others, we are unmoored by the experience of going *michutz lamachaneh* as a family member or as a patient. Our communities, our coworkers, and our families cannot help us if we present an image that is divorced from reality. We need boundaries that are protective and appropriate but mutable enough to allow us to receive support, as this vignette about a rabbi dealing with a health crisis in his own family illustrates.

Rabbi Bill Weiss's father was hospitalized suddenly and he and his family needed to fly out of town to be with him. Bill called his congregational president, Michelle, and told her that his father was ill, it looked pretty serious, and he didn't know what the next few days would hold. He asked Michelle to field anything that came up and to only call him about congregational business in an emergency. Bill went on to say that he would be grateful to hear from Michelle, as a friend, in the meantime. He was going to need all the support he could get, he said. Michelle asked if he would like to hear from other congregants. Bill asked her to relay the following message to the congregation: "Rabbi Weiss's father is seriously ill and he has gone to be with him. If congregants want to be in contact, Rabbi Weiss requests expressions of concern and support via e-mail, not phone. Rabbi Weiss hopes the community will understand that he will not be able to respond to each message." Bill and his family wanted congregants to be aware of what was going on; at the same time, they needed to establish some limits and realistic expectations. They knew that receiving supportive messages from the congregation would help buoy them in the days ahead, and that deeper contact with friends like congregational president Michelle would also bring sustenance.

The levitical priest teaches contemporary caregivers lessons about pacing, vulnerability, boundaries, and Special Appointments, themes that flow through the modern illustrations we have provided here. Numbers' account of Eleazar's *tamei* state after he came into contact with the *mei niddah* offers astute insights about multistage transitions that cannot be completed without the requisite passage of time. Ultimately, the levitical priest teaches us that our work—which is intended to bring transformation to others—also changes us. Our ability to integrate these changes is central to our self-care.

Integrating Transformation

A story is told of a Cherokee woman marching on the Trail of Tears. A few days out, she did not rise to join the march. The United States soldiers started prodding her with their gun butts, shouting at her to get up and start marching. With tears in her eyes, she looked up at them and said, "I can't move forward. My soul has not yet caught up with me."[21] To help our souls catch up with us, we can apply to ourselves the maxim that "every story needs a listener."[22] When we find confidantes with whom to share our experiences—whether they are colleagues, supervisors, or therapists—we have the opportunity to explore how our work with care-receivers affects us. In these safe spaces, we can express the jumble of emotions we experience, give voice to our own existential and spiritual questions, look at

---

21. Like many folk legends, this story has no single source and appears in multiple versions in many countries. While Nancy originally heard this told about the North American Trail of Tears, more contemporary versions set in Africa, the Amazon, and Thailand can be found on the Internet.
22. This is the motto of the Institute for the Healing of Memories, based in Cape Town, South Africa. For more information, see www.healing-memories.org.

the different ways we have come unmoored, and forge narratives through which we understand what happened. Holding our stories inside only compounds the disorientation and trauma our work lives frequently arouse. Healthy self-care practices require that we tell stories about our souls and our hearts, our bodies and our minds, describing how the full integrity of our beings is challenged and changed by the work we do.

In his masterwork, *I and Thou*, Martin Buber explains that in I–It moments we are not fully present. I–Thou moments, in contrast, are moments of true presence that are transformative for both parties. Buber teaches that, ultimately, real meeting between people is about engagement and change. In his words, "Relation is reciprocity. My You acts on me as I act on it."[23] In the hours and days following intense caregiving interactions, we are thrust into situations that demand more of us than we can give. This is because our thoughts, emotions, and souls have not had sufficient opportunity to sit with and integrate all that we heard and witnessed. When we avoid exploring the emotions that arise for us after we are exposed to others' *tumah*, it is perhaps because we fear the encounter will fracture us. Ultimately, this fear of change closes us off from the potential for transformation that such encounters hold.

While Leviticus's sacrificial system often seems obtuse and irrelevant to modern readers of the Bible, we propose that it has particular metaphorical resonance for caregivers who are seeking ways to attend to their own transformations. In the closing section of this chapter, we turn our attention to a modern interpretation of sacrificial rites, specifically the *chatat* offering. Jacob Milgrom makes

23. Martin Buber, *I and Thou*, A new translation with a prologue and notes by Walter Kaufmann (New York: Scribner, 1970), 67. The transformative impact of these meetings is clearer in Ronald Gregor Smith's translation, which uses "affects" in lieu of "acts on" (2nd ed.; New York: Charles Scribner, 1958), 15.

the case that, although *chatat* is generally translated as "sin offering," it should more accurately be called the "purification offering." He points out that the word *chatat* is derived from a verbal form unrelated to "sin" that means "to cleanse, expurgate, decontaminate." He also notes that many of the cases in which a *chatat* offering was brought stemmed from events unrelated to sin. The *metzora's* reentry into the community after his confinement *michutz lamachaneh* was one example of this.[24] In this spirit, we interpret the priest's *chatat* offering as an expression of his desire to wipe away *tumah*, to feel cleansed, and to restore himself to balance.

The priest's *chatat* offering consisted of a bull. After placing his hands on the bull's head, the priest slaughtered the animal and sprinkled its blood on the altar. Then the priest dug deep into the innards of the bull and removed the organs that were buried in fat in order to offer them to God.[25] This is a startlingly resonant metaphor for our own lives. When we address the imbalances caused by our boundary crossings, we must also dig deep to explore the inner parts of ourselves, the parts that are encased in layers of viscous fat that impede our view. These are the hidden parts of ourselves where we carry the weight of what we have seen and witnessed in the course of our work.

After this, the priest went *michutz lamachaneh* to dispose of the bull's remains. He placed unwanted viscera, body parts, internal organs, and excrement in a *makom tahor*, where he burned it on the ash heap.[26] This notion of an "ash heap"—a place to dispose of the burdens and imbalances we unwittingly carry—is rich in interpretive possibilities. Julie's "ash heap" is her therapist. For Jon, it's his supervisor. For Sasha, it's her weekly breakfast with close friends. For

---

24. Jacob Milgrom, "Sin-Offering or Purification Offering?" *Vetus Testamentum* 21 (1971): 237-39.
25. Leviticus 4:4-11.
26. Leviticus 4:11-12.

Sam, it's removing work clothes and showering before having a drink with his partner and sharing at least one story from his day. For Tina it's her meditation practice. Each of us benefits from a metaphorical (or real) ash heap where we dispose of the leftover pieces of the *tumah* that we have picked up in our daily work. After leaving these messy remains behind, we hope to move forward with a restored sense of wholeness and balance.

When the priest took the remains of his *chatat* offering to the *makom tahor*, we imagine the walk he must have made from the inner recesses of the *Ohel Moed*, through the tents of the camp, to a place beyond the borders of the camp. He made this walk in public, in full sight of the community, while hauling the burned, bloody remains of the animal he had just sacrificed. Far from being a secret, the reality of the priest's humanity was integrated into the very fabric of the sacrificial system. The priest exposed himself as someone who needed ritual, blood and guts, and ash heaps for his own restoration and wholeness. When contemporary caregivers lose sight of this truth, we create impossible standards for ourselves and pretend to the wider community that we are something we are not.

Without land of their own, the priests were dependent for sustenance on the meat, fruit, and grains that community members offered at the *Ohel Moed*.[27] However, the priests could not eat the remains of their own *chatat* offerings. In N. H. Snaith's straightforward words, "The priest could not eat his own sin."[28] For the purpose of this interpretation, the priest needed a clear separation between his typical activities and the rituals that fostered and bolstered his own well-being. In a similar way, we might acknowledge that our professional lives cannot possibly meet all of our emotional and spiritual needs. While our jobs might feed us

27. Numbers 18:8–20.
28. N. H. Snaith, "The Sin-offering and the Guilt-offering," *Vetus Testamentum* 15 (1965): 75.

in many ways, we also need set-aside activities through which we cleanse and tend to the most tender parts of ourselves, allowing others to provide for us and feed us. Indeed, once the priest had offered and disposed of his own *chatat*, he could then move on to the work for which the rest of the community so depended on him.[29]

The rules that framed the lives of the ancient priests provide us with wise instruction. In our daily work, professional caregivers are in intimate contact with people who are suffering and traumatized. We are exposed to tragedies and horrors that sometimes leave us shaken to our cores. In Leviticus's parlance, we are rendered *tamei*. We need to wait until nightfall; we need to allow our souls to catch up with us. We allow ourselves to be transformed when we enter into the presence of another human being and tell our stories. We also need to step into God's presence, inviting God to hear our prayers and hopes, our pain and sorrows. We need to step out of our comfort zones, remove our actual and metaphorical finery, and allow others to witness our human frailties and vulnerabilities. We benefit greatly when we look inside, remove what we no longer need, and find a safe place to dispose of these unwanted leftovers. In this way, we deepen our capacity to restore balance within ourselves—and, ultimately, within our relationships with other human beings, the transcendent, and the world. It is to this work that we now turn, focusing in the next chapter on professional caregivers' work with those who are ill.

---

29. Leviticus 4 describes how the priest had to bring his own *chatat* offering before he could offer any other person's *chatat*.

5

Outside the Camp: Patients and Their Loved Ones

> Illness is the night-side of life, a more onerous citizenship. Everyone who is born holds dual citizenship, in the kingdom of the well and in the kingdom of the sick. Although we all prefer to use only the good passport, sooner or later each of us is obliged, at least for a spell, to identify ourselves as citizens of that other place.[1]

Drawing on her own experience of living with cancer, Susan Sontag opens her essay "Illness as Metaphor" with these words. With her image of dual citizenship, Sontag evokes the experience of travel, reminding us that most of us, at some time in our lives, must pick up our second passport and journey to the "kingdom of the sick." Sontag describes the places where sick people reside as discrete geographic locations that are viscerally and concretely experienced by those who dwell there. She invites those who have not spent time there to imagine, through metaphor, what this "kingdom" might be like, implying that it is as real as the "kingdom" of the everyday life of those who are (temporarily, at least) in good health.

---

1. Susan Sontag, *Illness as Metaphor and AIDS and Its Metaphors* (1977; reprint, New York: Picador, 1988), 3.

Writing in part about his own experience of life after treatment for cancer, Arthur Frank extends Sontag's metaphor. He suggests that those who have dwelled in the "kingdom of the sick" and then returned to the "kingdom of the well" are, in truth, members of a separate "remission society," which is "either a demilitarized zone in between [the two kingdoms], or else it is a secret society within the realm of the healthy." He explains, "[M]embers of the remission society do not use one passport *or* the other. Instead they are on permanent visa status, that visa requiring periodic renewal."[2]

Lawrence Hoffman, writing about his experience of regularly visiting his chronically ill daughter in what he refers to as the "Land of the Sick," describes what is lost in translation when people from the two kingdoms come into contact with each other. He also describes how family members are dislocated and transformed by the experience of a loved one's illness. He gives stark, painful examples of the superficial conversations that ensure the "river" between the two worlds remains untraversable. He reaches the following conclusion:

> Old friends stop crossing the river to visit because they don't know what to say, and you stop crossing to their side, because they say what you cannot hear, and hear what you are not saying.[3]

These metaphors immediately resonate with those who have been, or are, patients. They capture the ways in which the experience of illness connotes travel, displacement, and a change in identity. They give expression to how illness dislodges both patients and family members from their moorings. They describe the feeling of losing one's "citizenship" and of needing to acquire new "travel documents."

2. Arthur W. Frank, *The Wounded Storyteller: Body, Illness, and Ethics* (Chicago: University of Chicago Press, 1995), 9 (italics in original).
3. Lawrence A. Hoffman, "Post-Colonial Liturgy in the Land of the Sick," in *CCAR Journal: A Reform Jewish Quarterly* (Summer 2006): 17, 19.

Although the verses that describe the *metzora*'s time *michutz lamachaneh* are sparse and terse, they provide us with some clear instructions for life in and between the two "kingdoms." While we are certainly not advocating for a return to biblical society, we present the experiences of Leviticus's "patients" because we believe Leviticus has something to teach us about identifying important sources of connection, including unmediated access to God and the experience of living outside quotidian time. These resources have the potential to anchor and guide us when we are in the kingdom of the sick and when we return again to the kingdom of the well. Leviticus's matter-of-fact approach to the inevitability of *tumah* is similar to Sontag's understanding that our bodies and our "passports" are stamped with the possibility of serious illness and the reality of mortality. In its accounts of the *metzora*, Leviticus presents a society that recognized and clearly named the need for transitional places and that offered maps and guidebooks about life there.

Life in and between Two Residences

Sontag, Frank, and Hoffman describe a terrain with two distinct locations: one for the sick and one for the well. The sick person becomes a traveler as she makes her journey to the kingdom of the sick. According to Sontag's metaphor, however, she is more than a mere tourist. By definition, a tourist makes a brief visit to a place that never loses its unfamiliarity and never becomes home. In contrast, the person who travels to the kingdom of the sick already holds a passport to this place. She is traveling to her second residence in a country of which she has always been a citizen, even if she is only now activating that citizenship. The journeyer to the kingdom of the sick becomes a sojourner in the second home she might never have known she had.

A person with dual citizenship understands the world through this lens of dual awareness and familiarity, but this can leave the patient's family and friends feeling confused and rejected. They may be resistant to the idea that their loved one now belongs to two places, and they may long for the time when she traveled on only one passport. Conversely, the patient's closest family members may have also been so profoundly shaped by the experience of caring for a seriously ill person that they, too, feel like they now reside in an in-between realm. Like anyone who has lived in two countries, those people who have spent time in both of Sontag's kingdoms are molded by two cultural and linguistic contexts, both of which are integral to their self-perception and to others' perception of them. Driven by an attachment to binary thinking, many of us want a person to fit neatly into one box or another. However, people who have lived in two places are, by definition, a product of their in-between-ness and thus defy easy categorization.

Family and friends may balk at hearing too many stories about their loved one's time as a patient, especially if he describes something he misses from his hospitalization, gives voice to the difficulties of his return, or describes how he has been transformed by the experience. Resistant to hearing the ex-patient's stories, family and friends wish the person they remember would reappear. Meanwhile, the returned sojourner wrestles with how to reconcile her two lives and homes as she slowly integrates the full import of her recognition that she is a dual passport holder. The inevitability of mortality, which might previously have seemed like an unnameable problem only known to other people, is now starkly real. Despite this, it is often an unwelcome conversation topic. When some conversations are too painful or confusing to initiate, silence and secrets become the order of the day. Frank's use of the term "secret society" to describe the fraternity of people who are in remission is apt.

Frank employs the metaphor of temporary or renewable visa status and describes the transformation and (at least partial) reorientation of the former patient who has spent time in the kingdom of the sick. Effectively, the former patient has lost her passport to the kingdom of the well and uses a visa to maintain her residence there.[4] These visa holders must periodically travel to the kingdom of the sick to renew their visas; ultimately, they fear they will lose this visa and possess only their passport to the kingdom of the sick. With this metaphor, Frank describes how members of the "remission society" continue to be monitored by healthcare providers. (Frank's construction of the remission society is most relevant to those with a chronic and/or life-threatening illness. Obviously, the metaphor is far less apt in the case of those who had a brief hospitalization for, say, elective surgery.)

Frank's image powerfully captures the monotony, disruption, and anxiety of appointments, tests, and waiting periods. Seemingly at the mercy of a bureaucracy beyond their control—and this bureaucracy could equally well be a hospital, a health insurance company, or the Department of Homeland Security—members of the remission society live with uncertainty about if or when their visa will be revoked. Alternatively, a person might make the decision to stop renewing his or her visa, choosing to let a terminal illness run its course rather than continuing with tests and treatment. If this happens, he will return to the kingdom of the sick to live out his remaining days. Some people choose to make this final part of their journey while receiving hospice services at home, rather than in an institutional setting. Arguably, the home temporarily becomes an

---

4. In real life, there are several ways in which one might lose the passport to one's country of birth. United States citizens, for example, risk losing their passports if they become naturalized citizens of another country, swear loyalty to another government, serve in the armed forces of a country that is at war with the United States, or formally renounce United States citizenship. For more information, see http://travel.state.gov/law/citizenship.

"outside-the-camp" location because it is set aside for the end-of-life journey.

Those who, like Frank, have written their own illness narratives and/or recorded others' narratives frequently describe how a sojourn in the kingdom of the sick entails rupture and displacement. Citing the experience of a woman with chronic fatigue syndrome, Frank writes, "Serious illness is the loss of the 'destination and map' that had previously guided the ill person's life."[5] At the same time, these writers attest to the transformative potential of illness. Each collapse carries with it the possibility of rebuilding, of reconstituting what initially seemed irreplaceable.

The two of us know from our own experiences as patients and as family members, as well as from our work as rabbis and chaplains, about the countless journeys to which illness and mortality, rupture and survival give rise. To travel from the kingdom of the well to the kingdom of the sick is to expand one's mental map—even as a sojourn in this second residence can be dissonant or worse. It is perhaps for this reason that, in their book about living with breast cancer, Susan Kuner, Carol Matzkin Orsborn, Linda Quigley, and Karen Leigh Stroup begin with the following dedication: "To our fellow initiates, whose spiritual paths have led them into strange, new lands: May this book serve as a companion and friend to you along the way."[6] The authors wrote this book because they wished they had had such a guide to accompany them through their breast cancer journeys. Like other illness narratives and like chapters 13 and 14 of Leviticus, their book is a guide for the sick and for the well as life's routines are disrupted by illness. In the following three sections, we

5. Frank, *Wounded Storyteller*, 1.
6. Susan Kuner, Carol Matzkin Orsborn, Linda Quigley and Karen Leigh Stroup, *Speak the Language of Healing: Living with Breast Cancer without Going to War* (Berkeley: Conari, 1999), dedications page.

delve into Leviticus's accounts of the *metzora* to imagine possibilities for healing and connectedness in contemporary *michutz lamachaneh* healthcare settings. We look first at the role of lament, then at ways of maintaining connectedness, and finally at the power of ritual.

Encountering and Lamenting over Mortality

The *Metzora* as a Mourner

> Mourners may tear their garments, put on sackcloth, weep, wail, toss ashes or dust on their heads, roll in ashes or dust, and sit or lie on the ground. They may fast, groan or sigh, move their bodies back and forth, utter dirges or mourning cries, avoid anointing with oil, lacerate themselves, and manipulate head or beard hair by means of shaving or depilation. Mourners have contact with the corpse and become polluted thereby. They may walk barefoot, strike the thigh, allow their hair to hang loose and uncovered, avoid washing themselves or their garments, abstain from sexual relations, cover or avoid grooming the moustache or face, and eat foods associated with mourning.[7]

Culled from biblical texts that describe mourning, this is Saul Olyan's list of mourning practices. He asserts that the mourner engages in these behaviors to separate himself from both the sacrificial cult and ordinary social activities.[8] The *metzora* also lived with these cultic and social restrictions, and Olyan's list includes several actions that are mentioned in Leviticus's discussion of *tzara'at*: rending the clothes, uncovering the hair, and covering the upper lip, all activities through which the *metzora* mimicked the social behavior of the mourner.

---

7. Saul M. Olyan, *Biblical Mourning: Ritual and Social Dimensions* (Oxford: Oxford University Press, 2004), 30–31. Ultimately, argues Olyan, these behaviors allow the mourner to rework his relationship with the deceased. By taking on the appearance and *tumah* of the deceased person, the mourner is able to establish "a new, mutually beneficial relationship" between himself and the deceased person. The mourner meets the needs of the deceased by invoking the deceased's name and bringing him food offerings. In return, the mourner perhaps hopes that the deceased will arrange for "beneficent intervention" on his behalf (p. 60).

8. Olyan, *Biblical Mourning*, 35.

Additionally, the *metzora* cried out two words: "*Tamei! Tamei!*"[9] The reasons for doing this are well established: *tzara'at* is, to once again borrow Jacob Milgrom's phrase, "an aspect of death."[10] In the levitical worldview, the breakdown of one's body is something that must be both mourned and publicly announced. Although still alive, the *metzora* mourned the loss of his bodily integrity and announced that his physical being was compromised. His announcement was essential for the broader community, the well-being of which was threatened by skin abnormalities that might not have been readily visible under the *metzora*'s clothing. It was also essential for the *metzora* because it allowed him to step into the social role of mourner and, we propose, to receive the comfort that was the mourner's due.

As already noted, we have adopted the Rabbis' reading of Leviticus, which claimed that both the suspected and the confirmed *metzora* were confined *michutz lamachaneh*. This means that, at the time of his announcement of mourning, the *metzora* was already removed from the community at large and was in contact only with the priest. The Hebrew Bible presents a paradoxical paradigm: the *metzora* had to separate himself from everyday life but, at the same time, mourning was a social activity that demanded accompaniment. Olyan explains, "A number of texts suggest that all mourners ought to have comforters, and [that] to be without a comforter is a particularly grievous thing." These comforters sat with the mourner and adopted his mourning rituals and sometimes his ritual pollution.[11] Although Leviticus does not prescribe a comforter for the *metzora*, several rabbinic *midrashim* offer an interpretation in which the *metzora*'s cry of "*Tamei! Tamei!*" is a signal to passersby that they should request

9. Leviticus 13:45.
10. Jacob Milgrom, *Leviticus 1–16: A New Translation with Introduction and Commentary*, Anchor Bible 3 (New York: Doubleday, 1991), 819.
11. Olyan, *Biblical Mourning*, 46–47.

God's compassion upon the *metzora*. The *metzora*'s cry, these *midrashim* teach, is a petition for consolation.[12] Since the priest's role encompassed presence, accompaniment, and witness, he arguably became the *metzora*'s comforter. While the biblical text provides us with no information about the emotional and spiritual lives of the *metzora* or the priest, it is a starting point from which we might reorder and reimagine our worlds by creating time and space in which to mourn the losses illness brings.

In Leviticus, the two words of the *metzora*'s mourning script—*Tamei! Tamei!*—are brief and terse. They lack the searing emotional content of Psalms and Lamentations, in which the speakers lament volubly over the fact that they are bereft and bereaved, shattered and suffering. The two words do, however, constitute the only biblical description in which mourning rites are used in the context of illness. As such, they tell us that sometimes we need to mourn the vagaries of the body. As Olyan demonstrates, biblical mourning is a social process that holds open the possibility to all parties of naming and adjusting to new realities.

In our own time, some patients take on physical markers that notify the wider community of their new status. These might include hospital clothing, loss of hair, a port for an intravenous line, use of a wheelchair or walker, a change in eating habits, or simply a different way of holding one's body. All of these are signs that things are not the same as they were before; they are reminders of the body's fragility and ultimate mortality, facts that seem more real than abstract during times of illness. Other patients, meanwhile, might show no outward signs of their illness. They carry their symptoms inwardly or, as was likely the case with many *tzara'at*-related skin

---

12. See Babylonian Talmud *Moed Katan* 5a, Babylonian Talmud *Niddah* 66a, and *Yalkut Shemoni* 13:45. This teaching appears to contradict the rabbinic claim that the *metzora* was *michutz lamachaneh*, where we imagine there were few passersby.

changes, under their clothes. In some cases, the ability to hide the symptoms of a disease might compromise when and how a person receives appropriate treatment or support. For this reason, the *metzora*'s public announcement is especially intriguing and compelling for modern interpreters of the text.

Illness is worth mourning over because, in Frank's words, it constitutes the "unmaking of a person's world."[13] With his call of "*Tamei! Tamei!*," along with his adoption of some of the signs of mourning, the *metzora* announced that his world was unmade, that everything was not the same as it once was, and that things had not turned out as he had hoped. By taking responsibility for breaking the news himself, rather than relying on the levitical priest, the *metzora* owned his condition and was forced out of any denial he might have had. It was this public announcement that allowed the *metzora* to enter into his mourning process, to invite others to mourn with him, and to begin the process of remaking his world in the light of these new realities.[14]

Leviticus makes no mention of the *metzora*'s loved ones. However, in our own time we know that these caregivers make frequent journeys between the kingdom of the well and the kingdom of the sick, sit for hours at patients' bedsides, attend meetings with doctors, anxiously wait for test results, and, ultimately, enter into a state of mourning along with the patient. As the *metzora* cries out *Tamei! Tamei!*, family members utter a parallel cry of, "My loved one is *tamei!*" Because family members share the patient's lament, they

13. Frank, *Wounded Storyteller*, 103.

14. For an exploration of illness and benefit-finding, see, for example, Charles S. Carver and Michael H. Antoni, "Finding Benefit in Breast Cancer during the Year after Diagnosis Predicts Better Adjustment 5 to 8 Years after Diagnosis," *Health Psychology* 23, no. 6 (2004): 595–98; and Donald E. Goodkin, "The Psychosocial Impact of Multiple Sclerosis: Exploring the Patient's Perspective," *Health Psychology* 18, no. 4 (1999): 376–82. For an exploration of the experience of caregivers, see Youngmee Kim, Richard Schulz, and Charles S. Carver, "Benefit Finding in the Cancer Caregiving Experience," *Psychosomatic Medicine* 69 (2007): 283–91.

cannot easily serve as the patient's comforter; in fact, they themselves are in need of a comforter. Often, they need comfort both when they are *michutz lamachaneh* visiting the patient *and* when they are back home. Like the levitical priests, healthcare workers travel between the camp and *michutz lamachaneh*. All of these workers, and especially clergy and chaplains, are especially well positioned to serve as comforter, witness, and presence for patients and their family members. Experienced in the art of boundary crossing, they can do this in all of the settings where patients and family members spend time.

Mixing Mourning and Rejoicing

According to Olyan, the rule of thumb is that in biblical passages mourning and rejoicing "are never combined in the same person."[15] One can be a mourner or a rejoicer, but one cannot be both on the same day—or, at least, this appears to be the general rule. Olyan points out, however, that this rule is "complicated by several texts that bear witness to the sanctioned fusion of rejoicing and mourning behaviors in the same individual."[16] In these verses, which date from the period after the destruction of the First Temple in 587 b.c.e., pilgrims participated in ritual rejoicing even as they mourned for the destroyed sanctuary. As Olyan explains, without the cultic center, the highly choreographed distinction between mourning and rejoicing collapsed.

> With the temple lying in ruins, such a loss of ritual distinctions, expressed as a fusion of normally separate ritual behaviors, is not difficult to conceive. . . . Movement between the ritual states of mourning and rejoicing is no longer possible, because a distinct sphere for rejoicing [that is, the Temple] has ceased to exist.[17]

15. Olyan, *Biblical Mourning*, 124.
16. Olyan, *Biblical Mourning*, 126. Olyan cites Jeremiah 41:4–5 and Amos 8:3.

Mary Douglas has argued that the entire book of Leviticus is a guide for pilgrims whose feet could no longer traverse the actual terrain of the Temple. Instead, these pilgrims made journeys to ruins or traced the steps of the journey in their imaginations.[18] Leviticus is a guide that is rooted in the reality of brokenness. Even though it describes strict separations between the sacred and the profane, it is set against the backdrop of a ruined temple. With the cultic center shattered, there was no means for the community to maintain *taharah* and *kedushah*. The sacking of Jerusalem was an ever-present reality and a loss that could never be adequately mourned. At the same time, the Israelites' lives continued to encompass the annual cycle of pilgrimage festivals, replete with their expressions of joy and celebration.

The Rabbis of the Talmud also acknowledged the truth of this paradox. In one of many passages devoted to this topic, Rabbi Yehoshua scolded ascetics who refused to eat bread and wine in the wake of the destruction of the Second Temple in 70 c.e. because they were part of the Temple's rituals. Rabbi Yehoshua counters that, according to this logic, Jews should also refrain from bread, fruit, and water. He concludes with these words:

> My children, come and I will say to you, not to mourn at all is impossible because the decree [of destruction] has already been decreed. But to mourn too much is also impossible because we do not place a decree upon the community unless the majority of the community is able to withstand it.[19]

Mircea Eliade's distinction between "sacred" and "profane" time,[20] helps contextualize Rabbi Yehoshua's teaching and the situation

---

17. Olyan, *Biblical Mourning*, 128. This refers to the destruction of the First Temple in 587 b.c.e.
18. Mary Douglas, *Leviticus as Literature* (Oxford: Oxford University Press, 1999), 230–31.
19. Babylonian Talmud *Bava Batra* 60b (authors' translation). We gratefully acknowledge Robert Tabak, who drew our attention to this teaching.
20. For a more detailed discussion, see chapter 2.

Olyan describes. In the wake of the destruction of the Temple, the Torah describes life that sits uneasily at the nexus of these two different types of time. (Rabbi Yehoshua describes a similar conflation of these two types of time after the second devastating destruction, centuries later.) On the one hand, the Torah's sacred story is embedded within the cycle of planting and harvesting to affirm God's power and beneficence. This time is cyclical. Simultaneously, the invading Babylonians arrived within the context of linear, profane time, sacked Jerusalem, and left behind a ruined city.

This confluence of mourning and joy in the same moment requires us to acknowledge that we cannot always make neat distinctions between the different temporal realities in which we live. While there are times when mourning or joy should be honored and elevated, most of our lives are lived in the terrain where gladness and sorrow, exaltation and heartbreak jostle up against each other. Indeed, it is not uncommon for chaplains to gather with family members at the bedside of an ill or dying patient to celebrate a wedding, a conversion, a baby naming, or other joyous occasion (in Hebrew, *simchah*). The plural of this word, *semachot*, is the name of a minor tractate of the Talmud that deals with the laws of funerals and mourning. It is generally accepted that this name is euphemistic, perhaps to ward off bad luck; indeed, Tractate *Semachot*'s official name is the straightforward *Evel Rabbati*, meaning "great mourning."[21] However, in our interpretation of the name, we see an almost playful allusion to the persistent reality of life's joyfulness in the context of a tractate dedicated to the topic of death.[22]

In a discussion that ranges over several pages in a different part of the Talmud, the Rabbis ponder the similarities and differences

21. Adin Steinsaltz, *The Talmud, The Steinsaltz Edition: A Reference Guide* (Jersualem: Israel Institute for Talmudic Publications, 1988; English translation New York: Random House, 1989), 46.
22. We are grateful to Alyssa Gray, whose thoughts on this topic were helpful to us.

between three different categories of people. They look at the person who is in mourning; the person categorized by the Bible as a *metzora*; and the person, known as a *menude*, who has been banned from the community for a transgression of some kind. According to this discussion, the mourner is required to suspend his mourning in order to participate in a communal festival. The *metzora* and *menude*, in contrast, must continue their period of separation from the community, regardless of where the community is in its observance of "mythical time."[23] Anyone who has been hospitalized during Passover or Christmas might well identify with how the significance of this obscure rabbinic ruling lives on in our own time. Without the requisite passage of "profane time," neither the *metzora* nor the contemporary patient can return to the community. However, family and friends bring strands and fragments of sacred time to the hospital bedside. This might take the form of songs, gifts, cards, special foods, or ritual objects, as we discuss later in this chapter.

This Talumudic teaching about the mourner reminds us that joy and the need for celebration persist, even in the midst of loss. The losses of illness and the mourning they engender are harsh reminders of the transience of life. Paradoxically, it is at precisely moments like these that we are also often reminded of life's transcendent elements—that is, of all that precedes us and all that outlives us. In his memoir of illness, *At the Will of the Body*, Arthur Frank describes one such moment. In the middle of the night, his body wracked with pain, he found a moment of "coherence" in the midst of suffering and "incoherence." In his words:

Making my way upstairs, I was stopped on the landing by the sight—the vision really—of a window. Outside the window I saw a tree, and the

23. Babylonian Talmud *Moed Katan* 14b. For the entire discussion, see 14b to 16a. See also David Kraemer, *The Meanings of Death in Rabbinic Judaism* (London and New York: Routledge, 2000), 117–32, for a fascinating discussion of this section of *Moed Katan*.

streetlight just beyond was casting the tree's reflection on the frosted glass. Here suddenly was beauty, found in the middle of a night that seemed to be only darkness and pain. . . . I was still in pain, but the pain had brought me to that landing, which was the only place I could be to see the beauty of that window. Coherence was restored. . . . At the moment when the incoherence of illness and pain makes it seem that all you have lived for has been taken away or is about to be lost, you find another coherence in which to live.[24]

As Frank describes, the experience of being ill might allow us to find meaning and purpose in the eternal cycles of life of which we are a part. The sight of a glorious sunset, flowers in the height of bloom, or winter's first snow all invite us to appreciate that which existed long before we ever did and will continue long after we are gone. We might also find transcendence in our connections to other people. This might include family and friends whom we have long cherished but have seen too infrequently and with whom we are suddenly in much more regular contact as we share unfolding news about the course of an illness. It might also include the new connections we forge along the way as we cross paths with those whom we meet in the kingdom of the sick.

Maintaining Connectedness

Michutz lamachaneh places are not inherently or singularly places of mourning. Rather, they give rise to rich and complex ranges of emotional experiences. They are deeply alive places that shape and form all those who pass through or dwell in them, offering opportunities to maintain connectedness to God, to people "back home" in the kingdom of the well, and to others who reside *michutz lamachaneh*. These places have their own rhythms and contours;

---

24. Arthur W. Frank, *At the Will of the Body: Reflections on Illness* (Boston and New York: Houghton Mifflin, 1991), 33–35.

ultimately, they have the potential to become "camps" in their own right.[25] In Larry Hoffman's metaphor, a "river" separates the two kingdoms. While it is always possible to take a boat from one shore to the other, Hoffman suggests that the inhabitants of the two lands rarely choose to board these boats and experience only limited contact and commerce. This is undoubtedly true, but there are also times of connection—because the river *is* traversable. Implicitly, no special travel documents are needed to cross from one side to the other, merely the willingness to make the journey regardless of how uncomfortable the visit might be. Family members like Hoffman make this journey endlessly, reminding us that, just as the water itself meanders from one shore to the other, so might we.

Similarly, the legions of people who work in the healthcare sector—from housekeeping and dining room staff to doctors, nurses, social workers, and chaplains—travel daily between the two kingdoms. In many cases, these workers have personal experiences of activating their own dual citizenship in the kingdom of the sick, providing them with a dramatically different perspective on the place where they make their living. In one contribution to this topic, Rebecca Dresser edited a collection of writings by medical ethicists who have all had cancer themselves or cared for a loved one with cancer. In her introduction she writes,

> Before cancer entered our lives, most of us had worked for years in the medical ethics field. You might think that a background in medical ethics is good preparation for dealing with cancer. We are not so sure about that. . . . [W]e quickly discovered we were not experts in real-world cancer ethics.[26]

25. In the Torah, the military camp described in Deuteronomy 23:10-15 is, by its very definition, a camp in its own right.
26. Rebecca Dresser, ed., *Malignant: Medical Ethicists Confront Cancer* (Oxford: Oxford University Press, 2012), 3–4.

Dresser and her co-contributors bring valuable voices to this conversation as they synthesize their professional and personal experiences of time spent in healthcare settings. Meanwhile, the two of us have observed how healthcare providers who become patients sometimes find—to their surprise—that "home" is a healthcare facility. In her work as a hospice chaplain, Jo met Mark, a retired doctor who could have received hospice services at home but elected instead to receive care during the last months of his life in a nursing home. Describing his arrival there as a "homecoming," he was intensely curious about how life functioned there and was pleased to cast his professional eye over the institution's systems and offer some small pieces of advice. From this place that felt more like "home" than his own house, Mark mourned over his approaching death and said his goodbyes. Mark's story, as well as those in Dresser's collection, illustrate that, by boarding a boat to cross the river between the two kingdoms, we might forge unexpectedly transformative connections to people and places.

The Tent of Special Appointments: Real and Imagined Possibilities

In a sweeping study of how the Torah encapsulates a multitude of sometimes contradictory voices and stories, Israel Knohl distinguishes between the two Tents of Meeting, which he refers to as the "inner" and "outer" tents. The "inner" tent, which we refer to throughout this book as the *Ohel Moed*, was at the center of the camp and was where God reliably and permanently dwelled. In this tent, the priests managed and mediated all cultic activities. Ordinary Israelites brought their offerings to the entrance of the tent but could go no farther. In contrast, the "outer" tent, which we call the Tent of Special Appointments, allowed all people to have immediate and unmediated access to God. According to Knohl, the "outer" tent was open to everyone but was not God's dwelling place. Instead, God visited briefly and then returned to God's permanent abode in the heavens above. For Knohl, "The power of [this] religious experience lies not in its constancy, but in the intimacy of the fleeting encounter."[27]

A visit to the Tent of Special Appointments required leaving the camp. For some people—those who were *tamei*—this departure was involuntary and non-negotiable. For others, it was a choice freely made. If such a tent exists in our own time, we, too, must leave our comfort zones to go there. We must cross the boundaries of ordinary life and loosen our grip on the mental maps that typically guide us. If we make this journey, we do so with the Torah's assurance that God spends time *michutz lamachaneh* but that God's presence there is flickering and inconsistent. While *michutz lamachaneh*, we likely cannot access God in the ways to which we are accustomed—by going to a place of worship, for example, or by taking a favorite hike. We must, instead, find new ways of communicating with God. However, we are invited to bring our full selves into this conversation because the usual intermediaries, the priests, do not work in this tent. Here, each person is responsible for his or her own communication with God.

Implicitly, to encounter holiness at the Tent of Special Appointments we must be open, vulnerable, engaged with the present moment, and intentional in our search. This is perhaps a fitting description of how many of us experience the sacred. Most of us can access or create this state of being some, but not all, of the time; for most of us, it is an intermittent rather than a permanent encounter. Holiness is more of a flickering presence than a static resident, more like the God of the Tent of Special Appointments than

---

27. Israel Knohl, *The Divine Symphony: The Bible's Many Voices* (Philadelphia: Jewish Publication Society, 2003), 76. Almost all biblical verses that reference the Tent of Meeting refer to the "inner" tent. The "outer" tent, which we call the Tent of Special Appointments, is mentioned in Exodus 33:7-11 and in several passages in Numbers 11–12.

the God of the *Ohel Moed*. Martin Buber captures the nature of such encounters with his description of "the grace of [their] advents and the melancholy of [their] departures."[28] Life everywhere incorporates both grace and melancholy but the Torah's description of the Tent of Special Appointments suggests that this is especially true *michutz lamachaneh*.

The Torah teaches that the Israelites could make a physical journey to the Tent of Special Appointments at any time. It also describes a second type of journey that the Israelites could make to this tent, one that took place in the realm of the imagination. The Torah tells us how Moses would make the journey out to the tent to speak face to face with God.[29] As Moses traversed the land between the camp and the tent, the people stood in the doorways of their own tents gazing after him. When Moses reached the tent and entered it, God would descend in a pillar of cloud to speak to him. The watching people would prostrate themselves in the doorways of their tents, entering into their own private space of what Avivah Gottlieb Zornberg calls "reverie." In her words, the doorway of each person's tent represented a "transitional space between inside and outside." As the people stood in this space, they "imagine[d]" Moses' connection with God.[30] This description of the people standing in their doorways underscores that one way of accessing God involves being simultaneously inside *and* outside or, conversely, of losing a sense that there is a real distinction between inside and outside.[31]

The people's imaginative journey is, in and of itself, a form of connection with divinity, and these verses invite us to explore the

28. Martin Buber, *I and Thou*, A new translation with a prologue and notes by Walter Kaufmann (New York: Scribner, 1970), 84.

29. Exodus 33:8-11.

30. Avivah Gottlieb Zornberg, *The Particulars of Rapture: Reflections on Exodus* (New York: Doubleday: 2001), 349.

31. This hearkens back to our description in chapter 1 of neuroscientists' accounts of how religious experiences create a temporary breakdown in the barrier between self and world.

power and significance of our own remembered and imagined journeys. For many months, Nancy visited Sol, a resident at the nursing home where she worked. Every Friday afternoon, Nancy led Shabbat services at the home and Sol was a faithful attendee. With their full-time work schedules, Sol's children were rarely able to attend services. However, they had each attended once or twice, had met Nancy, and were familiar with the time, place, and general tone of the services. They knew that Sol left his room every Friday at 3:25, made his way down to the main floor, and took his seat in the community room. His family could not physically join Sol, but they accompanied him in their imaginations, sharing at some level in the experience that was unfolding in the facility. As they remembered and imagined Sol's weekly journey, they found comfort in their "reverie." Each week, within minutes of returning to his room, Sol answered his phone and heard the voice of one of his children or grandchildren wishing him a "Shabbat Shalom," the greeting they would have exchanged had they been sitting together at the service.

As Sol lived his life "outside the camp," his family continued to live almost all of their lives inside the camp. In this way, his family is similar to the community that waited for Miriam during her confinement outside the camp as her *tzara'at* healed. After Miriam and Aaron criticized Moses, God punished Miriam by covering her skin with *tzara'at*. She was then shut outside the camp for seven days and the community did not march on from the camp until she was gathered back to them.[32] Acutely aware that one of their number was missing, the community was depleted by Miriam's absence. The camp was changed as its members' hearts tarried with a loved one who was confined *michutz lamachaneh*. Whether literally or metaphorically, ordinary daily life—for the wilderness generation, for

32. Numbers 12:1–16.

Sol's family, and for all those who are waiting for a loved one to return from a *michutz lamachaneh* place—is at least partially suspended during this time.

Building an *Ohel Moed* outside the Camp

The experience of entering a contemporary *michutz lamachaneh* setting such as an acute care hospital, a nursing home, or a psychiatric hospital is often characterized by rupture and loss. Frequently, people in these situations lose their orientation to person, place, and time, as well as to their usual ways of accessing the transcendent. At the same time, these experiences open up new possibilities for connection—with God, with other people, and with the environment that now constitutes home. For the two of us, this experience of connectedness is at the heart of any definition of spirituality, which we understand as the experience of being connected to something larger than ourselves. This could be a transcendent relationship with a deity or with nature, music, art, tradition, community, family, or anything else that gives our lives meaning. Writing at the intersection of neurobiology and psychology, Daniel Siegel describes the sense of "interconnection" that arises when we "become aware that [we] are part of a much larger whole." Siegel uses the image of "transpiration" or "breathing across" to capture the gentle and embodied experience of connection to something beyond ourselves, and he goes on to suggest that "this sense of interconnection seems to be at the heart of living a life of meaning and purpose."[33] Implicitly, it seems this is something with which we can connect even when we are displaced from home.

33. Daniel J. Siegel, *Mindsight: The New Science of Personal Transformation* (New York: Bantam, 2010), 76.

Clergy, chaplains, and other professional caregivers accompany patients, residents, and staff who live and work *michutz lamachaneh*. This accompaniment includes being present with others as they name, access, and celebrate their own sources of connectedness. Facilities and institutions generally arrange formal opportunities for this type of connectedness by creating or temporarily repurposing spaces for accessing the transcendent. These spaces might be used for collective worship or for private meditation. While they are modeled on synagogues, mosques, and churches, they lack the formal institutional structures of the houses of worship that lie within the boundaries of the camp. In this way, they mimic the flexible and impromptu nature of the Tent of Special Appointments.

Curtis Hart writes about the practical steps involved in the creation of sacred spaces in institutions such as hospitals, describing them as places

> where beauty and the holy embrace each other. Sacred space is in a temporal location. And yet it also exists outside the bounds of time and history. Sacred space opens out into the world while at the same time remains safe for the inner life and its secrets. . . . Those who suffer and serve need this space more than words can express.[34]

When institutions schedule worship services within their walls, they connect patients and residents to communities, music, liturgy, traditions, and cycles of time *beyond themselves*—to that which transcends time and place. At the same time, services such as these connect patients and residents *to the present moment and the present place*. In the words of Peter Yuichi Clark, who writes about leading services in an inpatient geriatric psychiatric unit, "[W]orship is the work of creating a place—a place to commune, a place to play, a place

34. Curtis W. Hart, "Sacred Space," in *Professional Spiritual and Pastoral Care: A Practical Clergy and Chaplain's Handbook*, ed. Stephen B. Roberts (Woodstock, Vt.: Skylight Paths, 2012), 421, 430–31.

to act, and a place to struggle."[35] Clark understands that sacred space is portable and can be re-created anywhere with words, intention, and love. He describes how, at the beginning of each service, he would introduce himself and invite participants to do the same. "My hope," he writes, "was to model hospitality and acceptance of each person as a human being, rather than simply as a patient."[36] In this way, Clark and his fellow worshipers built an *Ohel Moed* in the unit's television bay and turned an institutional space into a sacred place.[37]

Because many hospitalized patients are unable to leave their beds to attend worship services, some hospitals televise their services, broadcasting them on patients' private television sets. Services might be truncated to accommodate patients' and residents' needs, might be scheduled around the larger rhythm of life in the facility, and might use simple, large-print booklets that are easy to hold and read. While we are unable to find any studies of worship services in acute care medical settings, a number of spiritual care providers (including Clark) have documented the goals, structure, and outcomes of services in in-patient psychiatric settings and in facilities serving geriatric populations. In an exploration of their efforts to lead Christian worship services with the "confused elderly," James W. Ellor, John Stettner, and Helen Spath point out that worship is often "an emotional and sensory experience," meaning that people who were active churchgoers are frequently "able to recall many of the repetitive or rhythmic aspects of worship that were memorized when they were young." In this spirit, they suggest creating services that incorporate "favorite hymns," familiar verses of Scripture, "patterned liturgical responses," and prayer.[38]

---

35. Peter Yuichi Clark, "A Liturgical Journey at Wesley Woods: Worship Experiences within an Inpatient Geriatric Unit," *Journal of Pastoral Care* 47 (1993): 389.
36. Clark, "Liturgical Journey," 407.
37. Clark, "Liturgical Journey," 409.

Participation in such services has the potential to unlock deep-seated memories of prayer's sounds and motions. Indeed, chaplains and others who work in long-term care facilities tell stories about people "who could remember the prayers, hymns, and liturgies of their faith even when they did not know the time of day." They also recount how even residents labeled as "difficult" or "disruptive" can benefit from participation in such services. Marty Richards and Rabbi Sam Seicol tell the following story:

> [A] male resident . . . in the advanced stages of Alzheimer's Disease . . . was brought to weekly Jewish Sabbath services at the insistence of the chaplain. He was generally non-responsive except for occasional outbursts, and was considered by staff to be inappropriate for group programs due to this disruptive behavior. After several weeks of quiet attendance, half-way through one service he shouted "Amen" at an appropriate point in the service, and continued for one more line of the prayer in Hebrew.[39]

Because many patients and residents are physically unable to attend services, chaplains often find creative ways to bring the cycle of liturgical and mythical time to the bedside. When Nancy worked in a nursing home, she constructed a diorama of a *sukkah*[40] and carried it from bedside to bedside, inviting residents to decorate it with paper cut-outs of fruits and vegetables. The facility also built a full-size *sukkah* on the roof of the building and held a Sukkot service there for ambulatory patients. At the beginning of this service, Nancy placed the diorama inside the *sukkah* and told attendees that it had been decorated by residents unable to join them on the roof. In an echo of

---

38. James W. Ellor, John Stettner, and Helen Spath, "Ministry with the Confused Elderly," *Journal of Religion and Aging* 4 (1987): 21–33, especially 28–31.

39. Marty Richards and Sam Seicol, "The Challenge of Maintaining Spiritual Connectedness for Persons Institutionalized with Dementia," *Journal of Religious Gerontology* 7 (1991): 31.

40. A *sukkah* (pl: *sukkot*) represents that temporary huts in which the Israelites dwelled during the harvest season. During the holiday of Sukkot, Jews build *sukkot* and eat and sleep in them for the duration of the holiday.

the tradition of inviting *ushpizin* ("guests") from biblical stories into the *sukkah*, Nancy symbolically welcomed the diorama decorators into the nursing home's roof *sukkah*.

Chaplains and other staff in institutional settings create sacred space for patients, residents, and workers. These spaces can be concrete and permanent, like hospital chapels. They can be improvised and temporary, as when an Ark containing Torah scrolls is wheeled into a dayroom for the brief duration of a service. And they can rely on memory and imagination, as in the example of the tiny, portable *sukkah* that Nancy brought from bed to bed and then up to the roof. Regardless of the physical space in which they are metaphorically raised, all of these tents depend on the compassion and generosity of leaders and attendees to construct walls and roofs of loving welcome. It is through these acts that we stumble upon Tents of Special Appointments and encounter God's flickering presence in what might at first seem unlikely places. It is also through these acts that *michutz lamachaneh* places become camps in their own right.

In Richards and Seicol's words, many people experience "God's love" when another person reaches out to them.[41] In our work in healthcare settings, we have observed how patients sometimes find solidarity, sustenance, and comfort in the relationships they form with their roommates—with people who had been strangers but now become compatriots sharing in the dislocation of life in the kingdom of the sick. While acute care hospitals offer few formal opportunities to name, deepen, or explore these relationships, long-term care facilities and in-patient psychiatric hospitals often do. In psychiatric settings, spirituality groups are an important venue in which this can happen. Lynne Mikulak writes that the "sharing of narrative" in such groups allows for "broader dimensions of insight

---

41. Richards and Seicol, "Challenge of Maintaining Spiritual Connectedness," 29.

about self-care, compassion for others, and awareness about illness and the human experience."[42] These groups also allow for the universalizing of suffering that is often stigmatized and poorly understood by people outside the walls of psychiatric hospitals. Such groups also present opportunities for caring connections as patients "give each other feedback, share their emotional responses to each other's stories, describe and explore common experiences, and help each other out with problem-solving."[43]

With or without the formal mechanism of a spirituality group, the drive to forge connections with others is clearly visible among people who are multiply displaced from the lives, places, and people they used to know. In an ethnographic study of a community-based residential facility for people living with mid- to late-stage dementia, Susan H. McFadden, Mandy Ingram, and Carla Baldauf paint a picture of residents who are busy, engaged, caring, funny, and happy. They attribute this to the intentionally supportive environment in which the residents live.[44] They describe how residents take care of each other, which meets a core human need to act virtuously toward others. They write, "[The residents] sought to comfort one another and to behave compassionately. Though their thoughts are scattered, their memories are gone, and their language is distorted, still something remains of their essential goodness that enables them to show virtue as best they are able." Through these acts, report McFadden et al., the residents repeatedly encountered their own and others' humanity.[45]

---

42. Lynne Mikulak, "Spirituality Groups," in Roberts, *Professional Spiritual and Pastoral Care*, 195.

43. Jo Hirschmann, "Psychological and Theological Dynamics in an Inpatient Psychiatric Chaplaincy Group," *Journal of Religion and Health* 50 (2011): 968.

44. Susan H. McFadden, Mandy Ingram, Carla Baldauf, "Actions, Feelings, and Values: Foundations of Meaning and Personhood in Dementia," in *Viktor Frankl's Contribution to Spirituality and Aging*, ed. Melvin A. Kimble (New York: Haworth Pastoral Press, 2000), 67.

45. McFadden et al., "Actions, Feelings, and Values," 80–81.

During her many years of work with elders living in nursing homes, Dayle Friedman developed what she calls the "*Mitzvah* model*," which "provides spiritual resources that can empower the Jewish person to meet the key challenges of aging." Focusing on "fostering a life of meaning, facilitating a life of celebration, and enabling a life of connection," this model might include creating opportunities for participation in religious services, offering adult education, forging intergenerational connections, creating volunteer and social justice opportunities for elders, and holding a space for life review and storytelling.[46] With Friedman's model, residents can connect with their own and others' essential humanity and goodness. While the kingdom of the well might be the camp we know best, the kingdom of the sick is a camp that we can come to call home and within which we might foster connections to God and people. As all of these examples show, there are multiple creative means through which we forge connection to our own selves, to other people, to places, and to God. These are all ways of mapping strange new worlds and adding new chapters to our narratives.

Transitions and the Rituals that Mark Them

The Significance of Time, Space, and Objects

In chapter 1, we described what neuroscientists have learned about what happens to people's brains when they participate in rituals. According to these understandings, rituals offer all-encompassing sensory experiences that allow for integration between different areas of the brain, a heightened sense of unity within oneself and between oneself and others, and a "de-centering" of the self that opens up

---

46. Dayle A. Friedman, "Letting Their Faces Shine: Accompanying Aging People and Their Families," in *Jewish Pastoral Care: A Practical Handbook from Traditional & Contemporary Sources,* ed. Dayle A. Friedman, 2nd ed. (Woodstock, Vt.: Jewish Lights, 2005), 346–63.

possibilities for the re-creation of the self. In the case of the *metzora* who is returning home from *michutz lamachaneh*, or a contemporary patient who is returning home from the kingdom of the sick, these brain changes mirror the physical journey of the *metzora*/patient. The patient's usual world has been unmade; now he is in the process of remaking it and of integrating the experiences he had *michutz lamachaneh*. Rituals to mark the end of a period of isolation, the body's repair, and the patient's return home give visceral, kinesthetic expression to the transition. They also allow for the brain—and, thus, the person—to adjust and change too.

The book of Leviticus prescribes a fascinating array of rituals that enable individuals to transition from being *tamei* to once again being *tahor*. In addition to bringing assorted sacrifices to the entrance of the *Ohel Moed*, ancient Israelites who had suffered from *tzara'at* were required to bathe and launder their clothes, shave their hair, receive blood and oil on their right extremities, have oil placed on their heads, wait for night to fall, and wait for a week in the entrance of their tents. As chaplains, we are often asked to collaborate with patients and families to mark transitional times in their lives. We may do this with words, silence, fixed liturgy, spontaneous and tailored prayers, or with ancient or new rituals.

As we work with patients and family members to identify and acknowledge transitional moments in the healthcare life cycle, Leviticus is a rich repository of ideas about the actions, objects, and media that symbolize change, loss, and restoration. Leviticus's usefulness to us is twofold, lying first in its recognition of patients' and caregivers' spatial and temporal journeys, and second in its utilization of objects from everyday and sacred realms. Ultimately, rituals are powerful because they ascribe sacred meanings to at least one of the following: objects, space, time, and/or a person or group of people. This is true for the formal rites that constitute communal religious practices and for the ad hoc rituals we create in our individual lives on an as-needed basis.

The first day of the *metzora*'s eight-day purification process was a private affair involving only the *metzora* and the priest. It took place outside the camp, away from the formal cult and the broader community, and it involved an intimate ritual in which the priest sprinkled a mixture of blood and fresh water over the *metzora*'s body. To perform the sprinkling, the priest used a bundle of cedar wood, hyssop, and crimson material—all of which were associated with the cult. In this way, the priest brought the cult to the *metzora*, allowing him to reacquaint himself with the sights and smells of the *Ohel Moed* and reunite his body with the cult.[47] Writing about a different *michutz lamachaneh* ritual, that of the *mei niddah*, Adriane Leveen points out that this watery mixture belonged outside the camp yet was the vehicle through which the individual was restored to his proper place within the camp.[48] The displacement of these materials from their usual context allowed for another "displacement" to happen as the *metzora* was "re-placed" home.

Upon the completion of this ritual, the *metzora* could begin the multistage process of his journey home. First he returned as far as the doorway of his tent, where he sat for seven days.[49] This liminal

---

47. Leviticus 14:4.
48. In her commentary on the use of *mei niddah* in Numbers 19:9, Adriane Leveen notes that, when used in the Bible, the word *niddah* has at least three possible meanings: "menstrual impurity (the most frequent meaning), indecency, and purification (the present case)." Referring to the root *n-d-d* that means "to depart, flee, wander," Leveen suggests that in Numbers 19 "*niddah* conveys the nuance found in the term's original meaning—being set apart—since the watery mixture is to remain *outside* the camp. Yet through purification it restores the individual to her or his proper place *within* the camp." The *mei niddah* mixture functions in a similar way in our story: it belongs to the world beyond the camp, yet it is one of the vehicles that enable an individual to return to the community. (Adriane Leveen, note on "water of lustration . . . for purgation," in *The Torah: A Women's Commentary*, ed. Tamara Cohn Eskenazi and Andrea L. Weiss [New York: Women of Reform Judaism and URJ Press, 2008], 919 [italics in original]).
49. Leviticus 14:8.

space provided a visual representation of the *metzora*'s own liminal state of being in which he was physically back within the camp but not yet integrated into home or communal life. Framed by both the doorway and the seven-day period, the *metzora* reminds us of the contemporary person sitting *shiva* after a burial.[50] Indeed, in Barbara Mann's construction, *shiva* is defined by both temporal and spatial boundaries. In her words, "Though the shiva is an institution essentially defined by temporal boundaries, it may also be considered a kind of 'space,' in which mourning is enacted and evolves."[51] These boundaries remind us of the power of setting aside both time and space for integration and transition.

This is relevant in the case of both the biblical *metzora* and the contemporary patient—for example, a person who returns home after surgery but whose physical space is changed and disrupted by the presence of a hospital bed, commode, and daily visits from a nurse. Not until the completion of physical therapy—a metaphorical seven-day waiting period in which the patient sits only in her "doorway," not fully in her home—are this person's routine and home restored to what they used to be. Indeed, on the eighth day, the former *metzora* could both enter all the way into his tent and bring his own offerings to the entrance of the *Ohel Moed*.[52] Having transitioned through both time and space, the *metzora* had now achieved full integration into his family and home as well as into the community as a whole.

Our experiences of time are subjective and shaped by many factors. For example, at the onset of an illness or the beginning of a hospitalization, patients and family members begin to count time differently, using admission dates, discharge dates, and other markers

---

50. *Shiva* refers to the seven-day period following a funeral, during which mourners receive visitors at home and refrain from everyday activities.
51. Barbara E. Mann, *Space and Place in Jewish Studies,* Key Words in Jewish Studies 2 (New Brunswick, N.J.: Rutgers University Press, 2012), 13–14.
52. Leviticus 14:10-20.

associated with illness and recovery to mark changes in time. In institutional settings, time is determined by staff's shift changes, the rhythm of doctors' rounds, and the availability of the staff people who bathe patients, tend to wounds, and take X-rays. Rather than living according to her own habits and biorhythms, a patient will eat, take her medications, and sleep according to the hospital's understanding of time. In windowless ICUs, a patient's ability to remain attuned to the passage of time is further disrupted. The patient's disconnection from her typical schedules and routines, which includes the observance of workdays and rest days, further compounds this. This is also true for family members, whose routines are now determined by visiting hours, as well as numerous other appointments and errands related to the patient's hospitalization.

Leviticus's spatial map of the camp, the area *michutz lamachaneh*, and the transitional space of one's own doorway provide guiding images that help us to imagine, and gain insight into, our own spatial and temporal journeys. These maps and time frames invite us to notice changes in our bodies, spirits, daily activities, and relationship to familiar and unfamiliar spaces. Just as the *metzora* returned to the community slowly and by gradations, we too might find meaning in marking, naming, and honoring each step along the way. For example, a patient and her loved ones might choose to notice the different forms Shabbat takes when it is celebrated in a hospital setting, back home during one's recovery from a hospitalization, and then in synagogue when the person is well enough to begin returning to the contemporary *Ohel Moed*.

Renee was one of Nancy's congregants; her story is an example of how caregivers accompany people as they make their journeys through time and space, marking numerous stops along the way.

When Nancy first visited Renee in the hospital, she was hooked up to numerous machines. Renee had awakened from surgery following a stroke and was terrified to discover that she could neither move nor speak. Surrounded by her family, Renee and her loved ones waited anxiously and expectantly for signs that she would regain bodily sensation and mobility. After some days, when Renee began to respond to touch, everyone rejoiced with her in her victory. When she was able to voluntarily move her arm, their hopes rose exponentially. When Nancy brought an electric candelabra to her room on Friday afternoon, Renee stretched her right arm toward it as the candles went on, as if to bless them. There wasn't a dry eye in the room.

Renee's need for acute care passed, but she faced months, if not years, of rehabilitation. On the day that Renee moved from the hospital to a skilled nursing facility, her daughter Amy helped her to dress for the first time since her stroke. As Amy brushed out Renee's hair, her whole demeanor changed and it was clear to everyone in her family that she was taking her first steps toward reclaiming her identity. Renee made rapid strides at the nursing facility. Within a month, she was using a walker and was able to express herself with individual words and some simple sentences.

Throughout Renee's time in rehabilitation, members of the synagogue faithfully visited her. Each Friday, a group came in the late afternoon to welcome Shabbat with her. When Renee returned home, congregants continued to come every Friday for this communal welcoming of Shabbat in Renee's home. Eventually, after many months, Renee was ready to return to synagogue. When Renee looks back at that time, she still comments that nothing will ever compare to how she felt that first Friday as she walked into her synagogue to be greeted by familiar sights and sounds and by the love and warmth in her fellow congregants' faces. There was no doubt that she was back in her spiritual home. Surrounded by her community, she had returned to the place that had always contributed to her sense of wholeness and well-being. While she would always be grateful that the community consistently and lovingly came to her, she was now, finally, back where she belonged. The next morning, when she went forward to stand before the community and recite *Birkat Hagomel* (a prayer said following a life threatening incident), Renee offered God her deeply heartfelt thanks.

Renee's family, rabbi, and synagogue community accompanied her from one stage of recovery to the next, affirming each step in the process. Similarly, Leviticus 13 proceeds from the understanding that each step is important and must be named and recognized. Its complex flow chart includes cases of suspected *tzara'at* that ultimately turned out to be *tahor* affections of the skin. We learn from these verses that many people who were not ultimately diagnosed with *tzara'at* nevertheless spent one, two, or many weeks in isolation as the priest watched over the progression of their skin lesions. In our own time, many of us have personal experience of anxious periods of time as we await diagnostic appointments, test results, doctor's appointments, and approval from insurance companies. We may also experience uncomfortable waits for a doctor to arrive at a bedside, or for the day later in the week when the hospital's social worker will once again be in her office. These stressful waiting periods alter our routines and our experience of time, bring us face to face with the reality of fragility and/or mortality, and require us to travel to healthcare settings to which we might not ordinarily go.

In Leviticus, if a person was pronounced *tahor* upon completion of the seven-day period of waiting and isolation, he had then to wash his clothes before returning to the community.[53] This simple cleansing ritual acknowledged the end of one phase of time and the beginning of another. For modern readers, it offers a compelling alternative to the frequent expectation that, after such experiences, we sigh with relief, regain our composure, and move seamlessly back to our normal routines. Contemporary life does not provide any formal means of marking the transition from hospital to home, hospital to rehabilitation facility, hospital to home hospice care, or assisted living facility to nursing home, to name just a few examples of the types of

53. Leviticus 13:6, 34.

transitions contemporary patients and residents make from one type of caregiving setting to another. However, chaplains are uniquely placed to guide patients through these types of transitions. When Nancy worked with Louise, a woman who was preparing to make the transition from an acute care hospital to a rehabilitation facility, they discovered that a simple ritual allowed Louise to free herself from one setting so she could enter another.

Nancy first met Louise after she had been rushed to the hospital following the sudden loss of use of one side of her body. Her doctors found that she had a brain tumor that needed to be removed but the surgery posed the risk of additional damage. Fortunately, the surgery was effective: the tumor was removed without further damaging Louise's brain tissue and movement and sensation returned to her body.

However, when it was time for Louise to transfer to a rehabilitation facility, the healthcare team noticed she was emotionally distant and reluctant to talk about moving on. As Nancy explored this with her, Louise described how she wanted to give voice to her gratitude and wonder that, against some considerable odds, her body had emerged intact from this experience. A retired teacher, Louise decided she would like to return to her old school and find creative ways through which her students could develop gratitude for their bodies' capabilities. With Nancy's support, Louise gathered her family around her. She told the story of the trauma, fears, surprises, and triumphs of the past few weeks; offered a prayer of thanksgiving; and described how she would express her gratitude by helping students to celebrate their bodies. After this, she readily and happily packed for her move to the rehabilitation facility.

Oil, Blood, and Water

The rituals that allowed for the purification of the *metzora* involved three items: oil, blood, and water. Rich with symbolic imagery, these were substances that allowed for re-creation and sanctification. Similarly, many of the objects and media we use in contemporary rituals are taken from ordinary life. James Dittes, writing about the contemporary practice of pastoral care and counseling, puts it this way: "[T]he materials of the priest's practice are almost always the most mundane and ordinary extracts of daily life, things like bread, wine, candles, sheep and words."[54]

Because oil is something that we make with our hands, it represents the parts of our lives that we mold and shape and over which we have a measure of control. The same can be said for multiple things that are the products of our hands, minds, or hearts. We might include in this category creating art, music, song, or dance; or intentionally extending ourselves into relationships and the wider world by deepening friendships, joining a congregation, giving money to charity, becoming involved with a volunteer project, growing vegetables, or caring for a pet. We also have control over how we choose to respond to painful and unwelcome events. Viktor Frankl's ability to make meaning out of the extraordinary suffering he witnessed and endured in Nazi concentration camps is a distinguished example of this. Determined to approach others with a love that allowed him "to grasp another human being in the innermost core of his personality," Frankl uncompromisingly believed that "meaning is possible even in spite of suffering."[55]

Blood represents both life's fragility and its continuity and renewal. It symbolizes all that is beyond our control and it invites us to

---

54. James E. Dittes, *Pastoral Counseling: The Basics* (Louisville: Westminster, 1999), 156.
55. Viktor E. Frankl, *Man's Search for Meaning* (New York: Pocket Books, 1959), 134, 136.

acknowledge that many aspects of life and death are not in our hands.[56] While we would rightly recoil from using blood in a contemporary ritual, we might instead choose to use an item that represents hospitalization and—as is often the case—its attendant loss of control and dignity. Taking off a hospital identification wrist band or changing from a hospital gown into one's own clothing is ostensibly a simple act that encapsulates the reclamation of our own humanity even in the midst of frighteningly unknowable situations.[57] In the ritual for the purification of the *metzora*, the priest brought items associated with the cult of the *Ohel Moed* to *michutz lamachaneh*. In our own time, family and friends similarly bring religious items to patients' bedsides and homes, as Renee's story powerfully illustrates. These items, and the rituals associated with them, provide a bridge between the different "kingdoms" in which each of us resides over the course of our lives. In particular, they bring aspects of the *machaneh*—of home and community—to *michutz lamachaneh* settings.

Water, meanwhile, connotes cleansing, a fresh start, birth, and rebirth. Water's symbolic use persists in contemporary life—for example, in many initiation rites to mark entry into a religious community, whether at birth, upon reaching adulthood, or for the purpose of conversion. In Jewish life, ritual baths (*mikveh* in the singular, *mikva'ot* in the plural) must be filled with *mayyim chayyim* (literally, "living waters," referring to fresh water) that can be either springwater or rainwater. As discussed earlier, *mayyim chayyim* is the term used to describe the water over which the bird was slaughtered in the *metzora*'s ritual. Traditionally, women immerse in the *mikveh*

---

56. S. David Sperling explains that blood represents, and therefore is equated with, life. It has the power to protect the living from death and to "change the status of affected [that is, *tamei*] persons and thus confer life." See S. David Sperling, "Blood," in *The Anchor Bible Dictionary*, ed. David Noel Freedman, 6 vols. (New York: Doubleday, 1992), 1:761–63.

57. We gratefully acknowledge Neil Gillman's reference, in his Foreword to this book, to the power of this familiar ritual in a patient's life.

after the completion of the period of *niddah* (which refers to menstruation plus another seven days). Immersion in the *mikveh* also marks a person's conversion to Judaism and the transition before marriage. Contemporary rituals offer numerous other uses for the *mikveh*, including marking transitions related to fertility and reproduction, surgery, cancer treatments, and sexual abuse.[58]

Rachel Adler describes blood and water as "nexus fluids" because they combine life and death.[59] The recognition of this ancient combination invites us to consider creating rituals that allow for the naming of fears and hopes, for what has been and for what we hope will be. In this spirit, Jo worked with Claire on a ritual that Claire initiated. Shortly before Claire's discharge home following a long psychiatric hospitalization for depression, Claire used markers to write on pieces of paper all the things she hoped to leave behind in the hospital. These were all themes she had explored in conversations with Jo and her in-patient therapists. She then placed these pieces of paper in a bowl of water. Together, she and Jo watched the water lift the ink off the paper where it mixed seamlessly with the water. Claire then filled more small pieces of paper with the personal qualities and supportive people and activities she knew would be essential as she returned home. She placed these pieces of paper in a box Jo provided and they closed their ritual with a recitation of *Tefillat Haderekh*, Jewish liturgy's prayer for travelers who are setting off on a journey.

Whatever media we choose to use, the underlying purpose of ancient and contemporary rituals is to give symbolic expression to transitions that have geographic, physical, social, emotional, and spiritual dimensions. In the Torah, the verb root *kaf-peh-resh* describes many such transitions. *Le'kaper*, the *piel* form of this root,

58. See, for example, the websites of Mayyim Hayyim Living Waters Community Mikveh (www.mayyimchayyim.org) or Ritual Well (www.ritualwell.org).
59. See chapter 3.

is generally translated as "to forgive, atone, or procure forgiveness." The noun form, *kapparah*, is generally translated as "atonement." In Leviticus 14, the *metzora* must bring a series of four sacrifices, each of which brings about a change in status that is expressed with the *piel* form of the verb and is generally translated as "expiation" or "atonement."[60] Other conjugations of the same verb root, however, have a wider semantic range. We are particularly interested in the following two meanings: "to wipe away" and "to cover."[61] Both of these activities involve physical touch—in the first case to wipe clean, which might also be associated with rubbing in and integrating the residue of the old experience, and in the second to offer protection.

Atonement as Wiping Away

In an exploration of the meaning of *le'kaper* in the transitions Leviticus prescribes for Yom Kippur, Stephen A. Geller suggests that the verb describes a process of re-creation. Juxtaposing Leviticus's prescriptions for Yom Kippur with the story of Noah and the flood,[62] and drawing on the meanings of *le'kaper* that are connected to erasing or wiping away, Geller suggests that the purpose of the Yom Kippur rituals is to "renew the pristine nature of the bond" that existed between God and humanity prior to the flood and the (inevitable) entry of *tumah* into the wilderness *Ohel Moed*. The annual arrival of

---

60. The four offerings are the *asham, chatat, olah* and *minchah*. Leviticus describes the effect of each sacrifice as follows: *ve'khiper alav ha'kohen lifnei YHVH* (*asham*, Lev. 14:18, "the priest shall make atonement on his behalf before the Eternal"); *ve'khiper al ha'mitaher mi'tumato* (*chatat*, Lev. 14:19, "he shall make atonement for the one to be purified from his impurity"); and *ve'khiper alav ha'kohen ve'ta'her* (*olah* and *minchah*, Lev. 14:20, "the priest shall make atonement on his behalf and he shall be clean"). Authors' translations.

61. Marcus Jastrow, *A Dictionary of the Targumim, the Talmud Babli and Yerushalmi, and the Midrashic Literature*, 2 vols. (1950; reprint, New York: Judaica Press, 1984), 1:666–67. For midrashic purposes, we are taking some literary license here and applying meanings from other *binyanim*, or conjugations, to the *piel le'kaper*.

62. Genesis 6–8. Scholars generally believe that both passages were authored by P, the Torah's Priestly voice.

Yom Kippur, then, became a predictable and reliable opportunity for renewal and restoration.[63]

From a pastoral perspective, Geller's notion of creation is fascinating. In the story of creation told in Genesis 1, creation does not happen *ex nihilo*. Rather, God creates dry land, sea, and sky from what existed before—from the waters of the deep.[64] In our own lives, we live in the perpetual ebb and flow of loss and rebuilding, of small and large destructions and small and large re-creations. We never build something from nothing. Instead, we use the broken or discarded pieces of what went before as the bricks of new structures and edifices. We combine these materials with our hopes for the next stage of our lives, building something new that never before existed. In this way, re-creation implies forward rather than backward motion as we create something new out of the materials of our past. It describes the types of changes to which initially unwelcome events can give rise as suffering people and/or their caregivers metaphorically pass their hands over hurt places. In so doing, we wipe away what is no longer needed. We also rub in what cannot be discarded so that it can be assimilated into our physical, emotional, and spiritual beings and into the stories we tell about our lives. With this wiping away and rubbing in, we create the page on which we can begin to make a new map with which to navigate our changed lives.

This is similar to Andrew Lester's understanding of how the construction of future stories allows us to articulate hope, rather than despair, about what lies ahead. In Lester's words, this process involves "accepting the givens imposed by time past, living with the freedoms provided in the present, and shaping the possibilities that the future

---

63. Stephen A. Geller, "Blood Cult: Toward a Literary Theology of the Priestly Work of the Pentateuch," *Prooftexts* 12 (1992): 108–9.

64. Genesis 1.

presents."[65] Ritual is one means by which we might use actions to tell the stories of our past and future lives. When Jo and a hospice social worker worked with Tom, a man in his twenties who had recently lost his sister, they created a ritual that took salvageable material from the past and molded it into a hopeful future story. Tom's grief over his sister's death was complicated by the fact that they had been unable to resolve a long-standing conflict before she died. Using several objects that represented his grief, Tom told the stories of the objects and described the brokenness they represented. At the same time, he acknowledged the new insights he had acquired through his bereavement journey, which included gratitude for his relationship with his sister prior to their conflict. As Tom expressed his hopes for the future, he watered one of his sister's plants that he planned to bring into his home. The water, the plant, and his own articulated hopes represented the possibility of a meaningful future beyond his sister's death.

In the Talmud, tractate *Berachot* presents a series of stories that involve pairs of rabbis, one of whom is ill and one of whom is making a *bikkur cholim* visit. The rabbis' vulnerability is underscored by the fact that they slip in and out of the roles of being the visitor and the visited, reminding us that over the course of our lives we are likely to be both the caregiver and the care-receiver. Through these stories, we learn that ill people need visitors and support because "a prisoner cannot free himself from jail."[66] The *metzora* needed a priest who daubed him with blood and oil and offered a series of sacrifices on his behalf; Tom needed a space in which he could tell old stories, imagine new stories, and give kinesthetic expression to both; Renee needed a community that visited her consistently, regardless of where she

---

65. Andrew D. Lester, *Hope in Pastoral Care and Counseling* (Louisville: Westminster John Knox, 1995), 22.
66. Babylonian Talmud *Berachot* 5b.

was. The patient cannot "free himself" without the help of another human being. Indeed, *kapparah* is effected by the intimacy to which these relationships give rise. By being vulnerable, we allow others to touch us—literally or metaphorically. This touch supports us in the continual process of recreating ourselves as we rub in or wipe away what went before.

Atonement as Covering

The idea of atonement as covering is intriguing because it speaks to the need for a second party to be involved in the process of purification. While it is often possible for us to cover ourselves (with shelter, blankets, clothing, jewelry, or make up, for example), it is far easier—and often more comforting—for someone else to do this on our behalf. When we allow someone else to cover us, we accept that we are vulnerable and in need of help and protection. We allow another person to extend to us an act and a sign of care. In other words, we accept that we are human. To be a human in need of covering is part of the *metzora*'s ritual for reentry. The recognition of our commonality with other vulnerable, fragile humans is often the most significant transformation for people who have spent time in a contemporary *michutz lamachaneh* setting.

On the first and seventh days of the purification ritual following a healing from *tzara'at*, the *metzora* shaved his hair and bathed.[67] This ritual underscored his vulnerability, his (literal and metaphorical) nakedness, and his "newness." It also provided a blank canvas of sorts to which a "covering" could be added that would "wipe away" the *tumah* of *tzara'at*. In her study of Leviticus, Mary Douglas concludes that the word *kapparah*, which is generally understood as atonement, is a synonym for covering. She explains that the chapters of Leviticus

---

67. Leviticus 14:8-9.

that deal with *tzara'at* in skin, cloth, and houses describe a series of covered items:

> The chapters about physical impurity of humans who had to be cleansed by atonement were arranged to present the body in a series of covers, the covering of skin, the garment covering the house, the house covering both. When we reach the end of the book [of Leviticus] we find that over the ark of the covenant is another cover, the throne where God sits. . . . [T]his is the case for arguing that the atonement rite affords a cover for the people of Israel.

She goes on to point out "the range of reference in English for cover: to get insurance cover [*sic*], to cover a debt, to stand cover for a friend. Soldiers take cover, everyone does in a storm and game animals take cover from hunters. A shield covers the body, cover is a lid of a pot, of a manhole, covering is clothing."[68]

All of this offers an interesting vantage point from which to consider the "covering" that the priest applied to the *metzora* on the eighth day of the ritual. In this covering, the priest took blood from one of the *metzora*'s offerings and daubed it on the *metzora*'s right extremities—the ridge of his right ear, the thumb of his right hand, and the big toe of his right foot. The priest then covered each daub of blood with oil and also placed oil on the *metzora*'s head. Leviticus tells us, "*Ve'khiper alav ha'kohen lifnei YHVH.*"[69] This is generally translated as "And the priest shall *make expiation for him* before the Eternal";[70] an alternative rendering is "And the priest *covered him* before the Eternal." The priest covered sites at the edges of the body that represent our most vulnerable and exposed places and are most in need of protection. By "covering" these exposed,

---

68. Mary Douglas, *Leviticus as Literature* (Oxford: Oxford University Press, 1999), 244–45.
69. Leviticus 14:18.
70. See, for example, *JPS Hebrew-English Tanakh* (Philadelphia: Jewish Publication Society, 1999), 238.

external places, the priest symbolically covered the entire body in all of its vulnerability. Ultimately, these coverings effected "expiation" in all of its meanings: purification, restoration, protective covering, wiping away, re-creation, and returning to balance. Interestingly, when Aaron ordained the priests he mimicked the ritual for the *metzora* as he daubed blood onto the priests' right extremities.[71] Covering is powerful, so much so that it can restore *taharah* and confer *kedushah*.

To feel another person's hands resting on the top of one's head—as the *metzora* would have when the priest placed oil there—is to be deeply comforted. This action recurs throughout religious rituals including, for example, in the weekly Shabbat evening blessing that parents offer to their children. When Jo worked with Richard, a hospice patient who was wracked with guilt, he described his metastatic cancer as "sin that is stuck to my insides." In a brief period of wakefulness a few days before he died, he said, "I just want someone to put their hands on my head and tell me everything will be okay." Jo reached out her hands, used them to cover Richard's head, and said to him the words he had asked to hear. She kept her hands there as Richard drifted off to sleep.

A teaching in the Babylonian Talmud suggests that covering and accompaniment are related acts. In the midst of a section dealing with the importance of accompanying a deceased person to his or her burial place, the Talmud draws a line of connection between the Hebrew word for funeral (*levayah*; literally, "accompaniment") and garland (*livyah*). In chapter 3, we explored the semantic, theological, and practical connections between the words for priest (*Levi*) and *levayah* (accompaniment, in the narrow sense of attending a funeral and the broader sense of walking with someone through life). Using

---

71. See Exodus 29:20 and Leviticus 8:23-24.

a verse from the book of Proverbs about a garland and a necklace, the Talmud's teaching suggests that the experience of being accompanied is similar to the experience of wearing a garland and a necklace: "[The accompaniers] are a garland of grace (*livyat chen*) upon your head, a necklace about your throat."[72]

Placing one's hands on another's head, or putting one's arm around another's shoulder, brings comfort, reassurance, and the simple reminder of presence. These acts are filled with the same care and generosity as placing a garland or necklace on another human being. On the most simple, visceral level, they are especially important types of touch for people whose primary contact with other human beings is clinical and mechanistic. They are acts through which we offer grace. And for the recipient of the "garland," being accompanied evokes the feeling that one is special, beautiful, and the recipient of unconditional love.[73]

These stories about *kapparah* invite us to find ways to transcend *and* integrate the pain of the past and of the present moment. In this way, we step into hopeful and newly fashioned stories and we connect to a sense of possibility. This sense of hopeful possibility is both deeply rooted in our own beings and swirls through all that is beyond us. Through conversation, prayer, solitude, ritual, gathering, or quiet contemplation, we might—as Eliade explains—notice that "[a]ll time of any kind 'opens' on to sacred time."[74] By this Eliade means that even "profane time," which we described earlier as the unfolding of

72. See Proverbs 1:9 and Babylonian Talmud *Sota* 46b. We gratefully acknowledge Nancy's teacher, Shlomo Fox, who compiled a selection of sources on accompaniment that includes this teaching from Tractate *Sota*.

73. This teaching reminds us of the *bedeken* ritual that is often performed before a Jewish wedding. Traditionally the time when the groom placed the veil over the bride's face, the ritual has been reimagined by egalitarian couples as an opportunity for each partner to place upon the other a piece of clothing, a ritual item such as a *kippah* or prayer shawl, a piece of jewelry, or a garland or corsage of flowers.

74. Mircea Eliade, *Patterns in Comparative Religion*, trans. Rosemary Sheed (New York: Meridian, 1958), 389.

our individual lives, can present us with opportunities to connect to something beyond ourselves. We turn our attention now to how this might play out for soldiers and others whose lives are touched by war.

6

The War Camp and the Returning Warrior

In this chapter, we turn to the book of Numbers to explore stories that shed light on military life, the trauma of war, the challenges of reentry for demobilized warriors, and the pervasiveness of war themes in civilian life. Following Leviticus's exploration of priestly and cultic life, Numbers picks up where Exodus leaves off: after crossing the Red Sea, the Israelites spent two years at the encampment in the Sinai, readying themselves for battle and conquest. The remainder of Numbers is devoted to the Israelites' travels through the wilderness. Throughout this time, the people swam in a sea of complaint, resentment, and rebellion as they longed for the perceived certainty of life under Egyptian slavery. They pined for the past, resisted the present, and regarded the future with terror. When twelve spies scouted out the promised land, ten of them returned with reports of formidable giants, which convinced the people that conquering the land would be foolish at best. God responded with an angry punishment: this generation would spend forty years in the wilderness, where they would die, and their children would inherit the land of Canaan.

Military realities pervade the book of Numbers. At the book's opening, the Israelites are arranged in tribal and military formation around the *Ohel Moed*, which was the centerpiece of the camp. This presented the community with a visual reminder that cultic and military life were inextricably intertwined. The census, from which the English name of the book is derived, counted only men over age twenty—in other words, those who could fight in the impending military conquest.[1] Even prior to the Israelites' arrival in, and conquest of, the promised land—which is not chronicled until the book of Joshua—Numbers documents military disaster in the form of a battle the people initiated without God's approval,[2] as well as a string of military victories against an assortment of kings and peoples.[3] The Israelites' campaign against the Midianites, in which they acted on God's command, is especially bloody, prompting instructions about how warriors, weapons, and spoils of war should make the transition back into civilian arenas.[4]

In the book of Numbers, the word *machaneh* takes on new meanings. As in Leviticus, *machaneh* refers to the domesticated sphere of settled Israelite life—to the times between travels when the people pitched their tents in a cluster around the *Ohel Moed*. Numbers includes many references to *machaneh* in this sense. Dew and manna fell upon the *machaneh*,[5] and God whipped up a wind that dropped quail onto the *machaneh*.[6] The priest left and then reentered the *machaneh* in order to prepare the *mei niddah* that dispersed the pollution of death.[7] Similarly, returning warriors purified themselves

---

1. Numbers 1:2-3.
2. Numbers 14:44-45.
3. See, for example, Numbers 21:21-35.
4. Numbers 31.
5. Numbers 11:9.
6. Numbers 11:31.
7. Numbers 19:7. See chapter 4 for a full description of this ritual.

outside the *machaneh* and then reentered it.[8] When God sent down a furious fire, it burned the edges of the *machaneh*, which tells us that the *machaneh* had clearly defined borders.[9] We also learn that, for the marching Israelites, the *machaneh* was both the place they had left behind and the place toward which they were heading. In the words of Numbers 10:33-34,

> They traveled from the mountain of the Eternal a distance of three days and the Ark of the Covenant of the Eternal traveled before them for a distance of three days to scout out for them a resting place [that is, their next encampment], and the cloud of the Eternal was above them by day as they traveled from the camp.[10]

In addition to these meanings, the *machaneh* now took on military connotations. As the tribes arrayed themselves around the *Ohel Moed*, they were clearly preparing to march into war. The second chapter of Numbers, in particular, is peppered with military language: for example, the repeated use of *le'tzivotam* ("according to their troop") and *u'tzeva'o u'fekudeihem* ("his troop and their enrollment").[11] Each tribe assembled under its *degel machaneh*, meaning the flag or standard of each tribe, suggesting the insignia of a warring group.[12] The *machaneh* had become both a temporary dwelling place and an army in waiting. As a result, the inescapable reality of war was woven into the fabric of everyday life. Indeed, the verb *linso'a*, used repeatedly to describe the Israelites' progress through the desert, can be equally well translated as "to travel" or "to march." These two meanings underscore how the Israelites' forward progress was intimately connected to the imperative to go to war.[13]

8. Numbers 31:24.
9. Numbers 11:1.
10. Authors' translation.
11. See, for example, Numbers 2:3-4.
12. See, for example, Numbers 2:3, 10, 18, 25.

Like any other army preparing for war, the Israelites had no control over when, or to where, they would journey. All soldiers depend on their superiors to make decisions about battle plans. While most armies turn to a hierarchy of human commanders, the ancient Israelites left their itinerary and battle plans to God. In both situations, soldiers on the ground find themselves in highly unpredictable circumstances beyond their control, needing to trust and depend on another's decisions.

In the case of the Israelites, a string of verses describes how God's cloud covered the *Ohel Moed* each day.[14] Whenever the cloud lifted, the Israelites knew it was time to break camp and resume their march. This happened *al pi Adonai*, according to God's word, order, or command. The use of this phrase reiterates the essential point that the Israelites were not in control of—and, indeed, had entrusted to a power beyond themselves—the most basic ability to determine their own geographic coordinates. Furthermore, they might wait several days, a month, or a year for the cloud to lift, never knowing for how long they could sink into a daily routine and sense of order. Like people across time who have lived in the midst of war, in war's aftermath, or with the anticipation of impending war, the Israelites continually drew and redrew their mental maps as they made sense of their shifting environs.

In addition to the ways in which the *machaneh* of the full community took on some of the characteristics of the war camp, a few brief verses in Deuteronomy describe a specific war camp—a set-aside place for soldiers who were engaged in the business of war. Although it is not explicitly stated, it appears that this camp was only for warriors. Underscoring the ways in which a camp could also be

13. According to *The Brown-Driver-Briggs Hebrew and English Lexicon* (Peabody, Mass.: Hendrickson, 2001), the verb's semantic range includes "move," "march," "set out," and "journey" (p. 652). In Modern Hebrew, in contrast, the verb primarily means "to travel".
14. Numbers 9:15-23.

an army, the section begins, "When you go out as a camp (*machaneh*) against your enemy . . . ."[15] In this war camp, military life took place in a theater of war that was separate from everyday life. For the Israelites, as in our own time, war was both integrated into daily life and fenced off from it.

Beginning in the immediate aftermath of the flight from slavery, Numbers ends with the community assembled on the steppes of Moab, overlooking Jericho and the promised land, poised for the battles they would have to fight to take possession of the land. The body of the book stretches between these two significantly traumatic events: slavery and flight on one end, bloody conquest on the other. In between, Numbers records stories of terrified complaint, psychological disintegration, divine punishment, and battles with various conclusions ranging from devastating defeat to glorious victory. Numbers can be read, among other things, as a book about trauma—the traumatic legacy of slavery, the trauma of living in a time of war, and the trauma of anticipating the battles that lay ahead. Whereas Leviticus offers a tightly controlled guide, Numbers—despite its attempts at orderly counting and assembling—is filled with chaos. Rachel Havrelock describes the book in this way:

> "Numbers," the English name of the book, alludes to the social organization of the Israelites and the two censuses that frame the book . . . ; the Hebrew title, *B'midbar* [In the Wilderness] . . . , highlights the transitory setting of the narrative. The contrast between these two titles reflects the tension between order and chaos, culture and nature, obedience and rebellion that characterizes the book and drives its plot.[16]

---

15. Deuteronomy 23:10-15.
16. Rachel Havrelock, "B'midbar: The Architecture of a Count and the Architecture of Account," in *The Torah: A Women's Commentary*, eds. Tamara Cohn Eskenazi and Andrea L. Weiss (New York: Women of Reform Judaism and URJ Press, 2008), 789.

With this description, Havrelock draws attention to the destabilizing nature of the Israelites' constant motion through the wilderness. Compounding this instability are the factors that gave rise to the movement in the first place: the Israelites' homelessness in the wake of slavery, and God's punishment that condemned the generation of slavery to forty years of wandering. Both of these experiences brought fearfulness and restiveness, which become dominant themes in the book.

Despite—and perhaps because of—the destabilization that is at the heart of the book, Numbers is nonetheless a guide. It is a guide when it offers an idealized vision of how to proceed into battle in an orderly and comradely fashion. And it is also a guide when its ruthlessly chaotic and blood-drenched pages describe how humans are psychologically undone by violence, how war calls upon us to transgress the boundaries of typical life, and how returning home might cause havoc for everyone involved. Indeed, for Adriane Leveen, it is precisely in the heart of this destabilization where Numbers functions as a "path." In *Memory and Tradition in the Book of Numbers*, she explores the interplay between Numbers' presentation of the unraveling of the past and its promises about the future. She writes, "Numbers' editors succeed in moving from the total breakdown of God's plan for one generation and the haunted arena in which they die to restored order and purpose in the next. They dare to narrate a path out of that unmarked wilderness into the promised land for all time."[17] Following Leveen's lead, we also seek the "paths" that lie within Numbers' painful chaos.

Contemporary war writers often turn to ancient battle myths to make sense of their own experiences as a soldier or as someone who works with soldiers. Notably, Jonathan Shay, a Veterans

17. Adriane Leveen, *Memory and Tradition in the Book of Numbers* (Cambridge: Cambridge University Press, 2008), 5.

Administration (VA) psychiatrist, has written two moving and powerful books that weave contemporary veterans' stories into the narrative rhythm of Homer's *Iliad* and *Odyssey*. Mining these ancient poems for universal truths, Shay proposes that the *Iliad* describes the "moral dimension of trauma" and the "dreadful, rabid state" of warriors who are damaged by war. The *Odyssey*, meanwhile, "may profitably be read as a detailed allegory of many a real veteran's homecoming."[18] Edward Tick, a psychotherapist who deals extensively with war trauma in his clinical work, adopts a similar approach. He seeks "universal stories" about war that help contemporary people—both military and civilian—understand their own lives. To do this, he draws widely from Native American traditions, Greek and Norse mythology, the Bible, and other sources. He explains, "Considered from the mythic point of view, our lives are individualized versions of universal stories."[19]

Like Shay and Tick, we seek guidance in communal, inherited narratives. We mine the book of Numbers, and also brief passages in Deuteronomy and Joshua, for stories that shed light on the disruptive transitions associated with going to war, living with war, and returning from war. In the first section of this chapter, we explore what it is like to live in the midst of war, focusing on biblical and contemporary manifestations of the "war camp," trauma, and encounters with the "enemy." We also explore soldiers' return home after war, looking at how ritual, storytelling, and forgiveness can support demobilized soldiers as well as the broader community through these difficult transitions. Because neither of us conducts our clinical work in military or VA settings, the case material in

---

18. Jonathan Shay, *Odysseus in America: Combat Trauma and the Trials of Homecoming* (New York: Scribner, 2002), xv. See also Jonathan Shay, *Achilles in Vietnam: Combat Trauma and the Undoing of Character* (New York: Simon & Schuster, 1994).
19. Edward Tick, *War and the Soul: Healing Our Nation's Veterans from Post-Traumatic Stress Disorder* (Wheaton, Ill.: Quest Books, 2005), 28, 218.

this chapter draws on interviews with five Department of Defense chaplains, all of whom are also rabbis, and a retired Veterans Administration social worker. These six people have all worked extensively with military personnel as they prepare for war, go to war, and return home from war.

The War Camp

In six terse verses, Deuteronomy 23 addresses the matter of holiness within the military camp. This camp was holy because God was immanently and intimately present in it. God is described in human terms as a being that walked around the camp. The Torah uses the word *mithalech*, the reflexive form of the verb "to walk," to describe God's movement around the camp. This is also the verb used to describe how God moved around the Garden of Eden,[20] as well as to describe how various humans walked with or before God.[21] While the reflexive form of the verb defies easy translation into English, it seems that these walking actions connote presence, devotion, and loyalty. The war camp—like any other camp—was a sanctuary from inhumanity, and a place to reassert one's humanity and reconnect with guiding coordinates, even while in a place where life and death met.

Because the war camp was holy, the soldiers had to protect it from anything that qualified as a *davar ra* ("unpleasant thing") or *ervat davar* ("shameful thing").[22] The text gives two explicit examples: the rules for a man who has had a nocturnal emission, and the proper arrangements for going to the bathroom. The first example concerns *tumah*, which is at odds with *kedushah*. Similar to the procedures for purification after healing from *tzara'at* or after contact with the

20. Genesis 3:8.
21. See Genesis 5:22, 24; 6:9; 17:1; 24:40; and 48:15.
22. Deuteronomy 23:10 and 15 (authors' translation).

mei niddah that dispersed death, the soldier who was rendered *tamei* by a nocturnal emission had to leave the camp, bathe, and then return at sundown. The second example concerns a substance—excrement—that is not *tamei*. Rather, because it is unpleasant, soldiers were instructed to dig a hole in an area outside the camp and then cover it again when they had finished. To us, the intention in both cases is clear: the war camp had to be preserved as a place where God could stroll (literally without treading in anything untoward!) so that God could be intimately present with the camp's residents.

The war camp was not a theater of war; rather it was the place where soldiers prepared for and rested from war. While battle didn't happen there, this camp was presumably filled with portents and echoes of war. We imagine that wounded soldiers spent time there regaining strength or slipping into death, and we picture warriors experiencing the immediate aftermath of battle's trauma and making plans for their next offensive. Against this backdrop, God visited this place in God's most humanlike form—a strolling being that was apparently attuned to a human pace of activity. Like the priest who spent time *michutz lamachaneh* with the *metzora*, and like contemporary pastoral and other professional caregivers, God altered God's pace and rhythm to match that of the people most in need of presence. We imagine that this intimate presence was reassuring and comforting. It seems to us that the author of the book of Numbers chose this manifestation of God because it was the form most needed in the camp that occupied the physical space between everyday life and the bloody battlefield. Indeed, Tick reports that he has heard many veterans describe themselves as so "tainted" by their war experiences that their "soul[s] feel banished from the divine presence."[23] The trauma of war, then, calls for nothing less than God's intimately loving presence.

Harold Robinson, a rabbi and retired rear admiral in the Navy, served as a military chaplain in the First Gulf War, and in Afghanistan, Iraq, and the Horn of Africa. He describes the period of training before being sent to war as a "time of enormous anxiety." With wrenching detail, he describes the state of mind of the young men with whom he worked in the Navy:

> They are asked to openly risk death, and to risk death not necessarily for personal gain. They have to be comfortable with death. There is also a sense of guilt that they have abandoned their loved ones. And all of that is mixed in with a kind of guilty pleasure that this is really exciting, this is an adventure. This is way beyond the ability of the average 20 year-old to articulate and integrate. Afterwards, [that is, when their deployment is over] there is another range of emotions: guilt about "Why did I live? Why do I get to go back and live a normal life? I killed people, and maybe he was just like me." Or "I didn't kill people and maybe if I *had* killed that guy my buddy would still be alive." They replay battles a thousand times in their heads. But the average 20 year-old doesn't have words for this. He only knows he is feeling enormous passions.

Describing the weighty emotional burdens soldiers carry, Robinson says, "There is something literally demonic about war. It reaches into human beings and has them do things that are literally inhumane. The inhumanity of it all is counter-positioned for me with the image of my fellow human beings walking in the camp like God." For Robinson, the line between God and soldier blurs. Since each human is created *betzelem Elohim*, in the image of God, "each soldier walking in the camp is really God walking in the camp." Not only do these soldiers have a profound need to feel anchored by an intimate, immanent God, they also "will potentially have godlike power over other human beings—the power of life and death—actions that only God should be taking." Within this framework, says Robinson, the

23. Tick, *War and the Soul*, 131.

role of the chaplain is to "keep reminding [soldiers] they are human beings in the divine image, loved and capable of loving."[24]

Emily Rosenzweig is a rabbi and a Navy chaplain who works at the Great Lakes Naval Station in Illinois. There she serves new recruits who are at Great Lakes to participate in basic training, an eight-week introduction to military life. Great Lakes is *michutz lamachaneh* in the sense not only of being physically removed from the zones and arenas of typical daily life but also because the recruits there are denied access to the relationships, electronic devices, music, and TV shows in which they previously found sustenance, solace, and diversion. In Rosenzweig's words, "If you got through high school listening to music and talking to your friends on the phone, you can't do those things here." Committed both to naming the recruits' reality and to finding usable material within Jewish tradition to support and comfort, Rosenzweig structures her sermons around the daily experience of boot camp. She describes her work this way: "I try to take universal Torah and bring it down to boot camp level." By way of example, Rosenzweig describes the sermon she gave on the Shabbat on which Jewish communities read the story of Nadav and Avihu.[25]

> I talked about the idea that Nadav and Avihu are killed because they offer this *esh zarah* [strange or foreign fire]. We don't know what *esh zarah* is but we know that it doesn't go by the order and doesn't follow the structure that things are supposed to—because if it did, they wouldn't have gotten in trouble for it. . . . Something is in chaos within them. I compare that with the idea of creation, which starts with this idea of chaos. So I suggested that the work of Jews, and the work of righteous people, is to build from that chaos, to take the world from chaos to structure. We do this through food laws, which are also in that Torah portion, and [we do this in] how we talk and how we treat one another.

24. Interview with Rear Admiral Harold Robinson CHC, USN, Ret., conducted by the authors by phone in New York City, May 20, 2013.
25. Leviticus 10:1-3.

Boot camp starts out in chaos. They are not in uniform yet. They don't know which way is up and they don't know who to talk to. And then, slowly, they learn this new way of doing things. More and more structure appears and they can do more and more. But graduation at boot camp is not the end, it's only the beginning. [So I concluded the sermon with] Rabbi Tarfon's teaching [from the Mishnah]: You don't have to complete the work but you can't not do the work. You have to do the work.[26]

Rosenzweig delivered this sermon in the chapel on the base, a place that is not unlike the Tent of Special Appointments. She reports that, in the period that stretches from Friday evening to Sunday morning, the chapel hosts seventeen different religious services. While the exigencies of basic training—restrictions on the recruits' movements and the need for recruits to appear emotionally tough—means that the chapel is rarely used for individual prayer or meditation, it is clear that this plethora of worship services fulfill an important need.[27]

In her sermon, Rosenzweig instinctively names recruits' former axes of orientation, while also proposing new axes—that is, the orders and structures specific to boot camp—to which they might orient themselves. This complete reorientation would not be necessary or possible if the recruits were not so utterly removed from the world they have left behind. No longer in control of when they eat or sleep, no longer able to wear their own clothes, and living time according to a twenty-four-hour rather than a twelve-hour clock, these recruits are experiencing a type of radical deracination.[28] Like patients and their family members, military personnel and their family members count time differently, using markers such as deployment, first mission, most recent mission, or anticipated return date to orient themselves to the passage of time. Military personnel might also find

26. *Pirkei Avot* 2:21.
27. Interview with Chaplain Emily Rosenzweig LT, CHC, USN, conducted by the authors by phone in New York City, May 21, 2013.
28. For a more detailed discussion of this sense of disorientation, see chapter 1.

that their relationship to the cycles of time in the natural world is disrupted as they stay awake for hours in windowless bunkers or as they use goggles to simulate day vision at night. Additionally, they are likely to be in direct communication with family around the world at all times of the day and night, fitting conversations into the rhythm of their work and the exigencies of time differences.

Military life requires a thorough reorientation, complete with new home, family, and community. This reorientation, which begins in boot camp and continues through deployment, is so comprehensive that even years later retired military personnel continue to find home on their old military bases. In this spirit, Heather Borshof, a rabbi and Army chaplain, describes life at Fort Belvoir in northern Virginia. She reports that retired military personnel who have made their home in the Washington, D.C. area continue to attend services at the base's chapel. This is a profound illustration of their ongoing sense of connection to this *michutz lamachaneh* place they have come to call home.[29]

Like Robinson, who sees God's presence in the faces of military personnel, Rosenzweig encourages recruits to see God wherever they happen to be. While she acknowledges that some chaplains, particularly those who are Christian, might see themselves as "God's representative," she says that her job is "less to be the presence of God than the keeper of human beings."[30] Numbers offers a powerful description of God's intimate presence in the war camp; through their daily work, these military chaplains do justice to that portrait as they bring reminders and assurances that love and connection are tangible entities in these *michutz lamachaneh* places. Indeed, in the absence of all other orientation markers, we can still access the

29. Interview with Chaplain (CPT) Heather Borshof, conducted by the authors by phone in New York City, May 21, 2013.
30. Rosenzweig, interview.

"A" of attunement to something beyond ourselves. This stands in stark contrast to the experience of being in battle, where fear and distrust predominate, social and spiritual connections crumble, and the possibility of meaning making frequently evaporates.

Grotesque Distortions

Millennia before the development of contemporary systems of knowledge that explain and categorize trauma, the Torah recorded profound observations about how people behave when they are under tremendous stress. Although the Israelites crossed the Red Sea with celebration—similar, perhaps, to the joy and relief that accompany modern soldiers' homecomings—they were a traumatized people whose lives were dominated by reactions and associations born in slavery. As Shay explains, for those living in the wake of war's trauma, "the voice of a wartime past [is] experienced as more real and meaningful than the present."[31] This is an apt description of the Israelites, for whom the travails of slavery felt more real and satisfying than their current lives. Viewed through this lens, chapter 11 of Numbers is a disturbing account of a traumatized people's inability to find satiation—literal or metaphorical—in the present moment.

The story begins with the Israelites' bitter complaint of having no meat to eat. They remember with longing the food they used to eat in Egypt, and they crave it with a deep hunger. They recall the fish they ate there "for free" and they make a mouth-watering list of the foods they miss: cucumbers, watermelons, leeks, onions, and garlic. They deride the manna, the only food available to them in the wilderness, claiming that it makes their throats dry up. They lament, "*Ein kol*!"—which is to say, "We lack everything! There is no bounty here!"—at which point the Bible's editorial voice interjects,

31. Shay, *Odysseus in America*, 89.

undermining the people's complaint with a reminder that the manna was actually a rich oily and creamy delicacy.[32]

In response to the people's complaint, God declares that tomorrow the people will have meat to eat. However, this will not be one modest meal; rather, the Israelites will eat meat every day for a month until it comes out of their noses and they are repulsed by it. God whips up a wind that scatters quail, two cubits deep, over the surface of the camp. The reader is left to imagine the Israelites wading through this scene of grotesque abundance. We do learn, however, that the people spent the subsequent two days gathering up the quail. The verb *asaf* ("to gather") is used twice, bringing to mind images of people scooping up great armfuls of (dead?) birds in an elaborately time-consuming process.[33] The verb "to gather" also implies an attempt to rein in, and impose order on, something hopelessly scattered and disordered, similar to how we might use the phrase "to gather one's thoughts." Earlier in the chapter, when the Israelites first gave voice to their culinary complaints, the people were described as *ha'safsuf*, meaning "the riffraff" or the "great multitude." Drawn from the same root as *asaf*, we learn that the Israelites gather to complain and to give voice to their insatiable cravings, and they also gather armfuls of meat, hugging it close to their bodies. Their gatherings are greedy and desperate, driven by distorted memories of the past rather than by an accurate appraisal of the present.

In the midst of this gluttony, an already disastrous situation further unravels. As the people are still chewing, swallowing, and picking the meat from between their teeth, God strikes them with a deadly plague. From this time forward, this encampment becomes known

---

32. Numbers 11:4-9.
33. The image of the gathering of the dead quails has resonance with the idea of the Patriarchs being gathered to their ancestors at the time of their deaths. The first example of this involves Abraham's death in Genesis 25:8.

as *Kivrot-Hata'avah*, meaning "the place of buried appetites" or "the graves of the craving." The Israelites, who were described at the beginning of this story as *hitavu ta'avah*—in other words, truly craving meat—are now buried, along with their unsatiated appetites, in the dry earth of *Kivrot-Hata'avah*. Driven by a sickeningly distorted sense of their own needs, the people are literally consumed by their own appetites.

Contemporary war writers frequently describe how "killing and death become a more manageable task" through the dehumanization of the enemy.[34] The proclivity to see others through a distorted and dehumanizing lens is particularly evident in this story of uncontrolled appetite and in the story of the spies' report. After scouting out the promised land, ten of the twelve spies conclude that the inhabitants of the land are *Nephilim*, which is generally translated as "giants." In contrast, the spies report that they appeared to themselves—and therefore, they claim, must also have seemed to the inhabitants of the land—as mere grasshoppers.[35] Referring first to the people whom they have seen as *anshei middot*, men of (great) measure, the spies then use the term *Nephilim*. While giants share some characteristics with humans, they are essentially nonhuman, which underscores the spies' perception that an untraversable barrier separates them from the *Nephilim*.[36] Deepening the process of dehumanization, the spies now regard themselves as tiny, vulnerable insects, unrecognizable to themselves and thoroughly nonhuman.

Chapter 14 of the book of Numbers, which immediately follows this account of giants and grasshoppers, describes the effects of this distorted view of the world on the people as a whole and on God.

34. See, for example, Raymond Monsour Scurfield, *War Trauma: Lessons Unlearned from Vietnam to Iraq* (New York: Algora, 2006), 10–11.
35. Numbers 13:32-33.
36. The word also appears in Genesis 6:4 to describe other nonhuman beings. Here, the *Nephilim* are the offspring of sons of gods and daughters of men.

Ready to believe the spies' reports, the people join the spies in sinking into despair as they weep the whole night long.[37] Beginning with the spies' name for the allegedly enormous *Nephilim*, which could be translated as "those-who-cause-others-to-fall," the chapter spins on the repeated use of the verb "to fall"—with its root letters *nun-peh-lamed*. Through these varieties of falling, the chapter offers insights into the tragic effects of despair and fear, and also into the role of forgiveness. As the chapter opens, the people have wept all night and are now complaining to Moses, claiming that it would be better to die in the wilderness or return to Egypt than to enter the dangerous land to which God is leading them. Indeed, they predict that in this land they will fall (*linpol*) by the sword.[38] Here, the verb is used to predict a future disaster that will be wrought by the terrifying inhabitants of the land of Canaan. Immediately, Moses, Aaron, Joshua, and Caleb fall (*vayipol*[39]) on their faces as they try to convince the people that the land is good and there is no need to fear its inhabitants.[40]

A furious God then enters the scene and declares to Moses that God will disown the people. Moses intercedes with God, reminding God of God's compassion and urging God to reconsider. God says to Moses *salachti kidvarecha*, "I have forgiven you as you ask."[41] Many centuries later, this phrase found its way into the Yom Kippur liturgy, meaning that, for many Jews, it has strong associations with divine compassion and forgiveness. We will explore this theme later in this chapter. For now, we stay with the story at hand in which God

---

37. Numbers 14:1.
38. Numbers 14:3. To draw on Andrew Lester's work on future stories, we can say that the people lacked a hopeful and viable future story. See Andrew Lester's *Hope in Pastoral Care and Counseling* (Louisville: Westminster John Knox, 1995), as well as chapter 1 of this book, for an exploration of Lester's use of the term "future story."
39. This singular verb is used to describe the action of all three men, as if they were a united entity.
40. Numbers 14:5.
41. Numbers 14:20.

decrees that the people as a whole will be punished. The entire generation of slavery, save Joshua and Caleb, will be denied entry into the land and their corpses will fall (*yipolu*) in the wilderness. When Moses tells the people that this will be their fate, they mourn greatly and then decide to take matters into their own hands. Despite Moses' warnings of impending catastrophe, and despite their full knowledge that God is not in their midst, they declare their intention to set off for the hill country[42] about which God has told them.

In a story about falling, the fact that the people head for the heights underscores their rash folly. Moses warns the people, you will fall (*unafaltem*) at the hands of the Amalekites and the Canaanites, which is precisely what happens. Paradoxically, in a literary unit shot through with the verb "to fall," the Israelites set off on this disastrous military adventure puffed up with reckless ambition (*vayapilu*). The Jewish Publication Society (JPS) translates this word as an adverb, "defiantly," and Everett Fox offers "recklessly." Brown-Driver-Briggs translates the verb as "be heedless, neglectful, inadvertent" or "to swell."[43] The root appears in one other place in the Bible in a verb form, in Habbakuk; JPS understands this usage to refer to a person with a puffed up, rather than an upright, spirit.[44] In its noun form, the root can mean "mound" or "hill" or "tumor," all of which suggest swelling, inflammation, and, in the case of tumor, something that is out of place or wrong.[45] *Vayapilu* alliterates with the words related to falling, which further underscores how the Israelites attempt to ascend but only descend further into disaster and tragedy.

The people's military expedition results in falling—in the form of their deaths at their enemies' hands—but it is motivated by a desire to

---

42. Adriane Leveen suggests that this refers to Mount Hormah (personal communication).
43. See JPS, 316; Fox, *Five Books of Moses*, 730; and *Brown-Driver-Briggs*, 779.
44. Habakkuk 2:4; JPS, 1365.
45. This offers a striking parallel to *tzara'at*, which is also an inflamed disturbance of an otherwise flat area.

achieve the opposite. It is fueled by ambition, pride, inflation, and the desire to ascend. In this chapter, the Israelites' view of themselves and others is refracted through the perversions of a funhouse mirror. In these mirrors, the Canaanites are giants and the Israelites themselves are first grasshoppers and then mighty warriors. The Israelites are presented as traumatized people who have lost the ability to see clearly—with devastating results. But, extraordinarily, this story appears in a biblical chapter that includes at least a thread of forgiveness. We will return later to the connections between distorted vision, excruciating guilt, and the persistent possibility of forgiveness.[46]

The Domestic Sphere

Each week of each year, Jewish communities around the world read the same Torah portion, beginning with the first chapter of Genesis on the same week in the autumn and completing the last chapter of Deuteronomy one year later.[47] Each of these readings is paired with a nonpentateuchal biblical passage that echoes themes of the Torah portion; these pairings were chosen and set by the Rabbis of antiquity. The story of the spies in Numbers is twinned with a story in which Joshua sent two spies to the city of Jericho.[48] This second story offers a very different perspective on how war changes our perceptions of ourselves and others, by offering a description of what happens when the "enemy" enters all the way into our homes. Rather

46. According to Shay, "[T]he *Iliad* emphatically portrays the enemy as worthy of respect, even honor." Indeed, in this story, both the Greeks and the Trojans acknowledge that the gods might favor the other side. In contrast, "[t]he Judeo-Christian (and Islamic) world view has triumphed so completely over the Homeric world view that dishonoring the enemy now seems natural, virtuous, patriotic, pious." For Shay, this has clinical implications because "[r]estoring honor to the enemy is an essential step in recovery from combat PTSD" (*Achilles in Vietnam*, 103, 106, 114–15).
47. A minority of communities completes a full reading of the Torah over a triennial cycle, reading each week only a piece of the section that other communities read in its entirety.
48. Joshua 2:1–24.

than being a story about hideously refracted giants and grasshoppers, this is a story about domesticity and red thread.

Much of this second story takes place in the home of Rahav, a prostitute who lives in a house hollowed out of the city wall. While war depends, to some degree, on the dehumanization of the enemy, it is in reality an experience of boundary crossing. War brings soldiers onto the home turf, and even into the domestic spheres, of the people who are too easily dismissed as the enemy.[49] In Rahav's story, she hides the spies, protecting them from their pursuers. In return, the invading Israelites spare Rahav and her family, who signal their presence to the soldiers with a strand of red thread dangling from the window of Rahav's home.[50] At the same time, Israelite fighting men enter the homes of Rahav's friends and community, bringing violence, destruction, suffering, and death to the world that had been Rahav's until now. Indeed this is a perpetual reality of war: that people's homes—their *mikdash me'at* or little sanctuary, to use the rabbinic term—become arenas of battle.

Rahav's red thread carries echoes of the crimson stuff used in the construction of the *Ohel Moed* and in the purification ritual for the healed *metzora*. It is also a symbol of domesticity, of the way that soldiers must inevitably come face to face with women, children, homemaking, needlework, and the ordinary items of the domestic sphere. Paradoxically, this happens when they feel most distant from their own homes. Jill Hammer has written a contemporary *midrash*

49. With regard to contemporary corollaries, this type of contact might be an explicit military strategy. *Army Times* writer Kelly Kennedy tells the story of the United States military unit that was posted in Adhamiya, Iraq, in 2007. She reports that, according to "the new counterinsurgency manual written by General David Petraeus and his aides," American soldiers "were supposed to spend just as much time in living rooms drinking sweet, strong tea and trying to make connections with Iraqi citizens as they did rolling down the narrow streets shooting insurgents." See Kelly Kennedy, *They Fought for Each Other: The Triumph and Tragedy of the Hardest Hit Unit in Iraq* (New York: St. Martin's Press, 2010), 2. This type of contact might also be an unintended consequence of entering into a war zone.

50. Joshua 2.

that elaborates on the Talmud's retelling of Rahav's story, in which Rahav converts to Judaism and marries Joshua. In Hammer's story, Rahav and Joshua are bound together—after having crossed literal and metaphorical boundaries to join their lives—by a deep love and a deep anger. Unable to confront the reality of the Israelites' bloody slaughter of Rahav's people under Joshua's leadership, they bicker over all manner of minor issues. At the same time, they build a home and a family together, bringing daughter after daughter into their home.[51]

In the Bible, in the Talmud, and in Hammer's *midrash*, Rahav presents a human side of war. On the one hand is the impulse to dehumanize the enemy; on the other is the reality that war can turn enemies into rescuers, lovers, spouses, and family. Titled "And the Walls Came Tumbling Down," Hammer's story refers obliquely to the details of the conquest of Jericho but, more directly, to war's propensity to bring opponents into intimate contact with each other. Needless to say, this is an enduring phenomenon described in English with the phrase "war bride."[52]

Inextricably intertwined with these love stories, however, are the accompanying stories about disruption, suffering, and trauma, stories

---

51. Jill Hammer, "And the Walls Came Tumbling Down," in *Sisters at Sinai: New Tales of Biblical Women* (Philadelphia: Jewish Publication Society, 2001), 147–53.

52. See, for example, the website www.uswarbrides.com, which explores the experiences of "foreign born GI brides of World War II." In 2007, Christopher Dickey reported for *Newsweek* on relationships between American soldiers and Iraqis. He described how, against great odds, U.S. soldiers stationed in Iraq continue to cross boundaries and play out stories not unlike that of Joshua and Rahav. He wrote, "What is striking about the Iraq War is not that couples have met and fallen for each other and succeeded . . . in getting married. It's that so few of them have. State Department records show that after more than four years of occupation, only about 2,400 visas have been granted to Iraqi spouses and fiancés. Many of those may be marriages to Iraqi-Americans. (Neither the State Department nor the Pentagon breaks down the figures in detail.) Among the rest—several hundred—the few love stories between American soldiers and Iraqi civilians that have happy endings are ones of enormous patience as well as the enormous passion needed to bridge chasms of language and history, politics, religion, insurgency and, yes, terror." See "Love and War," October 13, 2007, http://www.thedailybeast.com/newsweek/2007/10/13/love-and-war.html.

in which war literally comes home. A few verses in Deuteronomy capture a tiny measure of this rupture. In a troubling injunction about the proper treatment of women captured in war, Israelite men are instructed to allow captured women whom they wish to marry a one-month period to weep for their mothers and fathers. While this cursorily short period of time hardly does justice to the trauma these women were experiencing, it does acknowledge that such ruptures give rise to great mourning and loss.[53]

Contemporary Approaches to Trauma

These biblical stories reveal what contemporary soldiers and their professional caregivers know all too well: war can have a devastating impact on soldiers and civilians. Because returning home after war is so profoundly challenging, and because the Torah directly addresses this transition, we turn our attention to war's effect on soldiers. In its list of the symptoms of Post-Traumatic Stress Disorder (PTSD), the fifth edition of the *Diagnostic and Statistical Manual* (DSM) includes involuntary and intrusive memories of the traumatic event; dissociative states; negative expectations about oneself, others, and the future; a tendency to blame oneself or others for the traumatic event; and aggressive, reckless, and self-destructive behaviors.[54] Raymond Monsour Scurfield is a Vietnam veteran and a social worker who has worked for several decades with veterans with PTSD. Describing the magnitude of PTSD's impact on individuals' psyches and spirits, Scurfield's list of symptoms includes a damaged sense of self, which can include self-hatred; feelings of "existential malaise;" a disconnect between cognition, affect, physiological responses, and

---

53. Deuteronomy 21:10-14.
54. American Psychiatric Association, *Diagnostic and Statistical Manual of Mental Disorders: Fifth Edition* (Washington, D.C., and London: American Psychiatric Publishing, 2013), 275.

environmental cues; a preoccupation with blame of self and/or others; and the pervasiveness of rage, grief, and fear.[55]

While the DSM categorizes PTSD as a mental disorder, some experts in the field emphasize its spiritual dimensions. For Tick, PTSD's greatest impact is on the spirit and the personality. In his words, PTSD "is best understood as an identity disorder and soul wound, affecting the personality at the deepest level."[56] In another important contribution to this topic, Rita Nakashima Brock and Gabriella Lettini describe "a wound of war called 'moral injury,'" which they define as "the violation of core moral beliefs." They distinguish moral injury from PTSD, noting that veterans often begin to explore these moral questions when the acute symptoms of PTSD are sufficiently managed to allow for the construction of coherent memories of their war experiences. Brock and Lettini describe moral injury in excruciating detail, writing, "As memory and reflection deepen, negative self-judgments can torment a soul for a lifetime. Moral injury destroys meaning and forsakes noble cause. It sinks warriors into states of silent, solitary suffering, where bonds of intimacy and care seem impossible. Its torments to the soul can make death a mercy."[57]

In our clinical work, professional caregivers invite those in our care to describe experiences that wound or deaden—or, conversely, that elevate or heal—the soul. Trust, a basic spiritual category, is the glue that holds together relationships, and it is at the heart of many groups' relationship to the transcendent. In this vein, Jonathan Shay proposes that PTSD is an "injury," rather than a "disorder." In addition, he

---

55. Scurfield, *War Trauma*, 167. Writing in 2006, Scurfield uses the DSM, 4th edition, as his reference point.

56. Tick, *War and the Soul*, 5. For a helpful historical summary of how the symptoms we now call PTSD have been perceived and named, see Tick, 99.

57. Rita Nakashima Brock and Gabriella Lettini, *Soul Repair: Recovering from Moral Injury after War* (Boston: Beacon Press, 2012), xiii–xvi.

distinguishes between what he calls "simple" and "complex" PTSD, describing the former as "the persistence into civilian life of adaptations necessary to survive battle" and the latter as "simple PTSD *plus the destruction of the capacity for social trust.*"[58] He also summarizes all PTSD conditions in this way: the "persistence of *valid adaptations to danger* into a time of safety afterward."[59]

Shay's definition is particularly helpful to us as we imagine ourselves into the Israelites' biblical story. For example, it is perhaps not surprising that a recently enslaved people that had fled through the roaring waters of a parted sea regarded other humans as terrifyingly monstrous. These adaptations were responses to slavery and, by the time of the story that unfolds in Numbers 14, the Israelites had not yet found a way to unlearn them. Similarly, the Israelites struggled to trust God, Moses, and even themselves. They feared terrible deaths for themselves and their loved ones and they did not trust in the possibility of a reliable source of sustenance. In fact, of PTSD's many manifestations, unregulated appetite is one.[60] In his search for usable allegories in the story of Odysseus's homecoming, Shay makes the case that when Odysseus's crew ingested the lotus plant they were indulging in some form of narcotic that would bring on "chemically induced forgetting." For Shay, there is a clear parallel between this strand of the *Odyssey* and the alarmingly high rates of substance abuse among veterans with PTSD. According to Shay's statistics, almost three-quarters of veterans with PTSD abuse alcohol and more than 10 percent abuse drugs.[61]

Jess Goodell's memoir corroborates these descriptions of unregulated appetite, both in her choice of partner and in her use

58. Shay *Odysseus in America*, 4 (italics in original).
59. Shay, *Odysseus in America*, 149 (italics in original).
60. See DSM, 5th edition, 275, reference to "excessive alcohol or drug use."
61. Shay, *Odysseus in America*, 36.

of alcohol. In her memoir, she describes her time in Iraq, where she served as a Marine and worked in Mortuary Affairs handling the corpses of both Americans and Iraqis killed in the war. Upon her return home, she found herself in an abusive relationship. Holed up alone at home all day, she turned to alcohol. She writes, "I hid from it all by drinking, but I could still not mute the memories or quiet the doubts."[62]

For Goodell, as for so many others, the effects of the trauma of war had already sunk deeply into her soul by the time she returned home. When Goodell and others cross the boundary separating war from home, they return to a place that is spatially familiar. However, they have frequently lost their orientation to self, others, place, time, and the transcendent. As a result, reentering a store that is geographically familiar might trigger a memory of danger in a war zone filled with heavily armed insurgents, rather than serving as an opportunity to receive a warm welcome home from the familiar shopkeeper. War turns normative expectations on their head, transforming typically safe spaces like homes and marketplaces into catastrophic scenes of destruction. For the soldiers who cause this destruction, and who live with the minute-by-minute possibility of being killed themselves, it is hard to find anywhere that feels safe—in the country where the war is fought or back at home. War ruptures the coordinates and indices that kept soldiers alert and oriented prior to their deployments, leaving them with the feeling of being chronically unmoored.

In Goodell's harrowing account of her service in Iraq, she writes about another form of boundary crossing: the line between life and death that military personnel constantly traverse.

We could *feel* the souls of these civilians, and these mothers and children who died horrendous deaths. Their souls were on the land and all

62. Jess Goodell, with John Hearn, *Shade It Black: Death and After in Iraq* (Havertown, Pa.: Casemate, 2011), 163.

around us; they were in the bunker with us. . . . The line separating the living from the dead, once clear and indelible, became blurred. It often became even less distinct when we were processing remains. A string of lights ran along the periphery of the open bunker's ceiling, but the light by which we processed remains came from searchlights that surrounded our work tables. They sat atop five-foot-high stands and projected our shadows onto the walls of the bunker. There we were disembodied, ephemeral, growing and shrinking in an instant, passing through each other, disappearing and reappearing again and again.

It came to feel like we were living in two worlds or between two worlds, between the living and the dead. We were the living among the dead, living in their world more than they were in ours. We were the ones piecing together and shipping home the remains of the dead, but we were never sure what we were doing to the souls of the dead, or what they were doing to us.[63]

While in Iraq, Goodell encountered a profoundly disturbing arena in which life and death relentlessly mixed together, removing all normally expected boundaries between one realm and the other. As we have explored, the Torah's Priestly authors were acutely aware of death's inevitability and sought to set aside special areas for the containment of *tumah*. Contemporary war zones and war camps are a similar types of spaces—but they are not generally accompanied by clear instructions for how to remain alert and oriented while in contact with *tumah* and when returning home. To return to David Kraemer's understanding of death and *tumah*, death's *tumah* "leaks" onto all the people who come into contact with it—with serious consequences.[64] It is this sojourn in the liminal space between life and death that makes homecoming so extraordinarily challenging for combat veterans.

Goodell describes the dissonance she experienced upon her return to America. To her, it seemed as if people were constantly eating,

---

63. Goodell, *Shade It Black*, 81–84 (italics in original).
64. See chapter 4.

shopping, and moving through life at a breakneck and superficial pace. She notes, "Everyone was busy. Too busy to meet, to have dinner, to carry on an actual conversation." After the intensity and loyalty of life as a Marine, where she had "friends who would give their life to protect mine," she now couldn't trust that someone "would show up to an agreed upon lunch date or actually meet me at the library as we had planned."[65] Like the patient who has returned home with an acute awareness of her dual citizenship, or like the Emergency Medical Services (EMS) worker who moves from a trauma scene to his son's music recital, returning veterans are also familiar with two distinct and dissonant cultures and struggle to make a home in either place.

Goodell records that, to compound the problem, she and her fellow Marines did not receive adequate support to assist them with their transition home. She describes a cursory encounter with a counselor prior to her departure from Iraq. Beyond this, she writes,

> There was no debriefing. There was no attempt to communicate with us in a therapeutic way, or to encourage us to talk to each other. There was nothing. . . . [The counselor] didn't tell us that what we saw and did in Iraq we'd never forget. He didn't say that the images would keep us awake all night in a sweat or that we'd never fully rid ourselves of the smell of death or that we wouldn't be able to eat or leave our parents' house or our own apartments for months or that we'd shoot at neighbourhood kids from our windows or pop sixty pills a day or wander the streets of our hometown in a stupor. The counselor didn't tell us that whole spheres of our lives and basic aspects of our selves were gone. Obliterated. That friends and family members and spouses, good memories, sleep, fun, food, and clarity would all have to be shaded black. He didn't tell us that for several of us, our former lives would be shaded black. The counselor didn't say that for a couple of us, hope would be shaded black.[66] [*The term "shaded black" refers to the practice of Mortuary*

---

65. Goodell, *Shade It Black*, 128–30.
66. Goodell, *Shade It Black*, 131.

*Affairs workers to take a pencil to a diagram of the body and shade in black
missing parts of the corpses with which they were working.]*

After life and hope have been "shaded black," daily life back inside the camp is drained of meaning. The process of reentry is impossibly painful for an array of complex reasons. For the purposes of the present study, we identify three areas—ritual, storytelling, and forgiveness—that are especially crucial for a successful reentry. All three of these allow for the creation of new narratives and neural pathways that override those that formed after repeated exposure to the sensory overload and trauma of battle. Additonally, these are all activities and arenas in which professional caregivers in Defense Department, Veterans Administration, healthcare, long-term care, congregational, and other community settings play a critical role.

Ritual

For Shay, the problem of returning home is ultimately one of "blood pollution," to which "many cultures respond . . . with purification rituals."[67] Briefly citing the ritual for the returning warrior described in Numbers 31, Shay recognizes that the invisible miasma of death's pollution changes all those who come into contact with it. It is an inevitable outcome of war, and it creates an urgent—and generally unmet—need for rituals for purification and reentry. Numerous other war writers describe this lack of attention to soldiers' need to transition slowly and thoughtfully back into civilian society.[68]

---

67. Shay, *Odysseus in America*, 152.
68. See, for example, Goodell, *Shade It Black,* 56–58; Brock and Lettini, *Soul Repair,* xvii–xviii; and Scurfield, *War Trauma,* 184–85. See also Karl Marlantes, *What It Is Like To Go To War* (New York: Atlantic Monthly, 2011), 178–87, 202–7; and John P. Wilson, "Culture and Trauma: The Sacred Pipe Revisited," in John P. Wilson, *Trauma, Transformation, and Healing: An Integrative Approach to Theory, Research, and Post-Traumatic Therapy,* Brunner/Mazel Psychosocial Stress Series 14 (New York: Brunner/ Mazel, 1989), 38–71.

Numbers 31 provides one example of such a ritual and provides us with an instructive text on reentry in the wake of war.

In Numbers 31, God commanded the Israelites to launch a war of vengeance against the Midianites. At the end of the battle, every adult male Midianite was dead, including the five kings of Midian. The Israelite warriors then took the women and children captive and seized the Midianites' animals and wealth as spoils of war. This, however, was insufficient; Moses (speaking, presumably, for God) instructed the men of the Israelite army to kill from among the Midianite captives all the male children and all the women who had had sex. This task completed, Moses and Eleazar instructed the Israelites on the procedures for purification in the wake of battle. It is hard to imagine a more brutally excessive war that could serve as the introduction to this *chukkat haTorah*, this law of the Teaching. As readers/listeners who engage with these verses, we are required to enter into war's raging cruelty—and then, abruptly, to enter into the slow and ritualized pace of transition and reentry. Both phases are inescapably part of the story.

Quarantined *michutz lamachaneh* for seven days, every warrior and captive who had taken a human life or touched a corpse (which, presumably, was just about everyone who was involved in the war) had to cleanse his or her body on the third and seventh day, which was the same rhythm prescribed for the person who had been in contact with a corpse for reasons other than war.[69] This cleansing also extended to all objects made of cloth, skin, goat's hair, or wood, which would likely include clothing, tents, bedding, and some weapons and utensils. All metal objects (Numbers is specific here, listing gold, silver, copper, iron, tin, and lead) had to be passed through fire and then washed in the *mei niddah* (the waters of

69. See Numbers 19:11-12.

lustration made from the ashes of a red heifer and described earlier).[70] Any object that could not withstand fire had to be passed through water. Finally, on the seventh day, each person involved in this purification ritual had to launder his clothes, which was the sign that he was *tahor* and could enter the camp.

In its description of this multistage process, the passage repeatedly employs the verb *lehitchate*, meaning "to purify oneself from impurity."[71] The passage also twice uses the verb *ta'aviru*, meaning "you will cause to pass through" or "you will cause to cross over," to describe the action of putting objects from the war theater into purifying fire or water. Passing through fire or water, these instruments of war symbolically traversed the boundary that turned that back into domestic tools. With the root *ayin-bet-resh*, this verb is related to *Ivrim*, the boundary crossers we described in chapter 4. Nowhere else in the Torah is this verb used in relation to a purification ritual.

Whether as soldiers or as captives, the people referred to in Numbers 31 passed beyond the borders of what most of us can imagine. Indeed, both verbs have semantic ranges that include "transgression," which we understand to describe the passage between *tahor* and *tamei* and back again, between life and death and back again. We assume that the cloth objects listed in the Torah's cleansing instructions included the clothes that these warriors and captives wore in the midst of war and plunder. In this way, the clothes represented the people who had worn them—people who entered into an unspeakably violent realm. With the aid of this ritual, they passed out of it and back into life.[72]

---

70. For a fuller discussion, see chapter 4.

71. *Brown-Driver-Briggs Hebrew and English Lexicon*, 307. According to *BDB*, this verb appears with this meaning only in passages authored by P. See Numbers 19:12, 13, 20; and Numbers 8:21 for other Priestly uses of the verb.

For the Torah's Priestly writers, the essential problem with *tumah* is that it can be transmitted to other people and objects, which destabilizes people, communities, and God. It is for this reason that returning warriors could not immediately go home but had to wait *michutz lamachaneh* for seven days. Like the *av hatumah*, which we described in the context of professional caregivers passing on their trauma and grief to those around them,[73] returning veterans also profoundly alter the emotional lives of their families. Scurfield uses a fairly mild term, referring to the "ricochet effect" of PTSD on families.[74] Reporter Mac McClelland is far more pointed, opening her *Mother Jones* article on the transmission of trauma to veterans' families with the provocative heading, "Is PTSD Contagious?" In this article, she profiles Caleb Brannan, an Iraq combat veteran with PTSD as well as a traumatic brain injury (TBI) resulting from multiple concussions sustained during at least twenty explosions. With gut-wrenching detail, McClelland describes how Caleb's entire family—he, his wife, and his six-year-old daughter—exhibit symptoms of PTSD, despite the fact that only one of them went to war.[75] In contrast, the biblical book of Numbers recognizes the dangers war poses to those who stayed back in the camp—dangers that our own society still struggles to name, treat, and prevent.

Compounding the problem of reentry is the fact that those rituals we do have for returning veterans sometimes miss the mark by treating returning soldiers like heroes. According to Harold Robinson, this is at odds with these men and women's perception of themselves as people who have "done something demonic and been

---

72. For more on how we are symbolically represented by the garments we wear, see Norman J. Cohen, *Masking and Unmasking Ourselves: Interpreting Biblical Texts on Clothing and Identity* (Woodstock, Vt.: Jewish Lights, 2012), especially 115–29.

73. See chapter 4.

74. Scurfield, *War Trauma*, 77.

75. Mac McClelland, "Is PTSD Contagious?" *Mother Jones*, January/February 2013. www.motherjones.com/politics/2013/01/ptsd-epidemic-military-vets-families.

through something demonic."[76] Also exacerbating the issue is the physical means by which many military personnel return home from war. Bob Feinberg, a rabbi and retired Navy chaplain, points out that the long sea journey home after World War II gave many soldiers an opportunity to prepare for their return and reentry. While some military personnel still do return home as a cohesive unit, making the long journey on an aircraft carrier or amphibious ship, many others fly home alone to an airline terminal.[77] As Feinberg says,

> You are expected to go to a place where you kill people and break things and then return home and be a member of civil society as though nothing changed in you. . . . That image of the guy coming off the plane and waiting for his baggage—that will never be a helpful reentry into civil society. . . . That transition can't be done in isolation.[78]

While American society as a whole does not (yet) have purification and reentry rituals for returning warriors, Bonnie Koppell, a rabbi and chaplain serving in the U.S. Army Reserve, wrote a "Ritual of Transition" for soldiers ending a deployment to Afghanistan. This ritual has been used many times by army chaplains working with returning soldiers. It opens with the words "We come together at this time of transition, to the end of this deployment, and prepare for the journey home." The officiating chaplain then invites participants to write on pieces of paper "what you would like to leave behind here" and to "ritually burn [the pieces of paper] as a symbolic way of letting go." As the papers burn, the officiant shares these words:

> Dear God, as we watch these flames ascend to Your holy throne, our hearts are torn with grief for all our losses, for all the pain we have experienced and for the death and destruction we may have caused....

---

76. Robinson, interview. See also Tick, *War and the Soul*, 182.
77. See also Marlantes, *What It Is Like To Go To War*, 19, 25.
78. Interview with Bob Feinberg, CDR, CHC, Ret., conducted by the authors by phone in New York City, May 21, 2013.

Allow us to leave behind what needs to remain behind, and emerge from this deployment with peaceful hearts.[79]

This powerful ritual uses words, symbolism, and actions to give expression to the horror of war, the liminality of the end of a deployment, and the hope for a healthy reentry. Interestingly, the ritual echoes a verse in Numbers 31 that reads: Moses and Eleazar the priest and all the heads of the community went out to meet [the returning warriors] *michutz lamachaneh.*[80] When the Israelite warriors first returned from their campaign against the Midianites, they were greeted by the community's priestly and political leaders. Although this verse is immediately followed by Moses' angry injunction to return to war and shed more Midianite blood, it nonetheless provides a powerful image. The community's leadership left the camp to share an in-between space with the men who had been fighting on behalf of the community and at the behest of its leaders. We see an echo of this in how soldiers and chaplains use Koppell's ritual to join together and mark the end of a deployment. Indeed, the chaplains who lead this ritual offer words that echo—in spirit and in essence—Eleazar's words as he introduced the transition ritual for objects and clothing: "This is the law of the Teaching . . . ."[81]

We can also see how rituals such as Koppell's would carry even more weight and significance if they included communal and political leaders. By meeting returning soldiers at military airfields or domestic airports, local clergy and political officials would parallel the Torah's description of how the community's leaders traveled outside the camp. We can imagine how this could be even more effective if followed by the debriefing period for which Goodell pleaded. Indeed,

---

79. Chaplain (COL) Bonnie Koppell, USAR, "A Ritual of Transition," in *The Army Chaplaincy* (Summer–Fall 2010): 31–32. Koppell serves as a colonel in the U.S. Army Reserve and is the Command Chaplain of the 807th Medical Command (Deployment Support).
80. Numbers 31:13.
81. Numbers 31:21.

this offers a powerful future story, to once again borrow Lester's term, for soldiers who are away at war and for their families back home. Soldiers would know they had the security of a spatial and temporal buffer zone before returning to their homes. Meanwhile, families would know that their loved ones were safely ensconced in this zone, and community leaders would be required to acknowledge the soldiers who were preparing to return home to this local "camp."

This discussion of homecoming rituals raises questions about appropriate leave-taking rituals. Once again, the Torah provides us with usable material. As part of a larger discussion about the ethics of war, Deuteronomy 20 describes how the priests and the *shotrim* (communal leaders) addressed the troops before they left for war. This happened while the soldiers were still in the midst of the people. The priests addressed the troops, reminding them not to fear because God was in their midst. With this address, the priests acknowledged the terror that war engenders, using four different verbs to describe the full spectrum of emotions associated with anxiety, fear, panic, and dread.[82] In the Torah's theocratic context, war was inextricably connected to God's guiding hand. In our own contemporary political context, this continues to be the case, despite a putative separation between church and state. While a full discussion of these issues is beyond the scope of the present chapter, we acknowledge their thorniness. We also highlight how, in this piece of biblical text, the priests concerned themselves with soldiers' emotional and—in contemporary parlance—religious and spiritual well-being, which is strikingly similar to the role played by military chaplains.

After the priests' address, the communal leaders stepped forward and exempted from the current war anyone who had recently built a house, planted a vineyard, betrothed himself to another—or anyone

82. Deuteronomy 20:1-4.

who was truly filled with fear of war.[83] It is significant that this exemption was given *before* the troops left for war, making it possible for an individual to step away from the troops and back into the wider community without stigma. Significantly, being fearful—which we read in this context as being unable to access a connection to God—is grounds for staying home. It carries no more shame than having a newly built house or a newly planted vineyard; it is a simple fact of life. The Torah conveys a straightforward message: because war has a tendency to rupture axes of orientation, it is irresponsible to send into battle anyone whose connections are already frayed. Similarly, it is irresponsible to allow soldiers to engage in war without rituals of farewell and return conducted by God's designated leaders at the boundary between the camp and *michutz lamachaneh.*

Storytelling

Harold Robinson identifies another challenge of reentry into the community: the lack of people to whom veterans can talk about their experiences. For Robinson, this is exemplified by an incident almost twenty years ago during a visit he made to a nursing home for sailors and marines.

> Robinson arrived at the nursing home wearing his Navy uniform and struck up conversation with an elderly World War II veteran and his adult daughter. During the course of the conversation, the veteran told a story of how his ship was torpedoed. Struggling to climb a ladder to safety in pitch darkness and terrifying chaos, this man was responsible for closing the hatch. He knew there were more men below and they would never get out. Yet, by closing the hatch, he ensured that those who had made it up the ladder would be saved. At the conclusion of the visit, the veteran's daughter walked Robinson out of the facility. She said that, in the fifty years since the war had ended, no one in the family

83. *Deuteronomy* 20:5-9.

had ever heard this story. She asked Robinson why. He responded that the veteran most likely didn't believe that anyone in his family would be able to understand or identify with the story. However, when he saw Harold's Navy uniform, he knew he had found someone whom he could trust with his story.[84]

For those who work with veterans, this type of incident is very common. Too often, veterans hold their war stories inside, believing they cannot trust others to hear them. Feeling safe enough to finally tell these stories can bring healing, relief, and comfort to veterans. Shay describes the restorative power of narrative in this way:

> Severe trauma explodes the cohesion of consciousness. When a survivor creates fully realized narrative that brings together the shattered knowledge of what happened, the emotions that were aroused by the meanings of the events, and the bodily sensations that the physical events created, the survivor pieces back together the fragmentation of consciousness that trauma has caused.[85]

To do this, the storyteller needs a story listener who is "strong enough to hear the story without injury" and "without having to deny the reality of the experience or to blame the victim." The listener must also "be ready to experience some of the terror, grief, and rage that the [narrator] did," be open to being "changed by the narrator," and to listen without leaping to judgment.[86] This is reminiscent of the "presence" dimensions of the priest's role described in chapter 3, and it is a mutually transformative role that many professional caregivers assume. For Shay, this act of storytelling has significant therapeutic benefits for the storyteller. The veteran whom Robinson encountered clearly recognized Robinson as someone with a common training and background who could be trusted as a story listener. In the process of this, it appears that Robinson modeled good listening for

84. Robinson, interview.
85. Shay, *Achilles in Vietnam*, 188.
86. Shay, *Achilles in vietnam*, 188–89.

the veteran's daughter so that she, too, could hear her father's story and be changed by it.

For Shay, an additional aspect of storytelling is that it allows for the "communalization of trauma." In a society that likes to glorify war rather than engage with its realities, this communalization constitutes "being able safely to tell the story to someone who is listening and who can be trusted to retell it truthfully to others in the community."[87] For twenty years, Robinson has been doing exactly this. He has shared this particular veteran's harrowing story with countless others—including the two of us—as a reminder of war's gut-wrenching reality and of society's low tolerance for these stories. This spreads war's burden among more people so that it does not need to be carried by veterans alone. Ultimately, it allows for the communalization of trauma, rather than its privatization.

For Shay, Homer played an essential role in this communalization of trauma. As he explains:

> The ancient Greeks revered Homer, the singer of tales, as a doctor of the soul. In the *Odyssey*, Homer paints a (self)-portrait of the epic singer whose healing art is to tell the stories of Troy with the truth that causes the old soldier, Odysseus, to weep and weep again.[88]

The Torah takes its place among ancient texts that allow those with no personal experience of war to look into a reflecting pool that shows society replete with the gruesome agony of the wars that are fought in all of our names. The Torah tells stories that are bloody, bestial, and terrifying, underscoring how this violence has the potential to dislodge from their moorings all those who experience it. At the same time, the Torah offers an assurance that God is present with each person even in the midst of war's physical, emotional,

87. Shay, *Achilles in Vietnam*, 4.
88. Shay, *Achilles in Vietnam*, 188.

spiritual, and moral pain, and in the slow process of return. Finally, the Torah provides a guide for how to return home safely—with cleansing rituals, adequate time, and communal accompaniment.

Forgiveness

In his work on veterans' experiences with guilt, psychiatrist Robert Jay Lifton differentiates between "static" and "animating" guilt. He defines "static" guilt as a state in which people are frozen in self-condemnation and emotional pain. He describes this as living in "a closed universe of transgression and expected punishment, in which one is unable to extricate oneself from a death-like individual condition." Animating guilt, on the other hand, "is characterized by bringing oneself to life around one's guilt." He elaborates:

> This requires . . . active imagery of possibility beyond the guilt itself. Animating guilt and image beyond the guilt are in a continuous dialectical relationship, the one requiring the other. Thus, animating guilt propels one toward connection, integrity, and movement. But for this self-propulsion to occur, one requires prior internal images of at least the possibility of these life-affirming patterns, imagery that can in turn relate to something in the external environment. In this sense the imagery of possibility antedates the animating guilt, but it is also true that animating guilt can activate the individual to the point of virtually creating such imagery.[89]

These "image[s] beyond guilt" are similar to Andrew Lester's future stories in that both of them allow us to imagine ourselves out of despair. In the tender moment in the midst of Numbers 14's depravity, God says to Moses, *salachti kidvarecha*, "I have forgiven you as you ask." It is as if God says, "I heard you, I saw you for who you are. I wasn't looking at your reflection in the funhouse

---

89. Robert Jay Lifton, *Home from the War: Learning from Vietnam Veterans, With a New Preface by the Author on the War in Iraq* (New York: Other Press, 2005), 126–28.

mirror; I was looking at you." In a story about a people's distorted view of their military enemies, their view of themselves also becomes distorted; everyone's image is refracted through the perversions of a funhouse mirror. But God sees clearly and compassionately, offering forgiveness in the midst of transgression. Ultimately, this is what a multitude of religious and spiritual traditions offer: communal stories and a liturgical cycle of time that hold out the possibility of forgiveness. This belief in the human capacity for change and healing is embedded into collective treasuries that promote individual and collective resilience, especially during the times when our sense of self is most compromised.

For people who have fought in wars, the need for forgiveness—of and by oneself, others, and God—is a crucial element of recovery and healing. One retired Veterans Affairs social worker told us the following story, which represents just one among hundreds of thousands of journeys toward wholeness taken by veterans and their professional caregivers.

In the early years of the Vietnam War, Jim enlisted in the Marines at age 18. He was driven by a sense of patriotic duty and also by his belief that the Marines represented the best qualities to which a man could aspire. He became a squad leader and saw a great deal of combat. In one firefight, during which he and his squad were ambushed by Viet Cong guerillas, Jim accidentally killed a Vietnamese teenage boy. Wracked with guilt for this boy's death, as well for the people killed in other villages and towns he had identified for bombing strikes, Jim began drinking heavily.

After returning home to the United States, Jim got married and had a son with his wife. He continued drinking, had difficulty maintaining a job, and suffered from typical PTSD symptoms, diving for cover, for example, if he heard a loud noise. His sleep was disturbed by nightmares and, as his son grew older, he saw in him the face of the teenage boy he had killed in Vietnam. Jim's marriage collapsed under the weight of his PTSD and his alcoholism—as well as under the weight of his stultifying guilt, which was unnamed at that time. In the process of separating from his wife, Jim approached the VA for help with his drinking, which is when this particular therapist began working with him.

Jim participated in an out-patient alcohol program, attended individual and group therapy, and got and stayed clean and sober. Over time, Jim began to trust his therapist with details about his time in Vietnam. As Jim slowly told some of his war stories, his therapist showed sympathy, concern, and care—rather than expressing shock, horror, and judgment as Jim had expected. This was a turning point for Jim. As his therapist and the rest of the VA team treated him with respect and dignity, Jim was able to re-connect with his own, long-severed feelings of self-respect. By extending to Jim compassion and understanding, Jim's therapist helped him to access these things within himself. His therapist also connected him with the Catholic priest on staff at the VA hospital. This turned into another important avenue of self-forgiveness for Jim. He reconnected with his faith community and found profound solace in Catholicism's teachings about God's enduring graciousness.[90]

Jim's story, like those of innumerable other veterans, is a reminder that forgiving another human being, helping another human being to access God's forgiveness, and/or giving another human permission to forgive him or herself are often essential elements of homecoming after war. In his chaplaincy work with soldiers, Bob Feinberg was deeply influenced by Jonathan Shay. From Shay, Feinberg learned to extend this permission to soldiers who were struggling with guilt over what they had seen and done in the course of a war. He would say to them, "As a senior officer, I give you permission to forgive yourself."[91] Feinberg learned that, if delivered in the context of a long-term supportive and therapeutic relationship, this ostensibly simple statement has the potential to unlock guilt and shame.

While these efforts focus on work with returning veterans, Koppell calls for a proactive approach that begins before deployment.

90. Interview with an anonymous retired Veterans Administration social worker, conducted by the authors in New York City, August 19, 2013.
91. Feinberg, interview.

Describing the sometimes crippling guilt war engenders, Koppell imagines a deeper role for chaplains that would help prepare soldiers for the spiritual and moral minefields that await them. She explains:

> [Soldiers] feel guilty because they have souls and values and a foundation of respect for life. Guilt is an incredibly healthy response to killing another human being, even in a situation like war where it may be a necessary evil. The military does not do a good enough job of arming our soldiers with a moral framework before they go to war. This is a role that could be taken on by chaplains and structured into the mobilization, along with getting your shots and getting your family briefing and getting issued your weapon.[92]

As we described above, this could be integrated into leave-taking rituals that could be adapted from the Torah's blueprint. Without opportunities to make sense of their guilt and seek forgiveness, veterans hold their guilt deep inside themselves where it cannot be transformed—or, to use Lifton's term, *animated*—into something compassionate and hopeful. Furthermore, guilt that cowers and shudders deep inside one individual's psyche cannot be communalized. Just as, in Shay's words, we have a pressing need for the "communalization of trauma," so, too, do we have a need for the communalization of guilt. As Tick explains, without this, veterans carry a burden that rightfully belongs to all of society:

> Without this transfer of responsibility, the veteran becomes the nation's scapegoat and carries its secret grief and guilt for all of us. Psychologically and socially, veterans often crawl into the dark corners of our culture and collapse under the crippling effect of carrying the moral and spiritual burdens of an entire nation alone.[93]

---

92. Interview with Rabbi Bonnie Koppell, conducted by the authors by phone in New York City, August 15, 2013.
93. Tick, *War and the Soul*, 237.

While the book of Numbers is far from a full-fledged handbook for the treatment of war trauma, it does paint a picture in which civilian and military realms are intermingled and interdependent. Numbers names and describes the reality of war, allowing all community members to hold a mental map that incorporates this inescapable fact of their lives. We certainly live in a far more complex society than that described in the Torah, but it is worth noting that few of us have any notion of where soldiers train, how they travel between civilian and military zones, or how they come home again. Given this, the Priestly imagination has much to teach us about mapping, and living into, a world in which the *tumah* that flows from national violence is unequivocally present.

7

The Priest, Prophet, and Pastor in Each of Us

In order for the wheel to turn, for life to be lived, impurities are needed, and the impurities of impurities in the soil, too, as is known, if it is to be fertile. Dissension, diversity, the grain of salt and mustard are needed: Fascism does not want them, forbids them, . . . it wants everybody to be the same . . . [I]mmaculate virtue does not exist either, or if it exists, it is detestable.[1]

Primo Levi, philosopher and Auschwitz survivor, wrote these words. Like the levitical conception of *tumah*, his words acknowledge the persistent reality of "impurities" within the fabric of life. In Leviticus, powerful transformations involving the passage of time and the use of ritual allow for the integration of illness, death, and war into the lives of individuals and the community. Primo Levi similarly proposes that "impurities" are an inevitable element of growth, change, and the maintenance of the diversity that naturally exists in the world. Without this, the world is a place of repression, stagnation, and artificially imposed uniformity.

---

1. Primo Levi, "Zinc," in *The Periodic Table*, trans. Raymond Rosenthal (New York: Schocken, 1984), 34.

Both the Hebrew Bible and early rabbinic literature articulate the desire for integrity in a world fraught with ambiguities and uncertainties. Expressed as a past that future generations might aspire to recapture, Leviticus presents a detailed vision of what lay within the realm of possibility. With Leviticus as their guide, the Israelites remained alert and oriented to person, place, and time, while also retaining an attunement to the transcendent. They accomplished this through the precisely delineated geography of the camp and its environs, a highly stratified and organized social structure, and elaborately detailed rituals. Within this worldview, maintaining balance and access to holiness was dependent upon holding seemingly incompatible elements in a creative tension. These opposites included the following: that *tumah* and *taharah* are both ineluctably part of the world; that touching substances that bring about purification can render the handler *tamei*; that God could be accessed both from the most inner sanctum and from a makeshift structure on the periphery; that humans long to remain oriented along familiar axes but that life is constantly in flux; and that being knocked off our moorings can, paradoxically, give us an expansive sense of connection to all that is beyond us.

As they sought to understand their own circumstances and communities, later generations of Rabbis built on the text of the Hebrew Bible for clues to how they might reach a longed-for future of greater wholeness and holiness. In the early rabbinic period, this perspective informed a new reading of Psalm 34:15, "Depart from evil and do good; seek peace and pursue it." By the Mishnaic period, the rabbis had turned Aaron, the High Priest, into the paradigmatic pursuer of peace, a *rodef shalom*. In *Pirkei Avot*, Rabbi Hillel instructed his students to follow Aaron's example by becoming people who loved and pursued peace.[2] This theme became so important that the injunction to pursue peace pervades rabbinic literature.

The midrashic collection *Pesikta d'Rav Kahana* offers a series of examples in which *shalom* (peace) is defined as the coexistence and cooperation of apparently opposing forces or materials. The authors of this string of teachings begin by looking toward the heavens for guidance as they claim, "The firmament is water, and the stars are fire, yet they dwell with each other and do no harm one to the other." Describing one of the plagues God brought down on the Egyptians, Rabbi Nehemiah concludes that even hostile elements can work together. As he explains, "Fire and hail, mingling, were made to work together." Finally, Rabbi Hanin brings a teaching from the human realm in which he says, "Rabbi Nehemiah's explanation brings to mind a crystal lamp wherein equal amounts of water and oil work together to keep the flame of the wick burning above the water and oil."[3]

In each illustration, neither element or force negates or overpowers the other. Instead, each is free to be itself in its uniqueness and fullness. Water and fire, fire and hail, oil and water all coexist; apparent opposites, they occupy space and time together to make *shalom*. For the writers of these *midrashim*, *shalom* was intimately connected to *shleimut*, meaning wholeness. Sharing the same root as *shalom, shleimut* reminds us that a whole is composed of more than one substance or experience. *Shleimut* occurs when diverse forces knit together to create something new and complete.

In this book, we have devoted a great deal of attention to the priests' special roles, presenting these as priest, prophet, and pastor. Our interest in this topic mirrors the significant space the Torah dedicates to the priests and their functions. At the same time, the

2. *Pirkei Avot* 1:12. *Pirkei Avot*, sometimes translated into English as *Ethics of the Fathers*, is a collection of ethical sayings from the Mishnaic period.
3. *Pesikta d'Rav Kahana*, chapter 1:3 C, D, trans. William G. Braude and Israel J. Kapstein (Philadelphia: Jewish Publication Society, 1975), 8–10.

Torah contains another message in which God tells the entire people, "You shall be for Me a nation of priests and a holy people."[4] We are intrigued by these two seemingly opposing images: on the one hand, a divinely ordained group of cultic priests set apart from all others, and, on the other, an entire people tasked by God to live a holy life as a nation of priests. Holding these two threads at the same time, we can begin to see how a world with a rarefied priestly class *and* an entire nation of priests might be a source of inspiration for all those who seek *shleimut*.[5]

In our own time, "immaculate virtue [still] does not exist" and all living things, by nature, are constantly changing. Like our ancestors, we long for holiness, purpose, and balance. However, we often resist the world's troubling ambiguities and astonishing diversity. Our contemporary political and social conflicts reflect our reticence about drawing "we-maps" and telling future stories that present a whole, just, and integrated world. The stories we have retold in this book, along with some additional ones we will explore in this final chapter, offer guidance and insight to individuals and communities engaged in the endeavor of creating *shalom* and *shleimut*. We begin by taking a wide view of the social reality of stigma, and we explore collective responsibility through two biblical stories about social transgression. We then revisit the levitical priest, describing how his particular type of sight and insight offers guidance to contemporary readers of the Torah.

Finally, we return to the *metzora* and the priest, the dyad that has formed the centerpiece of this book. We conclude with a new

4. Exodus 19:6; *mamlechet kohanim*, which literally means "kingdom of priests." We have taken the liberty of articulating this as "nation of priests" to reflect contemporary sensibilities.

5. This democratizing interpretation of Exodus 19:6 is consistent with one of the ways commentators have attempted to resolve this apparent tension. For further information about this tension and its possible resolutions, see Daniel R. Schwarz, "Kingdom of Priests," in *Contemporary Jewish Religious Thought: Original Essays on Critical Concepts, Movements, and Beliefs,* eds. Arthur A. Cohen and Paul Mendes-Flohr (New York: Free Press, 1987), 527–34.

perspective in which the *metzora* is surrounded by fellowship. Although he is physically on the margins of society, he turns out to be essential not only to its well-being but also to its survival. The priest, meanwhile, is on the margins of society, living in a City of Refuge alongside the category of people whom the Bible calls unintentional manslayers. The social microcosm of the Cities of Refuge offers powerful lessons about compassion, reintegration, and rebalancing in the aftermath of *tumah*'s flow into society. These stories will bring us back to this chapter's starting points: the transformative power of *tumah*, the potential for coexisting opposites to create *shleimut*, and the necessity of living as a "nation of priests" composed of people who claim for themselves the roles of priest, prophet, and pastor.

Boundaries, Stigma, and Collective Responsibility

In biblical narratives, being categorized as a *metzora* and spending time outside the camp never jeopardized an individual's status as a human being, a member of the Israelite community, or a person worthy of an ongoing relationship with God and the world. In contrast, as Foucault has described, modern and postmodern societies persist in a long-held tradition of making the term "leper" synonymous with "nonhuman." This conception of the leper is so deeply ingrained in contemporary life that it is difficult for today's readers of the Torah to see the levitical *metzora*, who is often erroneously described as someone with leprosy, as anything but a social outcast. As Foucault explains, we have created "a narrative of assigning the nonreasonable—'poor vagabonds, criminals, and deranged minds'—to the regions of excluded nonhuman whose symbolic inhabitant is the leper."[6]

---

6. Miroslav Volf, *Exclusion and Embrace: A Theological Exploration of Identity, Otherness, and Reconciliation* (Nashville: Abingdon Press, 1996), 61. Volf cites and paraphrases Foucault's

Stories rooted in these belief systems break the relational ties that bind humans together. When we dehumanize others, we are not obligated to participate in their care and we do not see our own well-being as intimately tied to theirs. We are socialized to counter our brain's natural impulse to activate its mirror neurons, which interrupts our innate ability to resonate profoundly with others so that they feel felt. In the contemporary world, there is a gap between what we know intellectually and the stories we tell ourselves. Intellectually, we know that the created world is in a constant state of flux, that all living things must change and die, that nothing can stay the same and endure forever. We know we have little control over what occurs. And yet, in contrast to the Hebrew Bible's stories that present ambiguity and flux as givens, some of our contemporary American myths are that we are strong; we have control over our destinies; we are fundamentally happy; and we honor those who are able to move easily beyond grief and loss.

It seems that, in order to hold fast to these "truths" about who we are, we place the sick and the weak out of sight. We relegate the enfeebled to facilities where the majority of the population need not see them. We blame those who are ill or out of work or imprisoned, accusing them of creating their own problems. We shun or pathologize expressions of unhappiness. We let our military and their families carry our collective grief, and we promote the message that our public memorials and annual ceremonies will provide a satisfactory statement about the nature of war.

Stories such as these deny the richly variable nature of human existence, narrow the scope of our vision, and socially sanction the persistent stigmatization of individuals and groups. They erase the reality that we frequently experience apparently contradictory

Madness and Civilization: A History of Insanity in the Age of Reason (New York: Pantheon, 1965), ix ff., 7.

emotions simultaneously or in close succession to each other. This is how Israeli poet Yehuda Amichai expresses this in his interpretation of the third chapter of Ecclesiastes.

A man doesn't have time in his life.
He doesn't have seasons enough to have
a season for every purpose. Ecclesiastes
Was wrong about that.

A man needs to love and to hate at the same moment,
to laugh and cry with the same eyes,
with the same hands to throw stones and to gather them,
to make love in war and war in love.
And to hate and forgive and remember and forget,
to arrange and confuse, to eat and to digest
what history
takes years and years to do.

A man doesn't have time.
When he loses he seeks, when he finds
he forgets, when he forgets he loves, when he loves
he begins to forget.

And his soul is seasoned, his soul
is very professional.
Only his body remains forever
an amateur. It tries and it misses,
gets muddled, doesn't learn a thing,

drunk and blind in its pleasures
and its pains.

He will die as figs die in autumn,
Shriveled and full of himself and sweet,
the leaves growing dry on the ground,
the bare branches pointing to the place
where there's time for everything.[7]

Our time is limited; our experiences and emotions are varied. Human existence is a jumble of joy and sorrow, pain and pleasure—because life does not come with rigid boundaries and fixed categories. Regardless, we seek to impose clearly labeled borders on ourselves and others. Our desire to assert clarity when things are ambiguous, to compartmentalize when there are countless anomalies, leads us to perceive dichotomies that do not exist. As a result, we have a tendency to believe that we ourselves exemplify what is desirable and that others are the cause of our distress, discomfort, or dis-ease.

Virginia Satir coined the term "identified patient" to recognize the function of the individual who both conceals and reveals a family's unexpressed agenda.[8] Without external intervention such as family therapy to address the range of issues that are impeding their healthy functioning, other members of the family project their anxieties onto the identified patient. Regarded as "the problem" that the family must

7. Yehuda Amichai, "A Man in His Life," in *Yehuda Amichai: A Life of Poetry, 1948–1994*, trans. Benjamin Harshav and Barbara Harshav (New York: Harper Collins Perennial, 1995), 351. Reprinted with permission from the Estate of Yehuda Amichai.
8. Virginia Satir, *Conjoint Family Therapy: A Guide to Theory and Technique* (Palo Alto, Calif.: Science and Behavior Books, 1983), 2, 50.

fix, the identified patient is effectively distanced from the family and objectified. In other words, she is stigmatized.

Similarly, those whom society stigmatizes conceal and reveal the dominant collective's secret fears and longings. In his seminal work on stigma, Erving Goffman introduced the original ancient Greek meaning of the word, explaining that stigma refers to

> bodily signs designed to expose something unusual and bad about the moral status of the signifier. The signs were cut or burnt into the body and advertised that the bearer was a slave, a criminal, or a traitor—a blemished person, ritually polluted, to be avoided, especially in public places. . . . Today the term is widely used in something like the original literal sense, but is applied more to the disgrace itself than to the bodily evidence of it.[9]

Drawing on first-person narratives of disabled people, mentally ill people, prostitutes, incarcerated and formerly incarcerated people, and gay people, Goffman explored commonalities among people with socially marginal identities. Published in 1963, his work offered an early and compassionate window into life on the margins of society. He painted a nuanced and sophisticated picture, explaining that social identities are unstable and shifting. In this construction, the bearers of "deviant" identities sometimes have the capacity to "pass" as members of the socially normative group, or to hide or leave behind (for example, through healing, recovery, or denial) the stigmatized parts of themselves. As a result, there is considerable overlap between those who, on any given day, present themselves as "normative" and those who present themselves as "stigmatized."[10]

While the Hebrew Bible does not stigmatize those who resided outside the camp or those who were part of the military camp, it

9. Erving Goffman, *Stigma: Notes on the Management of Spoiled Identity* (New York: Simon & Schuster, 1986), 1–2.
10. Goffman, *Stigma,* 133.

does reflect anxiety about social disorder. As we have described, Mary Douglas explains that the margins of the body represent the margins of society. When the body's fluids and inner parts breach their proper boundaries, as in the case of the *metzora*, the health and well-being of society at large are threatened. Breakdown at the borders symbolizes disorder. Even if the center is perceived as intact, the margins of both the physical body and the body politic are dangerous, unreliable, and unstable places. Consciously or unconsciously, society's members know that the categories they utilize are subject to change. As Goffman puts it, this means that the "normal" ones fear they will shift into a stigmatized category and, conversely, that the stigmatized ones will break the bonds of their categorization and join the ranks of the "normal."[11] No matter how much we attempt to distance ourselves from those who are stigmatized, we cannot completely ignore the fundamental similarities we share with all humans.

The fluid boundaries of these stigmatized identities are much like the porous border between the kingdom of the sick and the kingdom of the well, as described by Susan Sontag. It is also similar to the territories perceived during one part of the Israelites' journey as *michutz lamachaneh* and then, in a subsequent leg of the journey, as the camp. Much as we might hope for rigid certainty, the boundaries of our bodies, our identities, and our communities are porous and subject to change. The words of Pastor Martin Niemoller, who lived in Germany during the Nazi period, starkly present this reality and the terror it engenders. He wrote:

> First they came for the communists, and I didn't speak out because I wasn't a communist.
> Then they came for the socialists, and I didn't speak out because I wasn't a socialist.
> Then they came for the trade unionists, and I didn't speak out because I

11. Goffman, *Stigma*, 135.

wasn't a trade unionist.
Then they came for me, and there was no one left to speak for me.[12]

As Niemoller passionately attests, his irrational belief that he inhabited a rarefied category of humanity did not protect him or anyone else from Nazi persecution. Rather, it only served to underscore how all members of society are inseparably connected to each other.

The biblical narratives we have explored are rooted in the understanding that all members of a community are affected by what happens to one of its number. The two biblical stories we introduced in chapter 2 highlight this notion of mutual responsibility. We will look first at the story of the woodchopper who desecrated Shabbat, and then at the story about the blasphemer. These are brutal stories about capital punishment and we do not introduce them lightly. We do not seek to glorify or justify these stories, but to mine them for what they teach us about an entire community's responsibility for the punishment of social transgressions and, by extension, about those who inhabit the margins.

Numbers 15 records an incident in which a group of community members witnessed a man chopping wood on the Sabbath. They brought the man before Moses, Aaron, and the entire community. Since no one was sure how to proceed, the man was placed in custody while God delivered instructions to Moses that the man was to be put to death. God instructed Moses that the entire community must take the man *michutz lamachaneh*, where he was to be stoned. The community then followed these instructions and the man died.[13] Levitcus 24 recalls a similar incident in which a man identified as the son of Shlomit the daughter of Divri was heard blaspheming

12. Martin Niemoller, "First They Came," Holocaust Encyclopedia of the U.S. Holocaust Museum, http://www.ushmm.org/wlc/en/article.php?ModuleId=10007392.
13. Numbers 15:32-36.

God's name within the borders of the camp. Again, the transgressor was placed in custody until God rendered a decision. Again, the punishment involved the community taking the blasphemer *michutz lamachaneh* to stone him to death. However, this case involved one significant additional detail: all those who actually heard the man pronounce blasphemous words had to place their hands upon his head before he was killed.[14]

While the second story proceeds from the understanding that Shlomit's son was guilty beyond doubt, we can only imagine that those who had been within earshot of the blasphemy had to be absolutely certain of the transgressor's guilt. The personal, intimate gesture of placing their hands upon another human being's head required nothing less. Furthermore, they understood that their act was the signal to the rest of the community to begin stoning Shlomit's son. The rest of the community had to trust and follow this, along with the accusers' verbal testimonies. The interdependence of the whole community was made visible by the laying on of hands.

The story of the blasphemer opens with biographical information about the transgressor himself. The narrator describes the blasphemer's Israelite mother and Egyptian father and provides us with his mother's name. The point is clear: the son of Shlomit daughter of Divri is a human being with a name and a story. Given this, the community carried a heavy weight when it burst into the flow of this man's life and caused his untimely death. No doubt, this served as a severe warning to all those who heard the blasphemer's story and its ensuing communal rules. The point is further underscored by the fact that the story of the son of Shlomit is interrupted by information about the penalties for murder and maiming, both of which were to be paid in kind and applied equally

---

14. Leviticus 24:10–15, 23.

to Israelites and non-Israelites.[15] Again the point is clear: the community members involved in accusing, touching, and stoning a blasphemer had to be absolutely certain they were not committing murder, because this would cost them their own lives.

In both of these stories, community members were intimately involved in the punishment of those who were sent *michutz lamachaneh*. The transgressors' departures didn't take place in secret; instead, the entire community felt their impact, tangibly and kinesthetically. As Abraham Joshua Heschel so passionately argued, in a free society not everyone is truly culpable for atrocities committed against other humans. However, as Heschel and the stories of the woodcutter and the blasphemer teach, everyone is responsible.[16] This notion of communal responsibility is etched into the heart of Leviticus, which presents *michutz lamachaneh* not as a stigmatized location but, rather, as the place a community member went when he needed to enter into God's realm—whether temporarily or permanently. *Michutz lamachaneh* was not a proscribed, excised location; rather, it was mapped into every community member's understanding of communal geography. Responsibility did not end at the border between the camp and *michutz lamachaneh*; instead, this was the point at which it truly began to flourish.

Seeing in New Ways

The biblical accounts of the *metzora* underscore James Diamond's observation that the body is a "parable" or "riddle" that can be read like a text.[17] With these words, Diamond conveys the multiple ways bodies hold stories that are sometimes in plain view and sometimes

15. Leviticus 24:17-22.
16. Abraham Joshua Heschel, "The Reasons for My Involvement in the Peace Movement," in *Moral Grandeur and Spiritual Audacity: Essays* (New York: Farrar, Straus and Giroux, 1996), 225.

inscrutable. In some narratives, including Leviticus's, physical breakdown is regarded as dangerous to the body in question, the bodies close to it, and the body politic in general. Just as the ancient priests looked closely at bodies to determine what the individual and community should do, we can learn to read bodies as well. We are called upon to do this not because the illnesses to which our bodies are subject are dangerous, but because our own illiteracy is dangerous. Each one of us has a body that is susceptible to disease, impairment, trauma, and eventual disintegration. Our ability to read bodies' parables and riddles can help us to know ourselves better, make ourselves more available to others, and learn from the wisdom of those whose physical and mental realities are little known or not yet familiar to us.

Memoirs and narratives (such as Susan Sontag's *Illness as Metaphor* about cancer, Joan Didion's *A Year of Magical Thinking* about mourning, Martha Manning's *Undercurrents* about depression, Mitch Albom's *Tuesdays with Morrie* about chronic degenerative illness, and Jess Goodell's *Shade It Black: Death and After in Iraq* about the trauma of war[18]) are powerful because they expand our knowledge, open our hearts, and ignite our empathy. Closing our hearts and minds to other people's stories of illness, trauma, and loss has serious implications for the affected person, all those who come into contact with her, and the community at large. In the Bible's candid stories about illness and loss, the priest interacted comfortably and competently with every Israelite. In the accounts of his comings and goings from the camp,

17. James Diamond, "Maimonides on Leprosy: Illness as Contemplative Metaphor," *Jewish Quarterly Review* 96 (2006): 105.
18. Susan Sontag, *Illness as Metaphor and AIDS and Its Metaphors* (1977; reprint, New York: Picador, 1988); Joan Didion, *The Year of Magical Thinking* (New York: Knopf, 2006); Martha Manning, *Undercurrents: A Life Beneath the Surface* (San Francisco: Harper, 1994); Mitch Albom, *Tuesdays with Morrie* (New York: Random House, 1997); Jess Goodell with John Hearn, *Shade It Black: Death and After in Iraq* (Havertown, Pa.: Casemate, 2011).

there is no implication that the priest felt fearful. Instead, he left us with a model for drawing closer to others, showing we care, and noticing what makes others uniquely themselves. This is an intimate approach to managing distance. This applies to the distance that arises when a person is geographically removed from her loved ones because of illness or war, and it applies to the social distance that our dominant narratives, societal customs, and even laws enforce.

As we discussed earlier, the verb "to see" appears repeatedly in the narratives related to the *metzora*. When we follow the priest's example of looking deeply and closely, we have a better chance of witnessing other people in their fullness. This gives our mirror neurons the opportunity to see the hair color we share, the tone of voice we recognize, or the gestures that feel familiar. As David DeSteno reported in his article "Compassion Made Easy," our capacity to empathize can be triggered by any number of small details that create a resonance between us and another person. Once we experience that resonance, our desire to care for and respect the other increases. DeSteno suggests that we try thinking of our neighbor as, say, the fan of the same local restaurant, rather than a member of a different racial or ethnic group.[19] This allows our hearts and eyes to work in tandem, rather than at odds with each other. As Heschel observed, this counters the tendency in which "[o]ur eyes are witness to the callousness and cruelty of man, but our heart tries to obliterate the memories, to calm the nerves, to silence our conscience."[20]

Central to the priest's work was his attention to the smallest of details. This invites us to wonder about the stories of love and longing, loss and luminosity that are embedded inside tiny things that might at first seem insignificant. When the *metzora* left the camp, Leviticus does not tell us whether or not he took any belongings

19. David DeSteno, "Compassion Made Easy," *New York Times,* July 14, 2012.
20. Abraham Joshua Heschel, *The Prophets* (New York: Harper & Row, 1962), 5.

with him. The two of us imagine that many of the things he used and cherished in daily life remained in his home, serving as daily reminders for his family and friends of who he was and what he valued. While not physically present, his importance to those who knew him was palpable and meaningful. Writing about an absent family member, Volf notes that "as long as what belongs to him is with [those back home], he is, in a sense, with them and they are with him."[21] As we mirror the ancient priests' ways of seeing, we might observe how those who are institutionalized, deployed, or deceased are still present for their loved ones who are left behind. We can listen to how the family refers to the absent person in conversation, and notice how his pictures and personal items remain part of their daily routines. We can observe the place he holds in his loved ones' hearts, and we can acknowledge the power of his absence.

We have already explored how, for professional caregivers, he demonstrated the need to handle asymmetrical relationships with great care. Now we look at what these relationships, such as the one between the priest and the *metzora*, teach us about social interactions that extend far beyond professional caregiving relationships. Earlier, we looked in depth at the value of mirroring; here, we explore what happens when mirroring is not reciprocal or not present at all. This perspective invites us to "see" what impedes our own willingness or capacity to approach someone, and simultaneously to "see" barriers to someone else's willingness to approach us. We can then decide if we want to wait for our actions to be mirrored before we engage or choose to jump in regardless. Volf advocates this latter approach and proposes that we adopt a "moral stance" that eschews the need for symmetry in relationships.[22] By dropping our expectation for

---

21. Volf, *Exclusion and Embrace*, 158. Volf is writing here about the New Testament story of the prodigal son (Luke 15:11-32).
22. Volf, *Exclusion and Embrace*, 146.

reciprocity, we will expand our sense of ethical responsibility to others.

Emmanuel Levinas sheds more light on this, explaining that we tend to avoid or limit contact with others when we believe they won't respond in kind or will rebuff us. He encourages us, instead, to proceed from our own sense of connectedness without making this dependent on others' actions. In his words,

> The knot of subjectivity consists in going to the other without concerning oneself with his movement toward me . . . in approaching in such a way that, over and beyond all the reciprocal relations that do not fail to get set up between me and the neighbor, *I have always taken one step more toward him.*[23]

Ultimately, Levinas calls upon us to feel *obligated* to look into the face of the other. It is this sense of obligation, he says, that makes us human.[24] In our daily lives, we make countless decisions about whom we will look in the eyes. For all the times we connect with other humans, our days are also filled with the choice not to connect. We avoid eye contact by hiding behind dark glasses, a newspaper, or the mask of preoccupation. We cast down our eyes or look beyond the face of a panhandler on the street. We avert our eyes because we don't want to see and we don't want to be seen. We seek a comfortable resting place for our gazes because we don't want to have to acknowledge our own embarrassment and guilt about not connecting.

In Hebrew, the word for face, *panim*, is a plural form. The singular, *pen*, is most often used to describe one surface of a multifaceted

23. Emmanuel Levinas, *Otherwise Than Being: Or, Beyond Essence* (The Hague: Kluwer Academic Publishers, 1991), 84 (emphasis added).
24. Leonard Grob, "The Jewish Roots of Emmanuel Levinas' Metaphysics of Welcome," in *Encountering the Stranger: A Jewish–Christian–Muslim Trialogue*, eds. Leonard Grob and John K. Roth, Stephen S. Weinstein Series in Post-Holocaust Studies (Seattle: University of Washington Press, 2012), 76.

object, perhaps like one of the multiple facets of our faces, souls, and beings. To look into another *panim* is an invitation to see each person in her variegated and radiant complexity. Just as faces are multifaceted, so too is the act of seeing. As we learn from the example of the levitical priest, to see is to witness, to accompany, to seek to understand, to cross a boundary, to be a visionary. In Leonard Grob's summary of Levinas's approach, to face another human being is to be "invested with the infinite task of being responsible to the Other."[25]

Shleimut: A New Take on the Margins and the Center

The Bible is peopled with characters who envisioned visions and dreamed dreams. In the chaotic wake of the destruction of the Temple, the levitical narrative offered a promise of restoration and balance in which priestly activities would ensure God's continued presence in the midst of the community. Speaking to a population that claimed to seek God yet cared more about business than people, Isaiah accompanied his words of chastisement with a vivid prophecy of a society in which everyone would feed the hungry, clothe the naked, and free the enslaved.[26] Our contemporary visions and dreams, like these earlier ones, are built on the realities we know and the deficiencies that exist within them. Imagination is central to the task of visioning these visions and dreaming these dreams. As Ann and Barry Ulanov write, "Imagination inspires a new way of seeing. . . . It weaves links between opposites, recalling wholeness where earlier only opposing forces had seemed to exist."[27] Rather than seeing the center as a fecund place and the margins as barren, we can employ

25. Grob, "Jewish Roots of Emmanuel Levinas," 85.
26. Isaiah 58:1–14.
27. Ann and Barry Ulanov, *The Healing Imagination: The Meeting of Psyche and Soul* (Einsiedeln: Daimon, 2008), 113.

our imaginations in the service of uniting these apparently disparate places into a whole that flows with *shleimut* and *shalom*.

The Rabbis organized the annual lectionary cycle so that each Torah reading is paired with a thematically related nonpentateuchal selection.[28] During the week in the spring when communities read the chapters of Leviticus that deal with the *metzora*, the Torah portion is coupled with a story from Second Kings about four *metzora'im*. This story is set against a backdrop of danger and suffering; the Israelites living in Samaria were under siege by the Arameans and were surviving in a state of famine. Ostensibly marginalized because of their *tzara'at*, the *metzora'im* lived together in friendship and ultimately saved the larger community from starvation. We regard the rabbinic decision to include this extraordinary story in the annual lectionary cycle as a creative assertion of the notion that the center cannot survive without the margins.

Living at the gates of the city, the *metzora'im* realized that they faced a grim set of prospects: they could stay where they were and starve to death or they could go into the town, where they would also starve to death. Refusing to accept either of these unhappy choices, they conferred with each other and decided to risk a third option: to go to the Aramean camp in search of food, despite the risk of being killed. Upon their arrival, they found the camp deserted, the Arameans apparently having fled in great haste and abandoned their food, tents, belongings, and animals. The story's editorial voice enters to tell us the Arameans only abandoned their encampment after God caused them to hear what sounded like the terrifying approach of a great army.

The *metzora'im* ate their fill and looted some silver, gold, and clothing, which they buried for later retrieval. However, when they

28. See chapter 6 for a full description of this.

paused from their plundering to confer with one another other, they turned their sights from themselves to the entire community. Collectively, they decided to go to the king of Israel (who is unnamed in this story) with the intention of sharing the "good news" about the empty Aramean camp. As they neared the town, they called to the gatekeepers, informing them that the Aramean camp had no more human inhabitants but was replete with livestock and goods. Upon hearing this news, the king gathered his councilors to determine if this was an Aramean-orchestrated ruse. One courtier convinced the king to send some men on a reconnaissance mission. When they returned, they reported that the Arameans had indeed abandoned their camp, leaving behind food and other goods. With this, the calamity of starvation was averted.[29]

The coupling of this story with the chapters of Leviticus dealing with the *metzora* is quite remarkable. The story of the four *metzora'im* highlights both the bonds of community among those required to spend time *michutz lamachaneh* and their ongoing connections to, and concerns about, the well-being of the community inside the camp. These four men were risk-takers who took advantage of their open access to areas and populations that others in their community perceived as a threat. After this, they risked reestablishing contact with the community that had placed them beyond its borders. Despite the physical and social distance imposed upon them, the *metzora'im* acted not only in their own interests but in the interests of the entire group to which they still felt bound, ultimately playing a definitive role in its survival during a time of war and famine.

In the many biblical stories we have explored, we primarily encountered the Priestly perspective. We heard the *metzora*'s voice only once, and then he spoke words given to him by the priest.[30]

29. 2 Kings 7:3-20.
30. Leviticus 13:45.

We can only begin to imagine what the levitical *metzora*'s own teaching—his own torah with a small "t"—might have been had anyone chosen to record it. However, the rabbis took the bold step of incorporating the voices of these four *metzora'im* into the lectionary cycle. In Abraham Joshua Heschel's words, each person and event that opens us up to hearing new voices and perspectives "demythologize[s] precious certainties." The story of the four *metzora'im* expands our understanding of the levitical map and shifts our perspective on the relationship between the center and the margins. This, says Heschel, is one element of acting in a prophetic manner.[31] As we tell and hear unexpected stories, we integrate new messages about suffering and restoration, rupture and connectedness. Whether we are the people in the stories, the story's listeners, or the storytellers, such stories allow all of us to broaden our vision and understanding. This, in turn, creates new narratives, mental maps, and neural circuitry.

Three times in this story, the *metzora'im* turned to each other to discuss their situation. The biblical phrases "they said, each one to his fellow" and "they said, each one to his brother" underscore the men's palpable sense of connection to each other.[32] Central to the accounts of the levitical metzora, the warrior in the wilderness, and the woodcutter and the blasphemer is the belief that we are never entirely alone. The Torah illustrates this with images of God strolling among the warriors and receiving questions in the Tent of Special Appointments, as well as in its accounts of the priest's steady presence with the *metzora*. Shocking and terrifying though the stories of the woodcutter and the blasphemer are, they seem to make the same point: that even as a biblical figure walked toward punishment by death, community members went with him, sometimes even placing

31. Heschel, *Prophets*, 12.
32. 2 Kings 7:3, 6, 9.

their hands on his head. As Miroslav Volf writes, "Every breach of the covenant still takes place *within* the covenant. . . . Nobody is outside the social covenant; and no deed is imaginable which would put a person outside of it."[33]

Nobody is outside the covenant: not the *metzora*, or the warrior, or the person who is to be punished with death. This assurance that we are always within the covenant adds a new perspective to the idea of de-centering. Originally introduced in the first chapter of this book as Patrick McNamara's means of describing unbounded experiences in neuroscientific terms, we come now to a new usage of the term. Volf uses the term to mean the "de-centering of the self," which, he says, allows for "a re-centering of that same self."[34] If we know we always remain within the covenant, then de-centering—whether it is sought out or imposed upon us—might unmoor us but will not completely rupture our sense of our own humanity. It is this unmooring, this need to reread and redraw the maps that guide our lives, that invites radical transformation. Ultimately, this is a transformation of the de-centered individual and the community at large. In the case of the four *metzora'im*, the transformations that flowed from their story continue to echo into our own lives every time we hear it.

Surprisingly, the levitical priests were also no strangers to this kind of de-centering. Despite their high status in Israelite cultic life, they were economically marginal, landless, and dependent on the rest of the community for life's basic necessities. Numbers 35 describes the apportionment of the forty-eight towns in which the Levites would live. In six of these towns, they would live side by side with another marginal group, unintentional manslayers who had fled to one of these six Cities of Refuge.[35] When they served in the *Ohel Moed*, the

33. Volf, *Exclusion and Embrace,* 156 (italics in original).
34. Volf, *Exclusion and Embrace,* 70.

priests were set apart from the populace, sanctified through special rituals, and allowed access to exalted rooms hidden behind layers of curtains. In stark contrast to this, they lived in ordinary towns alongside people who couldn't safely live anywhere else. Taken as a whole, the priests' lives spanned an unusually broad spectrum that incorporated both high and low social status.

The unintentional manslayer was a person who, without malice or intention, had accidentally caused the death of another person. Because blood had been spilled, the levitical world was now out of balance and some form of restitution was required. In the case of murder, this would have been accomplished by the victim's *goel ha'dam*—literally, "blood avenger"—who would take the murderer's life.[36] Cities of Refuge, in contrast, were intended to protect unintentional manslayers from this type of vigilante justice, as well as provide a means of bringing the world back into balance that depended on neither the unintentional manslayer nor his avenger. Instead, when the high priest, who had served at the time of the murder died, the unintentional manslayer's sins would be wiped away, the world would be back in balance, and the unintentional manslayer could return home.[37]

The Torah states that the unintentional manslayer could flee to these Cities of Refuge "and live."[38] Later rabbinic commentators elaborated on this injunction. They drew out the multiple possible meanings of "to live" and created a set of compassionate rules intended to allow for protection and rehabilitation. The Cities of Refuge were intended to be easily accessible safe havens that also allowed for ongoing contact with other people. Rabbinic law required that the Cities be connected to the rest of the Israelites'

---

35. Numbers 35:1-34. In Deuteronomy 19:1-10 and 4:41-42, there are only three Cities of Refuge.
36. Numbers 35:19, 21.
37. Numbers 35:22-28.
38. Deuteronomy 19:4.

territory by roads that were direct, wide, and regularly repaired. Every crossroad had to be marked with a sign reading "Refuge, Refuge." Furthermore, the community was responsible for ensuring a fresh water supply that was either naturally available or transported into the town, and the Cities had to abut communities with a sizable population. If the unintentional manslayer had been a Torah scholar, he was provided with a teacher, and some commentators interpret the Rabbis' laws about the Cities of Refuge to mean that his wife and children were expected to join him.[39]

For the protection of the unintentional manslayer, no weapons were allowed in the Cities of Refuge. Some Rabbis said there should be no weapons for war or hunting; others said there should be no traps, chains, or ropes. Either way, the point was to avoid providing tools or weapons that an avenger could use to murder the unintentional manslayer.[40] The message was clear: reintegration and repentance were the goals, not hardship and punishment. Removed from the threat of physical harm, the offender could lead a productive, meaningful life precisely because he was surrounded by people whose relationships to him were deep and whose skills and knowledge could contribute to his rehabilitation. While he lost his intimate connection to the geographic location in which the murder took place, he could retain his orientation to person and time, as well as his awareness of the sacred. Over time, as his familiarity and bond

39. Israeli Supreme Court Justice Menachem Elon suggested that the positive treatment of unintentional manslayers in the Cities of Refuge should serve as a model for contemporary decisions related to prisoners' rights, including conjugal rights. He wrote that a prisoner has the same physical and spiritual needs and rights as all other human beings and argued that honoring them is required by Jewish law and contributes to the person's rehabilitation. He concluded that the unintentional manslayer's wife and children must have joined him in the Cities of Refuge and used this interpretation as the basis for responding to contemporary prisoners' conjugal requests. See "Weill vs. the State of Israel," Rulings of the Israeli Supreme Court, Vol. 41, Part 3, 1987, 477–502.
40. For rabbinic elaborations on the Torah's laws about the Cities of Refuge, see Mishnah *Makkot* 2:4-5, Babylonian Talmud *Makkot* 10a-b, and Mishneh Torah, *Hilchot Rotzeach* 8.

with the City of Refuge grew, he could regain his orientation to place.

We tell this story about the Cities of Refuge because we are intrigued by the idea that the priests and the unintentional manslayer lived side by side in a town dedicated to two very different kinds of marginal people. We also tell this story because it is yet another biblical acknowledgment of *tumah*'s inevitable flow into the world. It is a reminder that when things did not turn out as expected and hoped, the community took responsibility for helping people maintain their humanity and their connectedness.[41] We live in an out-of-balance world that needs Cities of Refuge—places where individuals *and* the community take responsibility for spilled blood, bad luck, and all the ways people's lives come apart at the seams. We would do well to adopt the Bible's recognition that we are responsible for some of our mistakes but not for all of them; that priests and unintentional manslayers might thrive when they live together; that sometimes it is the people at the margins who bring new life to those at the center; that we cannot restore order on our own; and that we need help from the community around us.[42]

Our lives are fragile and not really in our control; we are prone to crises of body, mind, and spirit, to war and communal tragedy, to violence and incarceration. We possess passports to lands we have not yet visited; we become dual citizens when we are least prepared for it; we reluctantly hold visas for which we never formally applied.

41. The Cities of Refuge raise important themes about contemporary criminal justice policy that are beyond the scope of the current project. For a related exploration of this topic, see Maurice D. Harris, *Leviticus: You Have No Idea* (Eugene, Ore.: Cascade Books, 2013). Harris devotes a chapter to the *metzora* and the priest, proposing that the *metzora* is analogous to a contemporary prisoner, and the priest to a "spiritual mentor" who assists the prisoner with his rehabilitation. See pp. 42–49.
42. Some of this material about the Cities of Refuge is drawn from Jo Hirschmann, "Parshat Mattot-Masei," sermon delivered at Congregation Beth Simchat Torah, New York, NY, July 9, 2009.

And, yet, we are inheritors of the ancient proclivity to find the transcendent in unlikely places, to seek out comforters when we are in mourning or in pain, to delve into the most hidden parts of ourselves and find the transformative truths that reside there, to hang from our window a red thread of impossible friendship in the midst of a war, to offer covering and protection to each other, and to endeavor to re-create ourselves when the onrushing enormity of life calls for nothing less. We are, in short, people with a great capacity to create new maps when our old ones no longer serve us.

Rachel Adler once rhetorically asked, "What does it take to see a leper as a son of Aaron?"[43] One way to see the *metzora* and the priest as one—and to see ourselves in each of them—is to mine the Bible for its lessons about the margins and the center, about the elite class of priests and the nation of priests. These are not two pairs of dichotomies but, rather, shifting categories that complement and highlight each other to create a new *shleimut*. The margins and the center are eternally bound together by us, human beings who inhabit both of these places, and all the places in between, over the course of our unpredictable lives. The levitical priests served as priest, prophet, and pastor in a community that both needed a special class of people to do this *and* was peopled by an inherently holy community.

For those of us who chafe at descriptions of the hereditary, hierarchical, and male priestly office, we might take comfort in the Bible's parallel strand that is democratizing and egalitarian. Leviticus instructs the priests that their task is to distinguish between *kodesh* and *chol* and between *tamei* and *tahor*. Beyond this, they must teach the people all of God's laws.[44] We take this to mean that the priests

43. Rachel Adler, "Those Who Turn Away Their Faces: Tzaraat and Stigma," in *Healing and the Jewish Imagination: Spiritual and Practical Perspective on Judaism and Health*, ed. William Cutter (Woodstock, Vt.: Jewish Lights, 2007), 159.
44. Leviticus 10:10-11.

were responsible for wise discernment. Just as the priests determined the meaning of multiple different types of *nega'im*,[45] so too might we. These *nega'im* might be *tzara'at* lesions, or physical blows, or spiritual injuries; they might be our stories of illness, or our stories of combat, or our stories of searching for a Tent of Special Appointments. The priests were witnesses of all these types of *nega'im* and we can be too.

Each of us can choose to serve as priest, prophet, and pastor in our moment-to-moment lives. We can do this by serving as the lantern that illuminates paths for others in the midst of changing selves, evolving relationships, shifting places, the vagaries of time, and the flickering but ever-present light of the transcendent. We can create new maps that correlate with a markedly different future story in which geographic, temporal, physical, and spiritual axes and boundaries are understood as fluid and expansive. In the face of the imbalances we see, we can ask "[t]he ultimately responsible question . . . not how I extricate myself heroically from a situation but [how] a coming generation is going to go on living."[46] We can actively contribute to a future that another generation will want to live into.

One final way that we might see the *metzora* and the priest as one: during liminal moments, each was anointed on his right extremities.[47] As the *metzora* stood on the precipice of *taharah* and the priest stood on the precipice of *kedushah*, the most vulnerable and exposed parts of their bodies were daubed and painted. This external mark signified a change that took place deep in their cores. This exterior covering offered protection and brought about transformation, allowing the *metzora* to go home and the priest to enter the *Ohel Moed*.

---

45. See chapter 3.
46. Dietrich Bonhoeffer, *Conspiracy and Imprisonment, 1940–1945,* ed. Mark S. Brocker, trans. Lisa Dahill, Dietrich Bonhoeffer Works 16 (Minneapolis: Fortress Press, 2006), 42.
47. Exodus 29:20; Leviticus 8:23-24; 14:17.

The *metzora* and the priest are in each of us. The *metzora* teaches us we are never alone and reminds us to take audacious risks. He reminds us that the margins are creative and life affirming. The priest is a revered *Moreh Derekh* who cannot live without the community's generosity and who is central to the communal project of protecting and rehabilitating those who make mistakes. In the dyad of the priest and the *metzora*, and also in the dyad of the unintentional manslayer and the priest, apparently dissimilar and even opposing types of people coexist and promote *shleimut*. Fueled by our imaginations and by the new neural pathways firing in our brains, we hold these bundled contradictions as one, living into new visions of *shalom*.

The priest leaves us with ancient words that might guide all of our journeys. Once said by the priests alone, these words now belong in the mouths of all who find comfort and guidance in these ancient stories. Wherever we find ourselves, however we orient ourselves, whatever future stories we most need to tell, may we all be bound together in our common pursuit of protection, presence, and peace.

> May God bless you and keep you.
> May God shine the light of God's countenances upon you and be gracious to you.
> May God lift God's countenances toward you and bring you peace.[48]

May this be so for all of us, now and always.

---

48. Numbers 6:24–26. Authors' translation.

Glossary

av hatumah (pl: *avot hatumah*)	a person who is *tamei* and then transmits that *tumah* to other people or things
bikkur cholim	visiting the sick
chatat	purification offering
chol	profane, ordinary; the opposite of *kodesh*
chol hamoed	times in the Jewish calendar that are in some ways holy and in some ways profane; the intermediate days of the holidays of Sukkot and Passover
Cities of Refuge	levitical towns that were also set aside as places of safety and protection for unintentional manslayers
ish tahor	a ritually pure man
Israelites	the people at the center of the Torah's narratives; also: ancient Israelites
Ivrim	Hebrew people; literally, those who cross boundaries
kadosh	holy
kapparah	atonement
kedushah	holiness
Kohen Gadol	High Priest
le'kaper	to atone for
levayah	literally, accompaniment; also, funeral
Levi	*See* Levites
Levites	the priests; descendants of Jacob's son Levi
levitical	pertaining to the priestly system described in sections of the Hebrew Bible, especially the book of Leviticus
machaneh	camp
makom tahor	pure place
mayyim chayyim	fresh water; literally, living waters

mei niddah	watery mixture made from the ashes of a red heifer and used to disperse the ritual impurity of death
metzora (pl. *metzora'im*)	person with the skin condition known as *tzara'at*
michutz lamachaneh	outside the camp
midbar	desert, wilderness
midrash (pl. *midrashim*)	interpretation, retelling, and reimagining of biblical stories; ongoing process begun in the rabbinic period
Moreh Derekh	A Guide for the Way
nation of priests	a means of referring to the entire Israelite people that emphasizes the holiness of all the people, not only the priestly class
nega (pl: *nega'im*)	a *tzara'at* lesion; a plague inflicted by God; a strike or blow inflicted by one human on another
Nephilim	giants
ohel	tent; habitation of an Israelite family
Ohel Moed	Tent of Meeting; used to refer to the Tabernacle inside the camp and the Tent of Special Appointments outside the camp
petach	doorway
p'nei hasadeh	literally, the face of the field; an uninhabited area beyond the camp
priestly	*See* levitical
Priestly	referring to the P tradition of the pentateuchal writings
rabbinic	referring to literature associated with the rabbinic period, which is generally understood to cover the period from the second to the sixth centuries
red heifer	cow that was slaughtered and burned to make the *mei niddah* used to disperse the ritual impurity of death
scapegoat	goat released on Yom Kippur to carry the community's sins away from the camp
shalom	peace
shleimut	wholeness
tahor	ritually pure
tamei	ritually impure
taharah	ritual purity
Tent of Meeting	*See Ohel Moed*
Tent of Special Appointments	the term used in this book for the Tent of Meeting located outside the camp
tumah	ritual impurity

tzara'at	skin condition often mistranslated as "leprosy;" also refers to something atypical (most likely mold) on the surface of buildings or fabrics

Bibliography

Abrams, Judith Z. "Metzora(at) Kasheleg: Leprosy Challenges to Authority in the Bible," *Jewish Bible Quarterly* 21, no. 1 (1993) 41–45.

Adler, Rachel. "Those Who Turn Away Their Faces: *Tzaraat* and Stigma," in *Healing and the Jewish Imagination*, (Woodstock, VT: Jewish Lights, 2007) 142–159.

Albom, Mitch. *Tuesdays with Morrie* (New York: Random House, 1997).

Alexander, Michele, *The New Jim Crow* (New York: The New Press, 2010).

Alter, Robert. *The Five Books of Moses: A Translation with Commentary* (New York: W.W. Norton, 2004).

American Psychiatric Association. *Diagnostic and Statistical Manual of Mental Disorders: Fifth Edition* (Washington, DC and London: American Psychiatric Publishing, 2013).

Amichai, Yehuda. "A Man in His Life," in *Yehuda Amichai: A Life of Poetry, 1948–1994*, trans. Benjamin and Barbara Harshav (New York: Harper Collins Perennial, 1995).

Avalos, Hector. *Illness and Health Care in the Ancient Near East: The Role of the Temple in the Greece, Mesopotamia, and Israel* (Atlanta: Scholars Press, 1995).

Balberg, Mira. "Rabbinic Authority, Medical Rhetoric, and Body Hermeneutics in Mishnah Nega'im," *Association for Jewish Studies Review* 35.2 (2011) 323–346.

Beentjes, Pancratius C. "'They Saw That His Forehead Was Leprous' (2 Chr 26:20): The Chronicler's Narrative on Uzziah's Leprosy," in *Tradition and Transformation,* Volume 52 in Studia Semitica Neederlandia (Leiden: Brill 2008) 79-90.

Begley, Sharon. "Religion And The Brain," *Newsweek,* May 6, 2001. www.newsweek.com/religion-and-brain-152895.

Bloom, Jack H. Ed., *Jewish Relational Care A-Z: We Are Our Other's Keeper* (New York: Haworth, 2006).

Bonhoeffer, Dietrich. *Conspiracy and Imprisonment, 1940-1945, Vol. 8,* ed. Mark S. Brocker, trans. Lisa Dahill (Minneapolis: Fortress Press, 2006).

Brock, Rita Nakashima, and Gabriella Lettini. *Soul Repair: Recovering from Moral Injury after War* (Boston: Beacon Press, 2012).

Breitman, Barbara E. "Wired for Connection: Contemporary Neuroscience, the Mystery of Presence and Contemplative Jewish Spiritual Practice," in *Seeking and Soaring: Jewish Approaches to Spiritual Direction,* ed. Goldie Milgram (New Rochelle, NY: Reclaiming Judaism Press, 2009) 374-385.

———. "Foundations of Jewish Pastoral Care: Skills and Techniques," in *Jewish Pastoral Care: A Practical Handbook from Traditional and Contemporary Sources,* ed. Dayle A. Friedman (Woodstock, VT: Jewish Lights, 2005) 95-124.

———, and Mychal B. Springer and Nancy H. Wiener. "*P'tach Libi B'Toratecha* (Open My Heart to Your Torah)," *CCAR Journal: The Reform Jewish Quarterly* (Summer 2012) 132-149.

Brown, F., S. Driver, and C. Briggs. *The Brown-Driver-Briggs, Hebrew and English Lexicon,* (Peabody, MA: Hendrickson, Sixth Printing, 2001).

Brueggeman, Walter. *The Prophetic Imagination* (Minneapolis: Fortress Press, 1978).

Buber, Martin. *I and Thou: A New Translation with a Prologue and Notes by Walter Kaufmann,* (New York: Scribner, 1970).

Carver, Charles S. and Michael H. Antoni. "Finding Benefit in Breast Cancer During the Year After Diagnosis Predicts Better Adjustment 5 to 8 Years After Diagnosis," *Health Psychology* Vol. 23, No. 6 (2004) 595-598.

Clark, Peter Yuichi. "A Liturgical Journey at Wesley Woods: Worship Experiences Within an Inpatient Geriatric Unit," *Journal of Pastoral Care* 47, no. 4 (Winter 1993) 388-403.

Cohen, Norman J. *Masking and Unmasking Ourselves: Interpreting Biblical Texts on Clothing and Identity* (Woodstock, VT: Jewish Lights Publishing and SkyLight Paths Publishing, 2012).

d'Aquili, Eugene and Andrew B Newberg. *The Mystical Mind: Probing the Biology of Religious Experience* (Minneapolis: Augsburg Fortress, 1999).

DeSteno, David. "Compassion Made Easy," *New York Times*, July 14, 2012.

Diamond, James. "Maimonides on Leprosy: Illness as Contemplative Metaphor," *Jewish Quarterly Review*, Vol. 96, No. 1, (Winter 2006) 95-122.

Dickey, Christopher. "Love and War," October 13, 2007, http://www.thedailybeast.com/newsweek/2007/10/13/love-and-war.html.

Didion, Joan. *The Year of Magical Thinking* (New York: Knopf, 2006).

Dittes, James E. *Pastoral Counseling: The Basics* (Louisville, KY: Westminster John Knox, 1999).

Doehring, Carrie. *Pastoral Care: A Postmodern Approach* (Louisville, KY: Westminster John Knox Press, 2006).

Donovan, Jane. "Battle Scars: Veterans Turn to Clergy for Counseling," *Christian Century*, February 8, 2012, 34-36.

Douglas, Mary. *Purity and Danger: An analysis of concepts of pollution and taboo* (London: Routledge, 1966).

———. *Leviticus as Literature* (Oxford University Press, 1999).

———. *In The Wilderness: The Doctrine of Defilement in the Book of Numbers* (Oxford University Press, 1993, 2004).

Dresser, Rebecca. Ed., *Malignant: Medical Ethicists Confront Cancer* (Oxford University Press, 2012).

Eliade, Mircea. *Patterns in Comparative Religion*, trans. Rosemary Sheed (New York: Meridian, 1958).

Ellor, James W., John Stettner and Helen Spath. "Ministry with the Confused Elderly," *Journal of Religion and Aging*, Vol. 4(2) (1987) 21-33.

Elon, Menachem. "Weill vs. The State of Israel," *Rulings of the Israeli Supreme Court*, Vol. 41, Part 3, 1987, 477–502.

Fontana, Alan and Robert Rosenheck. "Trauma, Change in Strength of Religious Faith, and Mental Health Service Use Among Veterans Treated for PTSD," *Journal of Nervous and Mental Disease*, 192:9, (2004) 579–584.

———. "The Role of Loss of Meaning in the Pursuit of Treatment for Posttraumatic Stress Disorder," *Journal of Traumatic Stress*, 18:2 (2005) 133–136.

Fox, Everett. *The Five Books of Moses: Genesis, Exodus, Leviticus, Numbers, and Deuteronomy: A New Translation with Introductions, Commentary, and Notes* (New York: Schocken Books, 1983, 1986, 1990, 1995).

Frank, Arthur W. *At the Will of the Body: Reflections on Illness* (Boston/ New York: Houghton Mifflin Company, 1991).

———. *The Wounded Storyteller: Body, Illness, and Ethics* (University of Chicago Press, 1995).

Frankl, Viktor E. *Man's Search for Meaning* (New York: Pocket Books, 1959, 1962, 1984).

Friedman, Dayle A. "Livui Ruchani: Spiritual Accompaniment," in *Jewish Pastoral Care: A Practical Handbook from Traditional and Contemporary Sources, 2nd Edition*, ed. Dayle A. Friedman (Woodstock, VT: Jewish Lights Publishing, 2005) xiii–xxv.

———. "Letting Their Faces Shine: Accompanying Aging People and Their Families," *Jewish Pastoral Care: A Practical Handbook from Traditional & Contemporary Sources, 2nd Edition*, ed. Dayle A. Friedman (Woodstock, VT: Jewish Lights, 2001 and 2005) 344–373.

Friedman, Richard Elliott. "Tabernacle," in *Anchor Bible Dictionary: Vol. 6*, ed. David Noel Freedman (New York: Doubleday, 1992).

Geller, Stephen A. "Blood Cult: Toward a Literary Theology of the Priestly Work of the Pentateuch," *Prooftexts* 12 (1992) 97–124.

Goffman, Erving. *Stigma: Notes on the Management of Spoiled Identity* (New York: Simon & Schuster, 1963, 1986).

Goodell, Jess, with John Hearn. *Shade It Black: Death and After in Iraq* (Havertown, PA: Casemate Publishers, 2011).

Goodkin, Donald E. "The Psychosocial Impact of Multiple Sclerosis: Exploring the Patient's Perspective," *Health Psychology*, Vol. 18 No. 4 (1999) 376-382.

Grob, Leonard. "The Jewish Roots of Emmanuel Levinas' Metaphysics of Welcome," in *Encountering the Stranger: A Jewish, Christian, Muslim Trialogue*, eds. Leonard Grob and John K. Roth (Seattle: University of Washington Press, 2012) 76-87.

Grosch, William N. and David C. Olsen. "Clergy Burnout: An Integrative Approach," *Psychotherapy in Practice*, Vol. 56(5), (2000) 619-632.

Hammer, Jill. "And the walls came tumbling down," in *Sisters at Sinai: New Tales of Biblical Women* (Philadelphia: Jewish Publication Society, 2001).

———. "Parashat Hukkat," ajrsem.org/2010/06/chukat577/.

Harris, Maurice D. *Leviticus: You Have No Idea* (Eugene, OR: Cascade Books, 2013).

Hart, Curtis W. "Sacred Space," in *Professional Spiritual and Pastoral Care: A Practical Clergy and Chaplain's Handbook*, ed. Stephen B. Roberts (Woodstock, VT: Skylight Paths, 2012) 421-433.

Havrelock, Rachel. "B'midbar: The Architecture of a Count and the Architecture of Account," in *The Torah: A Women's Commentary*, eds. Tamara Cohn Eskenazi and Andrea L. Weiss (New York: Women of Reform Judaism and URJ Press, 2008) 789-90.

Hendel, Ronald. "Mary Douglas and Anthropological Modernism," *Journal of Hebrew Scriptures* Volume 8, Article 8 (2008). ejournals.library.ualberta.ca/index.php/jhs/article/view/6205/5240.

———. and Saul Olyan. "Beyond Purity and Danger: Mary Douglas and the Hebrew Bible," *Journal of Hebrew Scriptures*, Volume 8, Article 7 (2008). ejournals.library.ualberta.ca/index.php/jhs/article/view/6205/5239.

Heschel, Abraham Joshua. *The Prophets* (Peabody, MA: Prince Press, 1962).

———. "The Reasons for My Involvement in the Peace Movement," in *Moral Grandeur and Spiritual Audacity* (NY: Farrar, Straus and Giroux, 1996).

Hirschmann, Jo. "Psychological and Theological Dynamics in an Inpatient Psychiatric Chaplaincy Group," *Journal of Religion and Health*, Vol. 50, No. 4 (2011) 964-74.

Hoffman, Lawrence, *Beyond the Text: A Holistic Approach to Liturgy*, (Bloomington and Indianapolis: Indiana University Press, 1987).

———. "Rabbinic Spiritual Leadership," *CCAR Journal: A Reform Jewish Quarterly* (Summer 2006) 36-66.

———. "Post-Colonial Liturgy in the Land of the Sick," *CCAR Journal: A Reform Jewish Quarterly* (Summer 2006) 10-35.

Hughes, Brian, and George Handzo. "Spiritual Care Handbook on PTSD/TBI: The Handbook on Best Practices for the Provision of Spiritual Care to Persons with Post Traumatic Stress Disorder and Traumatic Brian Injury," www.healthcarechaplaincy.org/docs/publications/landing_page/spiritual_care_ptsd_handbook1.pdf.

Hulse, E. V. "The Nature of Biblical 'Leprosy' and the Use of Alternative Medical Terms in Modern Translations of the Bible," *Palestine Exploration Quarterly* 107 (1975) 87-105.

Iacoboni, Marco. "Imitation, Empathy, and Mirror Neurons," *Annual Review of Psychology* 60 (2009) 653-70. www.nmr.mgh.harvard.edu/~bradd/library/iacoboni_annurevpsychol_2009.pdf.

Jastrow, Marcus. *A Dictionary of the Targumim, the Talmud Babli and Yerushalmi, and the Midrashic Literature*, (New York: Judaica Press, 1984).

Kaplan, Lawrence. "Hermann Cohen and Rabbi Joseph Soloveitchik on Repentance," *Journal of Jewish Thought and Philosophy* 13, no. 1 (2004) 213-258.

Kaufman, William E. "Time," in *Contemporary Jewish Religious Thought: Original Essays on Critical Concepts, Movements, and Beliefs*, eds. Arthur A. Cohen and Paul Mendes-Flohr (New York: The Free Press, 1987).

Kennedy, Kelly. *They Fought for Each Other: The Triumph and Tragedy of the Hardest Hit Unit in Iraq* (New York: St. Martin's Press, 2010).

Kim, Youngmee, Richard Schulz and Charles S. Carver. "Benefit Finding in the Cancer Caregiving Experience," *Psychosomatic Medicine* 69 (2007) 283-291.

Knohl, Israel. *The Divine Symphony: The Bible's Many Voices*, (Philadelphia: Jewish Publication Society, 2003).

Konnikova, Maria. "You're So Self-Controlling," *New York Times*, November 16, 2013.

Koppell, Bonnie. "A Ritual of Transition," *The Army Chaplaincy* (Summer-Fall 2010) 31-2.

Kraemer, David. *The Meanings of Death in Rabbinic Judaism* (London and New York: Routledge, 2000).

————. "The Logic of Impurity," *The Forward*, July 8, 2005, http://forward.com/articles/3783/the-logic-of-impurity/.

Kuner, Susan, Carol Matzkin Orsborn, Linda Quigley and Karen Leigh Stroup. *Speak the Language of Healing: Living with Breast Cancer without Going to War* (Berkeley, CA: Conari Press, 1999).

Lester, Andrew D. *Hope in Pastoral Care and Counseling* (Louisville, KY: Westminster John Knox Press, 1995).

Leveen, Adriane. *Memory and Tradition in the Book of Numbers* (Cambridge University Press, 2008).

Levinas, Emanuel. *Otherwise Than Being Or Beyond Essence* (Netherlands, Kluwer Academic Publishers, 1991).

Levine, Baruch. *Leviticus* (Philadelphia: JPS, 1989).

————. "Mythic and Ritual Projection of Sacred Space," *Journal of Jewish Thought and Philosophy* 6 (1) (1997) 59-70.

Levi, Primo. *The Periodic Table*, trans. Raymond Rosenthal (New York: Schocken, 1984).

Lewis, Joe O. "The Ark and the Tent," *Review and Expositor* 74 (1977) 437-46.

Lieberman, Matthew D. *Social: Why Our Brains Are Wired to Connect* (New York: Crown Publishers, 2013).

Lifton, Robert Jay. *Home from the War: Learning from Vietnam Veterans, with a new preface by the author on the war in Iraq* (New York: Other Press, 1973, 1985, 1992, 2005).

Lipskar, Sholom D. "A Torah Perspective On Incarceration As a Modality of Punishment and Rehabilitation," *Jewish Law Articles*, http://www.jlaw.com/Articles/PrisonerRights.html.

Mann, Barbara E. *Space and Place in Jewish Studies* (New Brunswick, NJ: Rutgers University Press, 2012).

Manning, Martha. *Undercurrents: A Life Beneath the Surface* (San Francisco: Harper, 1994).

Marlantes, Karl. *What It Is Like To Go To War* (New York: Atlantic Monthly Press, 2011).

Marx, Alfred. "The Relationship between the Sacrificial Laws and the Other Laws in Leviticus 19," *Journal of Hebrew Scriptures* Volume 8, Article 9 (2008). ejournals.library.ualberta.ca/index.php/jhs/article/view/6207/5241.

McClelland, Mac. "Is PTSD Contagious?" *Mother Jones*, January/February 2013. www.motherjones.com/politics/2013/01/ptsd-epidemic-military-vets-families.

McFadden, Susan H., Mandy Ingram and Carla Baldauf. "Actions, Feelings, and Values: Foundations of Meaning and Personhood in Dementia," in *Viktor Frankl's Contribution to Spirituality and Aging*, ed. Melvin A. Kimble (New York: Haworth Pastoral Press, 2000) 67-86.

McNamara, Patrick. *The Neuroscience of Religious Experience* (New York: Cambridge University Press, 2009).

Mikulak, Lynne. "Spirituality Groups," in *Professional Spiritual and Pastoral Care: A Practical Clergy and Chaplain's Handbook,* ed. Stephen B. Roberts (Woodstock, VT: Skylight Paths, 2012) 193-208.

Milgrom, Jacob. *The Anchor Bible, Leviticus 1-16: A New Translation with Introduction and Commentary* (New York: Doubleday, 1991).

———. "Sin-Offering or Purification Offering?" *Vetus Testamentum* 21 (1971) 237-9.

Miller-McLemore, Bonnie J. "The Living Human Web" in *Images of Pastoral Care: Classic Readings*, ed. Robert Robert C. Dykstra (St. Louis: Chalice Press, 2005) 40-46.

Newberg, Andrew and Mark Robert Waldman. *Why We Believe What We Believe: Uncovering our Biological Need for Meaning, Spirituality, and Truth,* (New York: Free Press, 2006).

Niemoller, Martin. "First They Came," Holocaust Encyclopedia of the U.S. Holocaust Museum. www.ushmm.org/wlc/en/article.php?ModuleId=10007392.

Nieuwsma, Jason A. and Jeffrey E. Rhodes. "Chaplaincy and Mental Health in the Department of Veterans Affairs and Department of Defense," *Journal of Health Care Chaplaincy*, 19 (2013) 3-21.

Olyan, Saul M. "Honor, Shame, and Covenant Relations in Ancient Israel and its Environment," *Journal of Biblical Literature*, 115/2 (1996) 201-218.

———. "What Do Shaving Rites Accomplish And What Do They Signal in Biblical Ritual Contexts?" *Journal of Biblical Literature*, 117/4 (1998) 611-622.

———. *Biblical Mourning: Ritual and Social Dimensions* (Oxford University Press, 2004).

———. "Purity Ideology in Ezra-Nehemia as a Tool to Reconstitute a Community," *Journal for the Study of Judaism* 35, no. 1 (2004) 1-16.

———. "Mary Douglas's Holiness/ Wholeness Paradigm: Its Potential for Insight and its Limitations," *Journal of Hebrew Scriptures*, Volume 8, Article 10 (2008). www.jhsonline.org/Articles/article_116.pdf

———. "The Ascription of Physical Disability as a Stigmatizing Strategy in Biblical Iconic Polemics," *Journal of Hebrew Scriptures* Volume 9, Article 14 (2009) 2-15. www.jhsonline.org/Articles/article_116.pdf

———. "What Do We Really Know about Women's Rites in the Israelite Family Context?" *Journal of Ancient Near Eastern Religions* Vol. 10 Issue 1 (2010) 55-67.

Rathje, William and Cullen Murphy. *Rubbish! The Archeology of Garbage: What Our Garbage Tells Us about Ourselves* (New York: HarperCollins, 1992).

Richards, Marty and Sam Seicol. "The Challenge of Maintaining Spiritual Connectedness for Persons Institutionalized with Dementia," *Journal of Religious Gerontology* 7, no. 3 (1991): 27-40.

Satir, Virginia. *Conjoint Family Therapy* (Palo Alto, CA: Science and Behavior Books, 1983).

Sawyer, John F. A. "A Note on the Etymology of Sara'at," *Vetus Testamentum* 26 (1976) 241-5.

Schiffman, Lawrence and Joel B. Wolowelsky. Eds. *War and Peace in the Jewish Tradition* (New York: Yeshiva University Press, 2007).

Schmitt, Rüdiger. "The Problem of Magic and Monotheism in the Book of Leviticus," *Journal of Hebrew Scriptures* Volume 8, Article 11 (2008).

Schwarz, Daniel R. "Kingdom of Priests," in *Contemporary Jewish Religious Thought*, eds. Arthur A. Cohen and Paul Mendes-Flohr (New York: The Free Press, 1987).

Schwartz, Joshua. "On Birds, Rabbis and Skin Disease," in *Purity and Holiness: the Heritage of Leviticus*, eds. M.J.H.M. Poorthuis and J. Schwartz (Leiden: Brill, 2000) 207-222.

Scurfield, Raymond Monsour. "Healing the Warrior: Admission of Two American Indian War-Veteran Cohort Groups to a Specialized Inpatient PTSD Unit," *American Indian and Alaska Native Mental Health Research*, 6:3 (1995) 1-22.

———. *War Trauma: Lessons Unlearned from Vietnam to Iraq: Volume 3 of A Vietnam Trilogy* (New York: Algora, 2006).

Shay, Jonathan. *Odysseus in America: Combat Trauma and the Trials of Homecoming* (New York: Scribner, 2002).

———. *Achilles in Vietnam: Combat Trauma and the Undoing of Character* (New York: Simon and Schuster, 1994).

Shoham-Steiner, Ephraim. "Al Tzara'at Naaman ve'Repuyah," in *Rishonim v'Achronim*, eds. Joseph Hacker, B. Z. Kedar and Joseph Kaplan (Jerusalem: Zalman Shazar Center for History, 2009) 213-236.

Siegel, Daniel H. *Mindsight: The New Science of Personal Transformation* (New York: Bantam, 2011).

Smith, Jonathan Z. *To Take Place: Toward Theory in Ritual* (University of Chicago Press, 1987).

Snaith, N. H. "The Sin-offering and the Guilt-offering," *Vetus Testamentum*, Vol. 15, Fasc. 1 (Jan. 1965) 73-80.

Solomon, Andrew. *Far From the Tree: Parents, Children, and the Search for Identity* (New York: Scribner, 2012).

Sommer, Benjamin. "Reflecting on Moses: The Redaction of Numbers 11," *Journal of Biblical Literature* 118, 4 (1999) 601-624.

———. "Conflicting Constructions of Divine Presence in the Priestly Tabernacle," *Biblical Interpretation: A Journal of Contemporary Approaches*, Vol. 9 No. 1 (2001) 41-63.

Sontag, Susan. *Illness as Metaphor and AIDS and its Metaphors* (New York: Picador, 1977, 1988).

Sperling, Shalom David. "Miriam, Aaron and Moses: Sibling Rivalry," *Hebrew Union College Annual* (1999-2000) 70-71.

———. "Blood," in *The Anchor Bible Dictionary:* Vol. 1, A-C, ed. David Noel Freedman (New York: Doubleday, 1992).

Steinsaltz, Adin. *The Talmud, The Steinsaltz Edition: A Reference Guide* (Jerusalem: Israel Institute for Talmudic Publications, 1988; English translation New York: Random House, 1989).

Stern, Sacha. *Time and Process in Ancient Judaism* (Oxford, UK and Portland, OR: Littman Library of Jewish Civilization, 2003).

Taylor, Jill Bolte. *My Stroke of Insight: A Brain Scientist's Personal Journey* (London: Viking, 2006).

Thomas, William H. *The Eden Alternative: Nature, Hope & Nursing Homes* (Sherburne, NY: Eden Alternative Foundation, 1994).

Tick, Edward. *War and the Soul: Healing Our Nation's Veterans from Post-traumatic Stress Disorder* (Wheaton, IL: Quest Books, 2005).

Ulanov, Ann and Barry. *The Healing Imagination: The Meeting of Psyche and Soul* (Canada: Daimon Verlag, 2008).

Volf, Miroslav. *Exclusion and Embrace: A Theological Exploration of Identity, Otherness, and Reconciliation* (Nashville: Abingdon Press, 1996).

Wenig, Margaret Moers. "Male and Female, God Created Them? The Intersex, Transgender and Transsexual in Jewish Tradition and in Our Lives," *CCAR Journal: The Reform Jewish Quarterly* Fall 2012, 130–42.

Wiener, Nancy H., Julie Schwartz and Michele F. Prince. "Seminary-Based Jewish Pastoral Education," eds. Jeff Levin and Michele F. Prince, *Judaism and Health: A Handbook of Practical, Professional, and Scholarly Resources* (Woodstock, VT: Jewish Lights, 2013) 108-127.

Wilson, John P. "Culture and Trauma: The Sacred Pipe Revisited," in John P. Wilson, *Trauma, Transformation and Healing: An Integrative Approach to*

Theory, Research, and Post-Traumatic Therapy (New York: Brunner/ Mazel, 1989).

Woolf, Virginia Woolf. *The Virginia Woolf Reader, Preface and Notes by Mitchell A. Leaska* (New York: Harcourt Brace, 1984).

Wright, David P. "Deciphering a Definition: The Syntagmatic Structural Analysis of Ritual in the Hebrew Bible," *Journal of Hebrew Scriptures* Volume 8, Article 12 (2008) https://ejournals.library.ualberta.ca/index.php/jhs/article/view/6210/5244.

———. "Holiness in Leviticus and Beyond," *Interpretation* 53, no. 4 (1999) 351-364.

———. *The Disposal of Impurity* (Atlanta: Scholars Press, 1987).

Yalom, Irvin D. *The Gift of Therapy: An Open Letter to a New Generation of Therapists and Their Patients* (New York: Harper Collins/ Perennial, 2002).

Yalom, Marilyn. *The American Resting Place: Four Hundred Years of History through our Cemeteries and Burial Grounds* (Boston: Houghton Mifflin, 2008).

Zornberg, Avivah. *The Particulars of Rapture: Reflections on Exodus* (New York: Doubleday, 2001).

Index of Subjects

9/11, 94–95

A&O, 7
  alert and oriented, 7, 9, 13
    times four (x4), 7
    times three (x3), 7, 20, 192,
      214
  aware and oriented, 9
    new pastoral
      understanding, 9
    to spiritual dimension,
      9–10, 216
  Leviticus as means of orientation
    for ancient Israelites, 192
Aaron, 34n, 37, 40, 55, 61, 66, 82,
  122, 192, 201, 216
  his breastplate, 55
  and Miriam's *tzara'at*, 40, 61
  with Moses and community,
    198
  with Moses and Miriam, 40,
    60–61, 165
  and ordination ritual, 144

  and the rituals for blasphemer
    and Shabbat desecrator, 201
  as *rodef shalom*, 192
  seeing the leper as a son of, 216
  and Yom Kippur ritual, 37, 66,
    82
Abraham, 70–71, 160
  model of caregiving for others,
    70–71
accessing God
  in the absence of the Temple,
    25, 208
  and caregivers, 87, 94
  in a city of refuge, 213–14
  through the covenant, 211–12
  through cultic ritual, 28, 34
  at doorway of one's tent, 40, 121
  by holding apparent opposites in
    creative tension, 192
  on the margins, 87, 189
  while *michutz lamachaneh*,
    38–40, 49, 66–67, 71, 105,
    120, 192

in the *midbar*, 37

in the midst of adversity, 42, 192

at military encampment, 28,
33–35, 38

by moving away from the
center of the camp, 37–39,
66–67, 192

through narrative, 26, 208

when neurologically de-
centered, 21–22, 48–49

at *Ohel Moed* in the camp,
33–35, 38, 192, 212, 217
prohibition for those with
or suspected of having
tzara'at, 64

at *Ohel Moed michutz
lamachaneh*, 38–40, 120,192,
211, 217

and *taharah*, 28

and the unintentional manslayer,
214–15

in unlikely places, 216

accompaniment, 145–46

biblical priest, 62–72, 77–78,
109–13

of blasphemer and Shabbat
desecrater, 39, 201–3, 211

contemporary pastoral
caregivers, 10, 52, 54, 71–72,
77, 86, 87, 91, 93, 110, 112,
205, 208

God and the Israelites, 25, 32,
208

God and those in military camp,
41–42

and Hebrew root, 70–71

priest and *metzora*, 68–73, 77–78

and the scapegoat, 37

spiritual, 49, 51, 71

of those who must spend time
away from community, 39,
201–3, 205, 207–8

ambiguities, 30–31, 59, 106,
192–95, 198

and desire to assert clarity, rigid
categories, 198

and holding them in creative
tension, 192, 196, 208

and integrity, 192

anointing

at liminal moment, 217

of *metzora*, 64–65, 68, 130, 142,
144, 217
priest in close physical
contact with, 68

of priest, 65, 217

ash heap, 99–101

atonement

as covering, 143–46

attunement, 9–10

and contemporary caregiver,
77–78, 80, 87

and "feeling felt," 19

between levitical priest and
metzora, 56, 63–64, 77

and the pastoral, 77

and the prophetic, 56, 77

comfort zones, 25. *See also* de-
centering; dislocation
connectedness, 11, 13
clergy role with others, 51–52
communal responsibility, 201–3,
207–8
definition of spirituality, 123
after disorientation, 25
while feeling unmoored, 21–22,
192
with God, 2, 10, 26, 39–40
interconnectedness, 9, 11, 48, 72
and "we-maps," 16
mirrored in brain function,
13
and interdependence, 11, 14, 16,
48, 72
with loss of sense of body's
boundaries, 22
of margins and center, 4, 195,
200, 208–9, 211, 215–16, 218
memory and, 8
and mirror neurons, 15–17
narrative and, 47
with place, 211
with others, 10–11, 15–16, 26,
48, 72, 207, 211, 215
after rupture, 211
with sacred, 9
with self, 10, 26
and sense of self, 8–11
with world, 2, 10, 11, 72
consecrate, consecration. *See*
Kedushah

corpses
contact with, 38, 41, 67
metzora considered like, 69
and *nega'im* in a criminal matter,
74–75
specially designated places for,
37, 41
and *tumah*, 38–39, 41, 60–61,
67, 80–81
correctional facilities. *See* prison
and prisoners
covenant
ark of, 34
breach of, 211
remaining inside, 211–12
covering, 143–46. *See also*
atonement; *Metzora*, at time of
diagnosis
creation, 140–43
from existing materials, 141
of sacred space in contemporary
life, 3, 123
recreation of self, 216
creating a usable future
through imagination, 24, 26,
192, 194, 217
through narrative or story, 24,
26, 42, 48, 195, 218
through theology, 10
crimson or scarlet material, 60, 64,
67, 131, 168, 217. *See also*
blood, blood symbolism

death penalty in the Bible

and "we-maps." *See* maps, "we-maps"

Numbers, Book of, 149–54, 190

nursing homes, 44, 119, 122, 125–29

Ohel Moed, 33–35, 69, 117
  in the camp, 33–35, 38, 82, 100, 192, 212
    and consecration, 33
    God's dwelling place, 33–34; conditions for indwelling, 33–34
  and cedar wood, hyssop, and crimson stuff, 67–68
  characteristics of
    kadosh, 34
    tahor, 34–35
  and contemporary corollaries, 122–29
  michutz lamachaneh, 38–40, 95–96, 119–29,192
  and military formation, 150–52
oil. *See* ritual
ontological mode, 49, 87

panim, 207–8
pastor, 51
  and ability to see and notice, 55, 68–69
  center and margins, 55
  characteristics of

guides and accompanies the collective and individuals, 52
offers support and accompaniment through life's transitions, 52
personal and collective, 55
as presence, 54–55, 71–72
walks with individuals as they map their inner and outer worlds, 52
works with individuals and families in intimate settings, 52
as diagnostician, 68–69
pastoral and spiritual care, 20, 56, 71. See also caregivers; pastor; priest; prophet
and awareness, 54
available to individuals, families, communities, 52
goals of
  assist people as they create new narratives, 20
  change of perspective and self-perception, 53–55
  move people toward holiness, 52
and imagination, 10, 52
and liturgy, 20
and mapping of mysterious or unknown territory, 54
and meaning making, 20, 71

Index of Authors

Index of Biblical and Rabbinic Sources

CPSIA information can be obtained at www.ICGtesting.com
Printed in the USA
LVOW10s0226020714

392527LV00003B/3/P